Korea 2012: Politics, Economy and Society

Korea 2012:
Politics, Economy and Society

Volume 6

Korea Yearbook

Edited by

Rüdiger Frank
James E. Hoare
Patrick Köllner
Susan Pares

Associate Editors

Stephen Epstein and Moon Chung-in

BRILL

LEIDEN • BOSTON
2012

This work was supported by the Academy of Korean Studies (publication grant AKS-2012-P-01).

Geographisches Institut
der Universität Kiel
ausgesonderte Dublette

ISSN 1875-0273
ISBN 978 90 04 23628 8 (paperback)
ISBN 978 90 04 24301 9 (e-book)

Copyright 2012 by Koninklijke Brill NV, Leiden, The Netherlands.
Koninklijke Brill NV incorporates the imprints Brill, Global Oriental, Hotei Publishing, IDC Publishers and Martinus Nijhoff Publishers.

All rights reserved. No part of this publication may be reproduced, translated, stored in a retrieval system, or transmitted in any form or by any means, electronic, mechanical, photocopying, recording or otherwise, without prior written permission from the publisher.

Authorization to photocopy items for internal or personal use is granted by Koninklijke Brill NV provided that the appropriate fees are paid directly to The Copyright Clearance Center, 222 Rosewood Drive, Suite 910, Danvers, MA 01923, USA.
Fees are subject to change.

This book is printed on acid-free paper.

Printed by Printforce, the Netherlands

CONTENTS

Preface xi

List of Refereed Articles Published since 2007 1
   South Korea 1
    1   Politics and foreign relations 1
    2   Economy 1
    3   Society 2
   North Korea 4
    1   Politics and foreign relations 4
    2   Economy 4
    3   Society 4
   The Two Koreas: Connections and Comparisons 5

Chronology of Events in the Korean Peninsula 2011 7
   South Korea 7
   North Korea 11
   Inter-Korean Relations and Six Party Talks 15

South Korea in 2011:
Domestic Politics, the Economy and Social Issues 21
   Patrick Köllner
    1   Introduction 21
    2   The April by-elections and their consequences 23
    3   The Seoul mayoral election and party mergers on the Left 27
    4   Parliament and the state budget 30
    5   After Fukushima: South Korea affirms
        increased reliance on nuclear energy 31
    6   South Korea's economy in 2011: the big picture 33
    7   Social issues 36

North Korea in 2011:
Domestic Developments and the Economy 39
Rüdiger Frank

1   Introduction 39
2   The 2011 joint New Year editorial 40
2.1 Key topic: improvement of the people's standard of living ... 40
2.2 Highlights of the editorial 41
2.3 Ideology 44
2.4 The leader(s) 45
3   The annual parliamentary session 48
3.1 Overview 48
3.2 Budget report 48
3.3 The work of the Cabinet 51
4   Death of Kim Jong Il 52
5   Other events 53
5.1 Trade and investment 53
5.2 Economic development 55
5.3 Mining and minerals 56
5.4 Telecommunications 57
5.5 Science and technology 59
5.6 Tourism 60
5.7 Environmental issues 61
5.8 Traditionalism 62
5.9 Administrative and personnel changes 63
6   Conclusion 63

Relations Between the Two Koreas in 2011 65
Sabine Burghart

Introduction 65
1   Kim Jong Il's death: a window of opportunity? 66
2   A change in the ROK's policy: principled flexibility? 67
3   A (w)hole of information? 69
4   Inter-Korean economic exchanges: a mixed picture 71
5   Mt Kŭmgang resort: lost forever? 74
6   Humanitarian aid further scaled down 75
7   Empowerment of ROK's second-class citizens 77
8   Defence, provocations and unification 78
9   Outlook 80

Foreign Relations of the Two Koreas in 2011 81
James E. Hoare

Introduction 81
1   Republic of Korea 81
1.1 Relations with the United States.. 81
1.2 Relations with China 83
1.3 Relations with Japan 86
1.4 Other relations 88
2   People's Democratic Republic of Korea 89
2.1 The Six Party Talks and relations with the United States 89
2.2 Relations with China 92
2.3 Relations with Russia 94
2.4 Relations with Japan 95
2.5 Other relations 95

KORUS, KOREU and beyond: South Korea's Free Trade Drive 97
Patrick Flamm and Patrick Köllner

Summary 97
1   Export dependence and increasing regional competition 98
2   South Korea's Free Trade Agreements 101
3   Economic expectations and concerns 101
4   Political dimensions of the trade agreements 104
5   Outlook 105

North Korea after Kim Jong Il:
The Kim Jong Un Era and its Challenges 109
Rüdiger Frank

1   Introduction 109
2   From death to funeral: events between
      19 and 31 December 2011 111
3   Does Kim Jong Un have the power, and will he keep it? 116
4   How is Kim Jong Un's legitimacy being built? 119
5   Do the Party and the military compete for power
      in North Korea? 122
6   How will China behave? 125
7   What will happen to North Korea's nuclear programme? 127
8   What will Kim Jong Un's policies be? 128

The Concept of Middle Power and the Case of the ROK:
A Review 131
Dong-min Shin

1   Introduction 131
2   Academic discourses on the concept of middle power 133
2.1 Early development 133
2.2 Trends in existing research 134
2.3 Limitations of existing research 135
3   The Korean context 138
3.1 The middle power discourse within ROK governments 138
4   The ROK's foreign and security affairs in context 142
4.1 Vital issues in the ROK's international relations 142
4.2 Existing research on the ROK from the middle power
    perspective 144
5   Conclusion 147

Northerners on Southern Screens:
From *Shiri* (1999) to *The Yellow Sea* (2010) 153
Mark Morris

Prologue 153
1   Introduction 154
2   Back story circa 2000 155
2.1 Shiri and Joint Security Area 156
3   The Sunshine years: Rom-com Northern spies, *t'albukja*,
    war comedies 159
3.1 Rom-com Northern spies 160
3.2 T'albukja: the coming of the defectors/refugees/migrants ... 161
3.3 War comedies 164
4   Contemporary visions, 2010-2011: war, life and
    death up North, refugees, *chosŏnjok* 166
4.1 War 167
4.2 Life and death up North 170
4.3 Refugees 171
4.4 Chosŏnjok 174
5   Conclusion 176

A New Deal: Graphic Novel Representations of
Food Issues in Post-famine North Korea 181
  Martin Petersen
  1 Introduction 181
  2 North Korean cultural production in the 2000s 183
  3 The representation of food in North Korean
     graphic novels 185
  4 *A Strange Letter* 188
  4.1 Meta-authorial reading 190
  4.2 Ironic reading 196
  4.3 Reader-recognisant meta-authorial reading 200
  5 Conclusion 206

Special Economic Zones, Trade and Economic Reform:
The Case of Rason Special City 209
  Bernhard J. Seliger
  1 Introduction 209
  2 Promises, unfulfilled dreams and failure 212
  2.1 SEZ: concept and practice 212
  2.2 Rason: early operations, early failures 215
  2.3 Rason's economic activities 217
  3 The rebirth of Rason as a transport corridor 221
  4 Does Chinese investment lead to sustained reform?
     Evidence from recent years 225
  4.1 The service structure for a special economic and
     transport zone 225
  4.2 The administrative response: Rason Economic
     Administration as a 'one-stop shop' 226
  4.3 Rason trade fair 227
  4.4 Rason agricultural research centre 228
  5 Conclusion 230

The North Korean Philosophy of Foreigners 239
  Tatiana Gabroussenko
  1 Introduction 239
  2 North Korean discourse of the foreign world:
     political roots, conflicting demands and challenges 241
  2.1 Soviet-style internationalism: a complex pattern 241

2.2	Political seclusion of the DPRK	243
2.3	'National solipsism' in the North Korean mono-ethnic mentality	244
2.4	The paradigm of unfinished war with the United States	246
3	Tales of 'good foreigners' as a special genre in North Korean fiction	249
3.1	Exoticisation of foreign friends	249
3.2	Koreanisation of foreign friends	250
3.3	Foreign friends versus North Koreans	252
4	Americans as 'good foreigners': case study of Kim Chun-hak's 'Enchantment'	254
4.1	The 'teenage girl'	256
4.2	A 'naughty boy'	258
4.3	Kim Il Sung and the fictional Carters—mutual sensuality	259
5	Foreigners as Korean heroes	260
6	Conclusion	262

About the Authors and Editors 269
Map of the Korean Peninsula 275

PREFACE

The editors of *Korea: Politics, Economy and Society* are proud to present the sixth volume of a series that has been published in this form since 2007. The year 2011, as covered in the first part of this volume, fortunately saw neither a nuclear test nor a military clash between the two Koreas. However, tension remained high and progress in inter-Korean relations was slow. While the South—the Republic of Korea—continued to prosper economically, the North—the Democratic People's Republic of Korea—was unable to achieve a major breakthrough in its economic development and has still not decided to resume the reforms that had started so hopefully at the beginning of the 21st century. Then, in December 2011, Kim Jong Il died, sending shockwaves through his country and putting North Korea into the spotlight of the international media. The new leader Kim Jong Un, his third son, has taken over a difficult and complex task.

As usual, the first part of the book consists of regular, standardised contributions that each cover a particular topic, including a chronology of events on the Korean peninsula, the domestic politics and economy as well as the foreign policy of each Korea, and inter-Korean relations. Keeping up with typically dynamic and multi-faceted Korea-related developments is not easy; the first part of the book thus provides an anchor and a record that sees its usefulness grow with time—in particular as popular search engines tend to ignore all but the most recent events. Our book series has thus become an indispensable reference source for scholars, journalists and policy-makers. This year, due to extraordinary events that deserve, we believe, particular attention, we have expanded this set of regular contributions by two more: one on North Korea and the death of Kim Jong Il, and one on South Korea and its drive to conclude free trade agreements.

The second, refereed part of the book brings together five specialised contributions on current affairs and developments in Korea, North and South. Dongmin Shin discusses the concept of 'Middle Power' and the case of South Korea, asking whether this concept is applicable to the ROK, and what the implications of doing so might be. Mark Morris explores the image(s) of North Koreans on the silver screen in the South, including such blockbusters as *Shiri* and *Joint Security Area*, but also smaller films which have looked at the society of South Korea through Northern eyes, adopting the point of view of North Korean refugees. Martin Petersen in his contribution on graphic novel representations of food issues in post-famine North Korea suggests that the North Korean graphic novel *A Strange Letter* from 2001 may be viewed as the regime striking a new deal with its citizens. Bernhard Seliger shares his vast experience on the ground as representative of the Hanns Seidel Foundation in his piece on Rasŏn Special City and the attached economic zone, arguing that the economic forces driving the development of Rasŏn as well as its geographic position will make it more viable and less inherently unstable than the other North Korean SEZs. Finally, Tatiana Gabroussenko examines the North Korean philosophy of foreigners and attempts to reconstruct a full version of the North Korean discourse of foreigners including its least studied part, internationalism.

Once again, the book has been supported by a generous grant from the Academy for Korean Studies (AKS), for which we are most grateful. Our thanks also go to our steady supporters at Brill in Leiden, in particular Albert Hoffstädt, Patricia Radder, and Dagmar Vermeer. We would also like to acknowledge the support by our associate editors Stephen Epstein of Victoria University in Wellington, New Zealand, and Chung-in Moon of Yonsei University in Seoul, South Korea. We remain grateful to Emeritus Professor Keith Pratt and the Design and Imaging Unit at Durham University for making available the map reproduced in the book. Special thanks are as always due to Siegrid Woelk, who has done more than a fine job producing the camera-ready copy.

Rüdiger Frank, James E. Hoare, Patrick Köllner and Susan Pares

Vienna, London and Hamburg, July 2012

LIST OF REFEREED ARTICLES PUBLISHED SINCE 2007

SOUTH KOREA

1   *Politics and foreign relations*

Online Grassroots Journalism and Participatory Democracy in South Korea (Ronda Hauben), 2007: 61–82

Fission, Fusion, Reform and Failure in South Korean Politics: Roh Moo-Hyun's Administration (Youngmi Kim), 2008: 73–94

Assassination, Abduction and Normalisation: Historical Mythologies and Misrepresentation in Post-war South Korea-Japan Relations (John Swenson-Wright), 2008: 95–124

The Disparity Between South Korea's Engagement and Security Policies Towards North Korea: The Realist-Liberal Pendulum (Alon Levkowitz), 2008: 125–147

The South Korean Left's 'Northern Question' (Joonbum Bae), 2009: 87–115

Conflict Management in Urban Planning: The Restoration of the Ch'ŏnggyech'ŏn River in Seoul (Annette J. Erpenstein), 2010: 85–112

The Role of Think Tanks in the South Korean Discourse on East Asia (Thomas Kern and Alexander Ruser), 2010: 113–134

Nation Branding in South Korea: A Modern Continuation of the Developmental State? (Alena Schmuck), 2011: 91–117

From 'Cold Friendship' to Strategic Partnership: The Transformation of South Korea's Political Relations with India (Niclas D. Weimar), 2011: 119–145

2   *Economy*

The Lone Star Scandal: Was it Corruption? (James C. Schopf), 2007: 83–111

Emergence of China and the Economy of South Korea (Joon-Kyung Kim and Chung H. Lee), 2007: 139–163

Changing Perceptions of Inward Foreign Direct Investment in Post-Crisis Korea (1998–2006) (Judith Cherry), 2007: 113–137

Dynamics of Korean Industrial Relations: Challenges for Foreign Invested Companies in the Metal Sector (Peter Kloepping), 2009: 143–175

Cheju Island as a Medical Tourism Hub in Northeast Asia (Jürgen Mühl), 2009: 177–204

South Korea's Economic Policy Response to the Global Financial Crisis (Werner Pascha), 2010: 135–164

'Green Growth': South Korea's Panacea? (David Shim), 2010: 165–187

South Korea's Economic Relations with India: Trends, Patterns and Prospects (Durgesh K. Rai), 2010: 189–215

Shopping Abroad the Korean Way: A Study in Resource Acquisition (Stefania Paladini), 2011: 147–174

3   Society

New Ancestral Shrines in South Korea (Heonik Kwon), 2007: 193–214

The Political Economy of Patriotism: the Case of *Hanbando* (Mark Morris), 2007: 215–234

Korean Modernism, Modern Korean Cityscapes, and Mass Housing Development: Charting the Rise of *Ap'at'ŭ tanji* since the 1960s (Valérie Gelézeau), 2007: 165–191

Higher Education Reform in South Korea: Success Tempered by Challenges (Peter Mayer), 2008: 149–170

The New Korean Cinema Looks Back to Kwangju: *The Old Garden* and *May 18* (Mark Morris), 2008: 171–198

Scapegoat, Beggar and President for the Economy: The Image of Lee Myung-bak as Seen through Political Cartoons in *Chosun Ilbo* and *Hankyoreh* (Katharina Polley), 2009: 205–225

The Korean Comfort Women Movement and the Formation of a Public Sphere in East Asia (Thomas Kern and Sang-hui Nam), 2009: 227–255

The Social Construction of North Korean Women's Identity in South Korea: Romanticisation, Victimisation and Vilification (Mikyoung Kim), 2009: 257–275

On the Trail of the Manchurian Western (Mark Morris), 2010: 217–246

Managing Labour Migration to South Korea: Policies and Problems Regarding Migrant Workers (Sarah Hasan), 2011: 175–205

Vil(l)e Encounters: The US Armed Forces in Korea and Entertainment Districts in and near Seoul (Elisabeth Schober), 2011: 207–231

A Trajectory Perspective Towards Return Migration and Development: The Case of Young Korean New Zealander Returnees (Jane YeonJae Lee), 2011: 233–256

Connecting East Asians in Europe: The Power of Korean Popular Culture (Sang-Yeon Sung), 2011: 257–273

NORTH KOREA

1 Politics and foreign relations

Negotiating with North Korea: Lessons Learned and Forgotten (Robert Carlin), 2007: 235–251

A Brief History of the Sino-Korean Border from the 18th to the 20th Century (Larisa Zabrovskaya), 2007: 283–297

The US–DPRK 1994 Agreed Framework and the US Army's Return to North Korea (C. Kenneth Quinones), 2008: 199–229

The International Community and the North Korean Nuclear Programme (Sebastian Harnisch and David J. Roesch), 2011: 333–360

2 Economy

Benchmarks of Economic Reform in North Korea (Patrick McEachern), 2008: 231–249

Beyond Lips and Teeth: The Economics of the China–North Korea Relationship (Tim Beal), 2011: 303–331

3 Society

Perilous Journeys: The Plight of North Koreans in China (Peter Beck, Gail Kim and Donald Macintyre), 2007: 253–281

Statistical Explorations in Terra Incognita: How Reliable are North Korean Survey Data? (Daniel Schwekendiek), 2009: 277–300

Migration Experiences of North Korean Refugees: Survey Evidence from China (Yoonok Chang, Stephan Haggard and Marcus Noland), 2009: 301–328

A Meta-Analysis of North Koreans Migrating to China and South Korea (Daniel Schwekendiek), 2010: 247–270

From the 'Soviet Era' to the 'Russian Renaissance': Evolution of the Narrative about Russia and Russians in the North Korean Cultural Discourse (Tatiana Gabroussenko), 2011: 275–302

THE TWO KOREAS: CONNECTIONS AND COMPARISONS

Trends and Prospects of Inter-Korean Economic Co-operation (Kyung Tae Lee and Hyung-Gon Jeong), 2008: 251–267

'Atoms for Sale': From 'Atoms for Peace' (South Korea) to 'Weaponized' Plutonium (North Korea), 1955–2009 (John P. DiMoia), 2009: 117–141

Playing the Game? Sport and the Two Koreas (Brian Bridges), 2009: 329–348

Textual and Visual Representations of the Korean War in North and South Korean Children's Literature (Dafna Zur), 2010: 271–303

CHRONOLOGY OF EVENTS IN THE KOREAN PENINSULA 2011

South Korea

11.01.11	ROK and Japan hold first-ever bilateral military conference in Seoul; conclude agreements on sharing military information and exchange of munitions and services.
13.01.11	ROK and United States (US) agree on a 10-year joint study to determine if ROK should be permitted to reprocess spent nuclear fuel using new, proliferation-resistant technology.
28.02–30.04.11	ROK–US annual joint military exercises Foal Eagle/ Key Resolve.
03.03.11	ROK and US begin 2nd round of talks on revision of bilateral atomic energy agreement set to expire in 2014.
12.03.11	5-member team from ROK's National Emergency Management Agency is first rescue team to reach Japan following Tohoku earthquake and tsunami of 11.03.11. Further 102 rescuers from ROK arrive in Japan, 14.03.11.
12–14.03.11	President Lee Myung-bak visits United Arab Emirates, secures oil development deal for export of 1.2 billion barrels of crude oil to ROK.
17.03.11	ROK and France sign agreement on transfer of Korean royal archives looted by French troops in 1866 back to Korea.
30.03.11	ROK protests to Japan over latter's claim to Tokto islands as Japanese territory in its revised middle school text books.
12.04.11	2-day meeting reported of ROK and Japanese nuclear safety experts after ROK had expressed concerns over release of more than 11,000 tons of water contaminated with radiation used to cool reactors at Fukushima nuclear power plant.

14.04–27.05.11	France returns 297 volumes of *Ŭigwe*, the Chosŏn royal protocol, to ROK in 4 shipments, on a 5-year renewable lease.
24.04.11	Trade ministers of ROK, China and Japan hold talks on trilateral free trade and regional economic co-operation in aftermath of Tohoku earthquake.
08–11.05.11	President Lee visits Germany; Denmark, 11–12.05.11; France, 12–14.05.11.
17.05.11	Michelin Guides publish Green Guide for Korea (in French).
21–22.05.11	President Lee, Chinese Premier Wen Jiabao and Japanese Prime Minister Kan Nato visit Fukushima, hold 4th trilateral summit in Tokyo.
25.05.11	ROK government minister visits Tokto islands. Japan protests to ROK.
25.05.11	Japan reported to have protested to ROK over visit by 3 ROK lawmakers to Kuril islands, with Russian permission.
30.05.11	ROK–US joint investigation begins of former US military bases, following claims by retired US soldiers that they helped to dump large quantities of Agent Orange inside US army Camp Carroll in 1978. 03.06.11, US 8th Army commander tells ROK environment minister that drums of chemicals were removed from ROK in 1982–83.
20.06.11	Outgoing commander of US forces in ROK says US will not deploy tactical nuclear weapons to ROK.
28.06.11	China sends first 120 government-brokered migrant workers to ROK.
29.06.11	15,000 protesters take to streets in central Seoul against ROK–US Free Trade Agreement (FTA) and rising costs of college tuition.
01.07.11	ROK–European Union (EU) FTA comes into implementation.
02–06.07.11	President Lee visits Republic of South Africa; 07–08.07.11, Democratic Republic of Congo; 09–11.07.11, Federal Democratic Republic of Ethiopia.
06.07.11	Pyŏngch'ang awarded 23rd Olympic Winter Games and Paralympics for 2018.

14–15.07.11	ROK and US hold 3rd round of talks on revision of bilateral atomic energy agreement.
24–27.07.11	President Patil of India visits ROK; bilateral nuclear co-operation agreement signed.
27–28.07.11	ROK and China hold their first defence strategic talks.
02.08.11	ROK protests against Japan's claim to Tokto islands in Japanese 2011 defence white paper.
16–26.08.11	Joint ROK–US military exercise Ulchi Freedom Guardian in ROK.
21–23.08.11	President Lee visits Mongolia; 23–24.08.11, Uzbekistan; 24–25.08.11, Kazakhstan. Discusses co-operation in energy projects.
30.08.11	ROK Constitutional Court declares unconstitutional ROK government's failure actively to conduct either diplomatic negotiations or arbitration to win compensation for 'comfort women'.
19.09.11	Speaking at the International Atomic Energy Agency (IAEA)'s general conference, the ROK announces it will increase its proportion of nuclear power generation to 59% by 2030, while enhancing its safety.
21.09.11	Construction of naval base commences at Kangjŏng village on Cheju island despite local opposition.
23.09.11	45-day festival to mark millennial anniversary of Tripitaka Koreana opens near Haein temple.
27.09.11	ROK, China and Japan open secretariat for trilateral co-operation in Seoul.
29.09.11	ROK foreign ministry reported to have set up task force to deal with issue of compensation for ROK women forced into sexual slavery during World War II. 03.10.11, Japanese foreign ministry states issue of compensation already fully resolved.
11–15.10.11	President Lee visits US. He and President Obama reaffirm US–ROK alliance, 13.10.11.
12.10.11	US Congress approves ROK–US FTA.
26.10.11	Park Won-soon elected mayor of Seoul in by-election, beating GNP candidate Na Kyung-won.
04.11.11	Around 1,000 people hold candlelight vigil in Seoul to protest against ROK–US FTA.
13.11.11	President Lee attends Asia–Pacific Economic Cooperation forum in Hawaii.

18–19.11.11	President Lee attends ASEAN+3 summit, East Asia summit and ROK–China–Japan trilateral meeting in Bali.
22.11.11	National Assembly passes ROK–US FTA.
23.11.11	US and ROK agree to seek improvements to the Status of Forces Agreement, following a series of crimes committed by US military personnel in ROK.
06.12.11	Japan returns 1,205 volumes of ancient Korean archives, seized during colonial period, to ROK under full Korean ownership.
12.12.11	Members of crew of Chinese fishing boat clash with 2 ROK coastguard vessels in Yellow Sea; one death, one injury. 15.12.11, protests outside Chinese embassy in Seoul.

NORTH KOREA

01.01.11	Joint new year editorial from *Rodong Sinmun*, *Chosŏn Inmingun* and *Ch'ŏngnyŏn Chŏnwi*.
12.01.11	Head of United States Joint Chiefs of Staff says DPRK missiles and nuclear technology pose serious threat to the US.
10.02.11	DPRK confirms outbreaks of foot and mouth disease.
16.02.11	Kim Jong Il's 69th birthday marked.
08–11.03.11	Thomas Curley, CEO of Associated Press, visits DPRK, seeks opening of AP bureau.
12–14.03.11	Extensive DPRK media coverage of Tohoku earthquake and tsunami of 11.03.11. DPRK Red Cross sends message of condolence to Japanese Red Cross, 14.03.11; donates US$100,000, 24.03.11.
14.03.11	NK arrests 2 Japanese in Rasŏn on charges of drug trafficking and counterfeiting. Confirms it will take legal action against them, 05.05.11.
19.03–03.04.11	12-member delegation of DPRK economic officials makes private visit to US to tour US industry.
24.03.11	Following fact-finding visit to DPRK, 21.02–10.03.11, United Nations World Food Programme (WFP), Food and Agriculture Organisation (FAO) and UN Children's Fund (UNICEF) publish rapid food security assessment.
03.04.11	DPRK condemns Japanese government's authorisation on 30.03.11 of school text books claiming Tokto islands as Japanese territory; and Japanese diplomatic Blue Book for 2011 for repeating claim on 01.04.11.
07.04.11	4th session of 12th Supreme People's Assembly (SPA) convenes in Pyongyang.
12.04.11	US reveals US citizen Jun Young-su under investigation in DPRK for 'crime against the regime'. Jun detained since November 2010. 14.04.11, DPRK announces it is preparing to indict Jun for unauthorised religious activities.
15.04.11	Kim Il Sung's 99th birthday celebrated.
26–28.04.11	Delegation of 'The Elders', consisting of former US president Jimmy Carter, former Finnish prime minister Martii Ahtisaari, former Norwegian prime minister Gro

	Brundtland and former Irish president Mary Robinson, visits DPRK as part of its tour to China, DPRK and ROK, 24–29.04.11.
29.04.11	WFP and UNICEF launch appeal for US$200 million for emergency aid for DPRK.
29.04.11	SPA announces establishment of special zone for international tours in Mt Kŭmgang area. Law to encourage foreign investment in the resort announced, 02.06.11.
20–26.05.11	Kim Jong Il makes unofficial visit to China; meets President Hu Jintao, 25.05.11.
24–28.05.11	Robert King, special US envoy on DPRK human rights, visits DPRK for consultation on 'humanitarian issues', expresses regret over Jun Young-su case. Jun released without charge, 28.05.11.
06–17.06.11	5-member team of EU officials visits DPRK to assess food needs.
08.06.11	Ground-breaking ceremony for DPRK–China joint economic zone at Hwanggŭmp'yong and Wihwa islands in Amnŏk river estuary. Law on Hwanggŭmp'yong–Wihwa economic zone adopted, 09.12.11.
20.06.11	KCNA reports DPRK working on developing rare earth minerals for economic growth.
23.06.11	President Obama extends national emergency in relation to DPRK. (First declared in 2008, has to be renewed yearly as legal basis for sanctions.)
23.06–01.07.11	KCNA director visits US at invitation of AP; signs agreement, 29.06.11, on opening of AP news bureau in DPRK.
25.06.11	Typhoon Meari hits western parts of DPRK.
27.06.11	Universities reported to be closing until April 2012 to allow students to undertake construction work.
04.07.11	EU announces it will provide DPRK with food aid worth US$14.5 million; insists on strict monitoring system.
04–05.07.11	Gazprom delegation visits DPRK, has talks with DPRK ministry of oil industry.
07.07.11	*Washington Post* reports claim by A. K. Khan, former Pakistani nuclear scientist, that DPRK paid US$3 million in bribes to Pakistani military officials in late

	1990s for nuclear technology. Pakistani government dismisses report.
09–12.07.11	China and DPRK mark 50th anniversary of bilateral treaty of friendship and mutual assistance.
12–15.07.11	Heavy rain floods 15,000 hectares (50,000 acres) of farmland; coal mines damaged.
16–30.07.11	Foreign Minister Pak Ui Jun visits Mongolia, Indonesia, Malaysia and Singapore; attends ministerial meeting of ASEAN Regional Forum in Indonesia.
24.07.11	Provincial and local elections held; 99.97% turnout, all candidates voted for.
28.07–08.08.11	KCNA reports severe damage caused late June–mid-July and late July–early August by heavy rain and typhoons.
06.08.11	ROK Red Cross reports US Red Cross and DPRK diplomatic mission in New York reached agreement in May on exchange of letters between DPRK residents and relatives in US.
07–09.08.11	Typhoon Muifa hits western coastal regions of DPRK, causing loss of life and injury.
08.08.11	Russia announces it will give 50,000 tons of food aid to DPRK through WFP. 1st shipment arrives in DPRK, 19.08.11; final shipment arrives 04.10.11.
18.08.11	USAID announces it will provide emergency aid worth US$900,000 from private organisations following floods in DPRK. Supplies arrive, 04.09.11.
20–25.08.11	Kim Jong Il visits Siberia and Far East region of Russia, meets President Medvedev, 24.08.11; visits northeast region of China, 25–27.08.11.
13–20.09.11	DPRK minister of oil industry leads delegation to Russia. 15.09.11, agreement between DPRK and Russia to set up joint working group to implement gas pipeline project.
14.09.11	*Izvestiya* reports Russia will write off most of DPRK debt owed to former Soviet Union.
13.10.11	Freight railway test run between Rasŏn and Khasan in Russia.
17–21.10.11	Valerie Amos, UN under-secretary-general and emergency relief co-ordinator, visits DPRK to assess humanitarian position; reports worsening situation.

18–21.10.11	US and DPRK hold working-level talks in Bangkok on resumption of Missing in Action (MIA) programme, following DPRK's acceptance of US request for talks, 19.08.11. Agreement to resume joint searches, 21.10.11.
21.10.11	French Prime Minister François Fillon, speaking in Seoul, announces France opened a cultural co-operation bureau in Pyongyang earlier in October.
10.11.11	2nd consignment of 50,000 tons of food aid donated by Russia to DPRK arrives in the country.
23.11.11	KCNA reports DPRK has adopted law on prevention of damage from earthquakes and volcanoes.
30.11.11	DPRK states construction of experimental light-water reactor (LWR) and of low enriched uranium for provision of raw materials is progressing.
04.12.11	Woodrow Wilson International Center for Scholars publishes dossier specifying DPRK participation in Vietnam War through dispatch of pilots for MiG fighter aircraft.
15–16.12.11	US agrees to deliver 240,000 tons of food aid to DPRK over coming 12 months.
17.12.11	Death of Kim Jong Il following a heart attack. 19.12.11, KCNA announces death. Mourning period of 17.12.11–29.12.11 is set.
19.12.11	DPRK test-fires 2 short-range missiles off east coast.
20.12.11	US Secretary of State Hillary Clinton expresses deep concern with well-being of people of DPRK in period of national mourning.
24.12.11	*Rodong Sinmun* refers to Kim Jong Un as 'supreme commander' of Korean People's Army (KPA).
28.12.11	Funeral of Kim Jong Il in Pyongyang. Live broadcast of ceremony.
29.12.11	Memorial service for Kim Jong Il in Pyongyang. Kim Yong Nam describes Kim Jong Un as supreme leader of party, army and people.
30.12.11	Political Bureau of Central Committee of KWP announces Kim Jong Un has assumed command of KPA in accordance with Kim Jong Il's behest of 08.10.11.

INTER-KOREAN RELATIONS AND SIX PARTY TALKS

03–07.01.11 Stephen Bosworth, US special envoy for DPRK, visits Seoul, Beijing and Tokyo to discuss next steps on DPRK policy.

05–14.01.11 DPRK–ROK exchange of proposals. DPRK government, political parties and social organisations propose unconditional reopening of dialogue to resolve current crisis between countries, 05.01.11; proposal repeated, 08.01.11 and 14.01.11, by Committee for Peaceful Reunification of Fatherland; ROK rejects DPRK's proposal, 10.01.11. Further exchange of proposals on specific issues, 10–12.01.11.

11.01.11 US Defence Secretary Robert Gates urges DPRK to impose moratorium on nuclear and missile testing.

13.01.11 ROK blocks access to internet sites using DPRK national web domain suffix .kp, as supplying 'illegal information'.

04.02.11 Russia confirms it does not oppose UNSC discussion of DPRK's uranium enrichment programme (UEP).

05.02.11 31 DPRK citizens reach Yŏnp'yŏng island by fishing boat. 4 ask to stay in ROK, despite repeated attempts by DPRK to get ROK to return them; remaining 27 return to DPRK, 27.03.11.

08–09.02.11 DPRK and ROK hold working-level military talks at P'anmunjŏm; end with no agreement on date for future talks.

23.02.11 China reported to have blocked UNSC from adopting report condemning DPRK's UEP.

26.02.11 ROK says it cannot agree to resume Six Party Talks on DPRK nuclear programmes until DPRK's UEP issue is defined as 'violation of Security Council resolutions that should be stopped'.

27.02, 01.03.11 DPRK threatens physical response to ROK and US annual joint military drills and against ROK facilities engaged in psychological warfare.

28.02.11 ROK says it has no plans to seek return of US nuclear weapons to peninsula, citing DPRK–ROK 1991 denuclearisation agreement. US National Security Council says it has no plans to reintroduce nuclear weapons.

10.03.11	DPRK official, speaking at Geneva Disarmament Conference, describes DPRK as 'nuclear weapons state'.
19.03.11	Kim Jong Il reported to have sent verbal message to family of Chung Ju-yung, former chairman of Hyundai Group, to commemorate 10th anniversary of his death.
20.03.11	DPRK military accuses US troops in ROK of trespassing into Demilitarised Zone on over 50 occasions between 01.03.11 and 08.03.11, threatens 'human damage' if such provocations continue.
24.03.11	UN Human Rights Council passes resolution deploring human rights abuses in DPRK. DPRK reacts angrily, 28.03.11.
29.03.11	DPRK and ROK geologists meet at Munsan (in ROK), agree on need for joint study of potential volcanic activity from Mt Paektu.
04.04.11	ROK approves donation of humanitarian food aid for DPRK children by 2 civic groups.
07–12.04.11	Kim Kye Gwan, 1st vice-foreign minister of DPRK, visits China for discussions with Wu Dawei, Chinese special representative for Korean peninsula affairs, on resuming Six Party Talks. China proposes nuclear delegates of DPRK and ROK first hold dialogue.
08.04.11	SPA formally annuls Hyundai Asan's rights at Mt Kŭmgang resort.
12.04.11	2nd session of talks between DPRK and ROK geologists at Kaesŏng; agreement to make on-site survey of Mt Paektu in June 2011.
22.04.11	DPRK military warn ROK they may direct fire at areas of leafleting from ROK side. Warning repeated, 30.05.11 and subsequently.
09.05.11	President Lee Myung-bak proposes inviting Kim Jong Il to Seoul for 2nd Nuclear Security summit in March 2012, if DPRK agrees to give up nuclear programmes. Repeats invitation, 13.06.11.
09.05.11	ROK permits 5 civic groups to deliver food and medical aid to DPRK worth US$769,000.
16–18.05.11	Stephen Bosworth visits ROK, meets Wi Sung-lac, ROK chief negotiator on Six Party Talks. 17.05.11, DPRK foreign minister says DPRK ready to honour

	19 September 2005 Joint Statement on denuclearisation of peninsula.
01.06.11	DPRK National Defence Commission reveals that DPRK and ROK held secret talks from 09.05.11, in which ROK proposed 3 summit meetings over the coming 9 months. No agreement was reached, since ROK insisted that DPRK apologise for Ch'ŏnan and Yŏnp'yŏng incidents. 02.06.11, ROK regrets that contacts have been made public.
03.06.11	KPA threatens military retaliation against ROK military for using pictures of 3 Kims as targets during firing drills.
10.06.11	US Assistant Secretary of State Kurt Campbell supports ROK view that an inter-Korean dialogue should take place before resumption of Six Party talks or US–DPRK talks.
17.06.11	DPRK announces it will dispose of ROK assets at Mt Kŭmgang resort under new law on resort; asks ROK companies to visit resort by 30.06.11 to discuss issue.
29.06.11	ROK team of officials and representatives of investors travels to Mt Kŭmgang, but meeting fails. 30.06.11, DPRK requests ROK firms with assets at Mt Kŭmgang to submit proposals on property adjustment by 13.07.11.
13.07.11	2nd meeting between DPRK and ROK on ROK assets at Mt Kŭmgang resort fails to make progress. DPRK asks ROK investors to provide plans by 29.07.11.
22.07.11	DPRK and ROK officials charged with nuclear discussions meet in margins of ASEAN Regional Forum in Bali, agree to further joint efforts. Foreign ministers of DPRK and ROK meet briefly, 23.07.11, in same forum.
26.07, 02.08.11	ROK civic group delivers 300 tons of flour aid on each date to DPRK. DPRK accepts video monitoring.
26.07–02.08.11	Kim Kye Gwan visits US, meets Stephen Bosworth, 28.07. and 29.07.11.
29.07.11	Arrest of 5 people in ROK alleged to be members of pro-DPRK underground group Wangjaesan.

29.07.11	DPRK notifies ROK it will dispose of ROK assets at Mt Kŭmgang resort, proposes alternatives for ROK investors, with deadline of 3 weeks.
01.08.11	DPRK repeats its commitment to early resumption of Six Party Talks without preconditions and to principle of simultaneous action.
03.08.11	ROK Red Cross offers humanitarian aid worth US$4.7 million to DPRK Red Cross in wake of floods. 04.08.11, DPRK asks ROK to provide food, cement and heavy construction equipment. ROK refuses request. In absence of response from DPRK, ROK cancels offer of aid, 04.10.11.
19.08.11	Hyundai Asan officials visit Mt Kŭmgang, but no outcome to visit. 22.08.11, DPRK says it will dispose of ROK property at resort, orders ROK-employed staff to leave. Staff leave, 23.08.11.
24.08.11	Kim Jong Il, on visit to Russia, says DPRK ready to return to Six Party Talks without preconditions and to impose moratorium on tests of nuclear weapons. DPRK and Russia agree on resumption of Six Party Talks.
03–07.09.11	ROK Buddhist delegation visits DPRK. 05.09.11, holds joint ceremony with DPRK monks at Myohyangsan, to mark millennium of completion of Tripitaka Koreana.
12–15.09.11	Chung Myung-whun, conductor of Seoul Philharmonic Orchestra, visits DPRK, reaches agreement on promoting joint performances.
21.09.11	DPRK and ROK chief nuclear negotiators meet in Beijing, but fail to agree on terms to resume Six Party Talks.
21–24.09.11	Leaders of seven major religions in ROK visit DPRK.
13.10.11	Kim Jong Il, in written interview with Itar-Tass, renews call for quick resumption of Six Party Talks without preconditions.
24–25.10.11	US and DPRK hold 2nd session of talks in Geneva to discuss resumption of Six Party Talks. Some progress noted, but no major breakthrough.

28.10.11 DPRK–ROK working-level meeting to discuss resumption of joint excavation of Manwŏldae royal palace in Kaesŏng.
02–05.11.11 Group of ROK Protestant church leaders visit DPRK.
08.11.11 ROK authorises donation of medical aid worth US$6.94 million to DPRK, to be directed through World Health Organisation.
14–23.11.11 Joint DPRK–ROK safety survey of site of Manwŏldae royal palace. 8 ROK experts and workers enter DPRK, 24.11.11, to participate in month-long preservation and restoration project.
21.11.11 UN General Assembly 3rd Committee adopts resolution on DPRK human rights' abuses. DPRK dismisses resolution, 24.11.11.
23.11.11 ROK military stages exercises near Yŏnp'yŏng island to mark 1st anniversary of Yŏnp'yŏng incident. 24.11.11, KPA supreme command threatens attack on ROK presidential mansion if any fire from ROK enters DPRK territory.
05.12.11 ROK announces it will donate humanitarian aid worth US$5.65 million to DPRK through UNICEF.
14.12.11 Coalition of ROK private civic groups delivers food aid across ROK–DPRK border. DPRK agrees to monitoring.
20.12.11 ROK government issues statement on Kim Jong Il's death expressing sympathy for people of DPRK, but sends no official condolence delegation; permits only the families of the late Kim Dae-jung and the late Chung Mong-hun to pay visit of condolence to DPRK.
26–27.12.11 Lee Hee-ho, widow of Kim Dae-jung, and Hyun Jeong-eun, chair of the Hyundai Group, visit Pyongyang to offer condolences on Kim Jong Il's death.

Chronologies prepared by Susan Pares from the following sources: Cankor (Canada–Korea Electronic Information Service), *Comparative Connections*, *DPRK Business News*, Korea Focus, Korea.net, *Korea: People and Culture*, North Korea Newsletter, *Vantage Point*. The assistance of J.E. Hoare is gratefully acknowledged.

SOUTH KOREA IN 2011: DOMESTIC POLITICS, THE ECONOMY AND SOCIAL ISSUES

Patrick Köllner

1 INTRODUCTION

Compared to preceding years, 2011 was a relatively quiet year in the Republic of Korea (ROK—South Korea) in terms of domestic politics and the economy. This is not to say that nothing exciting happened. For example, the Seoul mayoral election in October produced a major upset when disenchanted voters in the capital chose a non-party candidate to lead South Korea's centre of power and commerce. This event rattled both the governing Grand National Party (GNP) as well as the main opposition party, the Democratic Party (DP), both of which were deeply engulfed in factional struggles and presented themselves in a fairly uninspired manner to the public in 2011. In view of the upcoming parliamentary and presidential elections in 2012, the 'Seoul shock' of October 2011 created momentum in both the governing party and the opposition camp to close ranks—though whether both sides would be able to do so effectively remained an open question at the end of the year. Thus, even though South Korean domestic politics in 2011 lacked the big stories, such as mass protests or emotions running high over the deaths of former presidents, that had attracted international attention in preceding years, it offered interesting developments beyond the more tedious business—at least for the non-partisan observer—of cabinet reshuffles, parliamentary gridlock and the occurrence of more or less petty political scandals, of which there was quite a bit again. While domestic politics in South Korea are often not pretty, democracy as such is stable in the ROK, which is no small feat in a region in which there are only three other firmly established democracies: India, Japan and Taiwan.[1]

---

[1] The Economist Intelligence Unit (EIU) goes even further, judging Japan and South Korea to be the only two 'full democracies' in Asia. While the ROK was rated highly in the EIU 2011 Democracy Index with respect to the electoral process and

Turning to the national executive, 2011 saw President Lee Myung-bak enter his fourth and penultimate year in office—a constitutionally enshrined term limit bars the head of state from (immediate) re-election. Support for the incumbent hovered around 30-plus percent, which is not too bad for a South Korean president nearing the end of his stay in the Blue House. While many South Koreans do not question Lee's commitment to the job, his actual performance record has been a mixed one. While his administration has not been able to deliver on its ambitious economy-related campaign pledges, encapsulated in the immodest '747' vision,[2] the ROK mastered the financial and economic crisis, which started soon after Lee had taken office, remarkably well.[3] Moreover, while many South Koreas rightly bemoan increased social inequality and job insecurity as well as rising housing prices and education-related expenses plus growing living costs in general, it is also true that South Korea is beginning to catch up with Japan in terms of per capita income and is also doing well more broadly in macro-economic terms.

Finally, while inter-Korean relations have not made any headway under Lee's watch, South Korea has been able to raise its international profile in recent years. As part of translating the current government's 'Global Korea' vision into practice, the ROK has, among other things, engaged vigorously in summit diplomacy by staging the G20 Summit in 2010 and the Nuclear Security Summit in 2012, both in Seoul, and in between in 2011, in Busan (Pusan), the perhaps less glittery but nonetheless large-scale Fourth High-level Forum on Aid Effectiveness.[4] Also, despite not everyone in South Korea being happy about it,

---

pluralism, it did less well in terms of political participation—given, among other things, declining turnouts in national elections—and in terms of political culture— given the adversarial style of (party) politics. See the relevant report at: http://www.eiu.com/Handlers/WhitepaperHandler.ashx?fi=Democracy_Index_Final_ Dec_2011.pdf&mode=wp (accessed 6 June 2012).

[2] An annual economic growth rate of 7 percent, per capita income of US$40,000, and the ROK becoming the seventh largest economy in the world by 2012, see *Korea Yearbook 2008*, pp. 15–18.

[3] See Werner Pascha, 'South Korea's Economic Policy Response to the Global Financial Crisis', in: *Korea 2010: Politics, Economy and Society*, pp. 135–64; also *Korea 2011: Politics, Economy and Society*, pp. 31–32.

[4] For an official summary of this mega-event see the OECD's website at: http://www.oecd.org/document/12/0,3746,en_2649_3236398_46057868_1_1_1_1,00. html (accessed 6 June 2012). See also Philipp Olbrich and David Shim (2012), 'South Korea as a Global Actor: International Contributions to Development and Security', *GIGA Focus International Edition*, no. 2 (2012), for a brief overview and assessment of some aspects of the ROK's raised international profile. Online: http://www.giga-

the Lee Myung-bak administration has forcefully pushed the free trade drive started by earlier governments, culminating in 2011 in the entering into force of the Korea–EU Free Trade Agreement (FTA) and the ratification of the Korea–US Free Trade Agreement.[5] In sum, South Koreans by now know a lot about the strong and weak points of the incumbent administration.

Achievements in the area of free trade aside, officials in South Korea took pride in 2011 in the fact that the country's international trade volume passed the US$1 trillion threshold that year, making South Korea only the ninth country in the world to have managed this feat. Some other economic figures were also impressive, e.g. a nominal gross domestic product (GDP) of over US$1.1 trillion, putting the ROK's economy at 15th place in the word, just below Mexico's,[6] and a per-capita income of around US$30,000 in terms of purchasing power parity.[7] Driven by a strong trade performance and more modest growth in private and government consumption, the South Korean economy overall grew healthily by 3.6 percent in 2011. In spite of higher inflation and the growing overhang of household debt, consumer sentiment was good, not least due to robust job creation in 2011, bringing employment back to pre-crisis levels. These and other developments are covered in more detail in the following pages.

2 THE APRIL BY-ELECTIONS AND THEIR CONSEQUENCES

On 26 January, the Supreme Court confirmed an earlier verdict of a district court, which had sentenced the incumbent governor of Gangwon (Kangwŏn) province, Lee Kwang-jae from the DP, to a one-year prison term and a fine of 114 million won (US$102,000) for having been bribed by Park Yeon-cha, the CEO of the shoemaking company Taekwang Industry. The Supreme Court also upheld a ruling against a member of the National Assembly, Suh Gab-won (also of the DP),

---

hamburg.de/dl/download.php?d=/content/publikationen/pdf/gf_international_1202.pdf).

[5] On the ROK's free trade drive see the contribution by Patrick Flamm and Patrick Köllner to this volume.

[6] According to preliminary figures from the International Monetary Fund quoted on Wikipedia. Online: http://en.wikipedia.org/wiki/List_of_countries_by_GDP_(nominal) (accessed 6 June 2012).

[7] See EIU, *Country Report South Korea*, May 2012, p. 16. Online: http://www.eiu.com/public.

who had been given of a fine of 12 million won for having also received bribes from Park. The Supreme Court rulings marked another round in the so-called Shoegate scandal, which had started in December 2008, when Park was arrested for having evaded large amounts of taxes and for having engaged in bribery. Investigations eventually came to target a total of 21 people in politics and government, including former President Roh Moo-hyun, who amidst these investigations committed suicide in May 2009 (see *Korea 2010: Politics, Economy and Society*, pp. 14–16). Verdicts in the cases of Park himself and a few others were still pending as of early 2011. As a consequence of the Supreme Court ruling, Governor Lee and Representative Suh were stripped of their respective positions as their fines exceeded one million won, the legally relevant threshold triggering such consequences. Lee, a prominent liberal politician, was also barred from standing for public office for ten years (*Korea Herald*, 27 January 2011).

Lee's loss of office necessitated a by-election for the governorship in Gangwon province. This was held on 27 April, when by-elections for three National Assembly seats and for 28 seats in local assemblies also took place. These by-elections were seen as a barometer for the general political mood in South Korea. Overall, the ruling GNP did not do well in the by-elections, being able to win only one National Assembly seat and 14 of the local assembly seats. The Assembly seat won by the GNP went to the former governor of South Gyeongsang (Kyŏngsang), Kim Tae-ho, who had been nominated in August 2010 by President Lee as prime minister but had failed to obtain the job because of his shady ties to a corrupt businessman (see *Korea 2011: Politics, Economy and Society*, p. 28). After having kept a low profile for a few months, Kim, who had not so long before been seen as a possible presidential contender in 2012, was thus now able to re-enter South Korean politics as a national representative of Gimhae (Kimhae) in South Gyeongsang province.[8] Whether Kim's election to the National Assembly will also enliven his prospects to eventually assume higher political office remains to be seen. In the two other races for Assembly seats, opposition candidates prevailed, if only by a narrow margin. In South Jeolla (Chŏlla) province, a candidate from the far-left Democratic Labour Party (DLP) won against competition from six independents, five of whom had quit the DP to campaign for the

---

[8] In the by-election Kim beat Rhyu Si-min, leader of the small People's Participation Party.

seat—again underlining the fractious character of the main opposition party. The DP's leader, Sohn Hak-kyu, a former governor of Gyeonggi (Kyŏnggi) province, won a tight race in Bundang (Pundang), south of Seoul, against former GNP chairman Kang Jae-sup. The win bolstered Sohn's chances to become the main opposition party's candidate in the 2012 presidential election. Finally, the governorship in Gangwon went to Choi Moon-soon from the DP, the ROK's most northern province thus remaining in the hands of the main opposition party. Choi, in a curious set-up, beat Ohm Ki-young, who had been Choi's successor as head of the Munhwa Broadcasting Corporation, a major national broadcaster (EIU, April 2011, p. 11; and May 2011, p. 11).

In reaction to the poor faring of the GNP in the by-elections, President Lee partially reshuffled the cabinet in early May, with five new ministers being replaced. Bahk Jae-wan, for one, assumed the helm of the ministry for strategy and finance after having served before as labour minister. Such cabinet reshuffles take place quite frequently in the ROK in order to give the government a fresh coat of paint. As a consequence, ministers rarely serve for more than two years in office (EIU May 2011, p. 12, and June 2011, p. 11).[9] The ruling party also experienced changes in the aftermath of the by-elections, as the party's leadership resigned en masse to take responsibility for the defeats. An opinion poll taken in early May indicated that for the first time the DP had overtaken the GNP in terms of public support. Before the GNP leadership election, scheduled to take place on 4 July, GNP lawmakers chose Hwang Woo-yea, described in the media as a 'reformist', to become their new floor leader. The GNP's leadership had preferred a different candidate but did not prevail (EIU June 2011, p. 12). An emergency panel of the GNP took charge of preparing the party's national convention in July. Members of this panel agreed that 'factional disputes within the party [needed] to be eradicated once and for all in order for the party to truly renovate itself' (*Korea Herald*, 12 May 2012).

---

[9] A further cabinet reshuffle took place in late August, when three ministers were exchanged. Most notably, Hyun In-taek, the unification minister known for propagating a hard line towards North Korea, was replaced by Yu Woo-ik, a former geography professor, who had also served as the ROK ambassador to China. Yu subsequently called for a more flexible approach towards the North. In September, Choi Joong-kyu resigned as minister of the knowledge economy after two million South Koreans had suffered from temporary power blackouts during a heat wave (EIU, October 2011, p. 13).

The election of a new chairperson and new council members, however, nearly had to be postponed after a district court in Seoul had found the GNP's revised constitution unlawful—the revision, introducing new leadership election procedures, had lacked confirmation by the necessary quorum. Such a quorum was finally achieved in an emergency session of the party's national committee that took place on 2 July, i.e. only two days before the party convention. Out of seven contenders competing for the GNP's chairmanship, Hong Joon-pyo, a former prosecutor and four-term lawmaker, emerged victorious. Hong hailed neither from the president's camp within the ruling party nor from the anti-mainstream faction around Park Geun-hye, who in 2011 tried to consolidate her chances to become the ruling party's candidate in the 2012 presidential election. President Lee and Ms Park, who are not exactly close friends, had met in early June in what was their first official meeting in a year. At the end of the same month, Lee also met with opposition leader Sohn Hak-kyu in what constituted the first official get-together between the president and the head of the opposition in nearly three years. The two politicians remained apart on a number of issues, including the pending ratification of the free trade agreement with the US, but at least agreed on the need to cut university tuition fees, which had doubled in the past ten years to on average US$8,000, one of the highest levels among OECD nations. In fact, a day before the meeting between Lee and Sohn, the GNP had already announced plans to reduce tuition fees by 30 percent by 2014 (EIU, July 2011, pp. 11, 13).

In the course of the year, the new GNP chairman Hong Joon-pyo confirmed his reputation as a maverick politician when he repeatedly criticised the president and his policies. Among other things, Hong took issue with Lee's poor personnel choices (see *Korea 2011: Politics, Economy and Society*, pp. 27–29), the lack of a governmental 'control tower' to deal with crisis situations, and the president's hard-line stance towards North Korea.[10] It became ever clearer that Hong and the president were not reading from the same page, and more broadly, that President Lee was increasingly perceived even within his own party not only as a 'lame duck' but also a liability with a view to

---

[10] Hong himself visited the Kaesong Industrial Complex in late September and argued for a more flexible approach towards the North (see also the contribution by Sabine Burghart in this volume).

the GNP's prospects in the 2012 parliamentary and presidential elections (EIU, August 2011, p. 12).

3 THE SEOUL MAYORAL ELECTION AND PARTY MERGERS ON THE LEFT

Unexpectedly for everyone and certainly untimely for the GNP, another election took place earlier than that, a by-election for the mayorship in the capital of Seoul. This election had to be called after the incumbent, Oh Se-hoon from the GNP, had resigned on 26 August over a lost referendum. Oh had opposed the provision of free school lunches to all 810,000 elementary and middle-school pupils in the capital. He considered this practice an example of 'unaffordable populism' on the part of the DP-dominated Seoul City council and the city's progressive education superintendent Kwak No-hyun (who later lost his job over a bribery case). After having mobilised, with the help of conservative NGOs, the required 418,000 signatures (equivalent to 5 percent of Seoul's voters), Oh called a referendum on the issue with the aim of limiting free school lunch to pupils from needy families. Perhaps there was more at play than the provision of free school lunches in itself (for which there was support even within Oh's own party). Some observers at least saw Oh's move as a gambit to raise his profile in order to increase his chances for higher political office. Oh himself vehemently denied this and declared publicly that he would not seek the GNP's nomination for the 2012 presidential election. However, he upped the ante by declaring that he would resign as mayor if the referendum did not go his way. This in fact happened on 24 August, as the referendum failed when fewer than the required 30 percent of voters cast their votes. As a consequence Oh resigned (EIU, September 2011, p. 12, and October 2011, p. 13).

The necessary by-elections for the mayorship took place on 26 October. Using an intricate primary system, the progressive camp, consisting of the DP, the DLP and the splinter parties, the New Progressive Party and the People's Participation Party, chose a unified candidate. The chosen candidate, however, did not belong to the main opposition DP, much to the chagrin of the party's leadership. The DP's leader Sohn Hak-kyu even tendered his resignation but was persuaded—or so it was claimed on—to stay on. Park Won-soon, a human rights lawyer and social activist with no party affiliation (he had been a co-founder of the NGO People's Solidarity for Participatory Democracy), emerged victorious from the primary. Presenting himself as the 'people's candidate' and Seoul's first 'welfare mayor', he faced in the by-election Na Kyung-won, a female former judge and a rising star within the GNP, plus one other minor candidate. The election campaign itself involved quite a bit of mudslinging between the two main camps. It proved to be a close race that eventually tilted in Park's favour, when Ahn Chul-soo, a popular IT entrepreneur and dean of the graduate school of Convergence Science and Technology at Seoul National University, who himself had been rumoured to enter the mayoral race, threw his support behind the progressive candidate. Some polls indicated that Ahn might have won he had chosen to run himself. In the end he did not, and Park Won-soon won, gaining 53.4 percent (2.16 million votes) compared to 46.2 percent for Na (1.87 million votes). While Park did better among 20- to 40-year olds and in the northern and southwestern parts of the capital, Na received higher support from voters over 50 and in the southern parts (Seocho [Sŏch'o], Kangnam and elsewhere) of Seoul.[11]

While Park's election constituted of course a setback for the GNP and more specifically for Park Geun-hye, who had supported Na, the DP also emerged with a black eye from the mayoral election, not having been able to position its own initial candidate successfully. Furthermore, neither the GNP nor the DP could ignore the palpable disengagement of many voters from established parties, which manifested itself not only in the election of a candidate with no formal party affiliation but also in the public's interest in Ahn Chul-soo. Though it is unclear how deep-seated and sustainable the euphoria concerning him really is, Ahn might be tempted to join the 2012 presidential race. This in turn could significantly change that election's dynamics by adding a dark horse.[12] The ruling GNP inched closer to nominating Park Geun-hye by making her in December 2011 the chair of an emergency council to reform the party, and thus de

---

[11] See the *Economist*, 29 October 2011; EIU, November 2011, pp. 12–13; and Walter Klitz (and Sabine Burghart) (2011), 'Südkorea: Kommunale Nachwahlen mit nationaler Tragweite—Ohrfeige für das politische Establishment', in: Friedrich Naumann Stiftung für die Freiheit (ed.), *Bericht aus aktuellem Anlass*, no. 46 (2 November 2011).

[12] On the 'Ahn Chul-soo' phenomenon rocking South Korea in autumn 2011 see in somewhat more detail Daniel Schumacher (2011), 'Zwei politische Nobodys schockieren Koreas Regierende', Konrad Adenauer Stiftung (ed.), *Länderbericht Korea*, 28 October 2011; *Economist*, 1 October 2011; and EIU, October 2011, p. 12.

facto acting party leader. This step had been preceded earlier that month by the resignation of Hong as party chairman. Hong resigned amidst the continuing decline in the popularity of the governing party, which was also shaken by a number of scandals including the hacking into the website of the National Election Commission by the aide of a senior GNP parliamentarian on the day of the Seoul mayoral election. (It was reported that the aide, apparently acting on his own initiative, had wanted to prevent younger voters favouring Park Won-soon from locating their polling stations.) Hong had earlier on startled party colleagues by saying that he would resign if Park Geun-hye were to lead the party in the 2012 parliamentary election (EIU, January 2012, p. 14).

Elsewhere the 2012 parliamentary elections also cast their shadow ahead. Towards the end of 2011, the opposition camp moved closer together, if only somewhat. In one development, the Democratic Party, which at the time held 87 seats (out of a total of 299 seats) in the National Assembly, joined hands with the small, civic group-based Citizen Integration Party and with the Federation of Korean Trade Unions,[13] the larger and more moderate of two umbrella labour organisations in South Korea, to form on 16 December the new Democratic United Party (DUP, in Korean: Minju Tonghabdang [T'onghaptang]). A first party leader, to succeed the DP's Sohn Hak-kyu, was to be chosen at an inaugural congress of the DUP in January 2012. There were doubts though whether this merger would help to overcome the former DP's internal division between members hailing from the two southwestern Jeolla provinces, the party's heartland, and supporters of the late former president Roh Moo-hyun. Further to the left, after nearly a year of negotiations, three political entities merged to form the Unified Progressive Party (UPP, in Korean: Tonghapjinbodang [T'onghapchinbodang]). The UPP brought together the Democratic Labour Party (DLP), which is allied to the Korean Confederation of Trade Unions (see footnote 13), the People's Participation Party led by Rhyu Si-min, a health and welfare minister under Roh Moo-hyun, and a faction of the New Progressive Party, another small party that had split from the DLP in 2008 over a North Korea-related row.[14] At the time of the UPP's founding on 5 December, the party

---

[13] The other umbrella organisation being the more radical Korean Confederation of Trade Unions.

[14] See Joonbum Bae, 'The South Korean Left's "Northern Question"', in: *Korea Yearbook 2009: Politics, Economy and Society*, pp. 87–115.

held seven seats in the National Assembly (EIU, July 2011, p. 12, and December 2011, p. 12; *Korea Times*, 5 December 2012).

4 Parliament and the State Budget

When a governing party controls no less than 167 out of 299 seats in parliament, as the GNP did in the National Assembly in 2011, you might think that parliamentary affairs would run smoothly and very much reflect the government's agenda. Yet, the South Korean case confirmed again in 2011 that clear majorities do not easily translate into a smooth running of legislative affairs, especially if they are conducted in a climate of mistrust and adversity among the main parties. As in the preceding years of the 18th National Assembly, which started in 2008, parliamentary life in South Korea in 2011 was again characterised by a high degree of gridlock and impasses, punctuated by periods of hyper-activity when large numbers of bills were voted upon in rapid sequence. Only in mid-February, after a two-month hiatus, were the GNP and the DP able to agree on an extraordinary session of the National Assembly, which lasted for less than five weeks but saw the passing of 37 pending bills. At the end of June, the two main parties then agreed on a number of procedural reforms aimed at rationalising parliamentary proceedings and reducing related controversies. It was stipulated that the speaker of the National Assembly, a post given to the biggest party, was allowed to call for a vote without prior committee-based deliberation only in times of national emergencies. Also, according to the agreement, the budget bill for the following year was to be put before the full Assembly by 2 December. This is actually already mandated by the Constitution but has in practice never been achieved since 2002. There was also agreement on how to accelerate the handling of bills that languish in committees and how to block a filibuster (a tactic that is not, however, much resorted to in South Korea). Parliament was supposed to pass legislation on these procedural matters in September but, as in turned out, it eventually took until spring 2012 until relevant measures became effective (EIU, March 2011, p. 11, and July 2011, p. 12).

As an ordinary parliamentary session in June had left a number of important bills plus other contentious issues such as confirmation hearings and the parliamentary investigation of a banking scandal hanging up in the air, the GNP and the DP decided to convene another extraordinary session in August. Subsequently, in late November, the GNP used its parliamentary majority to ram ratification of the controversial free trade agreement with the US (plus related bills) through the National Assembly. Even though inter-governmental negotiations on the agreement had been started when Roh Moo-hyun was president (and a precursor of the DP had been in power), the DP effectively shifted course when Lee Myung-bak became president, using opposition to the agreement as a lightening rod for the opposition in the build-up to the parliamentary and presidential elections of 2012. A particularly discontented member of the socialist DLP even detonated a tear-gas canister inside the National Assembly to protest against the ratification. Fortunately, no one got hurt (EIU August 2011, p. 12, and December 2011, pp. 14–15).

Ill-will on the part of the main opposition party as a consequence of the railroading of the FTA ratification by the GNP nearly led to South Korea's entering the new year without a proper state budget. In that case the government would have needed emergency funding to pay government officials and so on. In the wake of Kim Jong Il's death, the two main parties, however, for once closed ranks and passed the budget (and related bills including a tax reform introducing a new income tax rate of 38 percent for income above the equivalent of US$259,000) on the very last day of 2011. The budget for 2012 saw a moderate overall increase in spending, especially on welfare issues— remember that 2012 was to be an important election year, bringing the overall budget to slightly over 325 trillion won (or US$290 billion). At an envisaged 1.1 percent of Gross National Product, South Korea's fiscal deficit however continued to be rather low in comparison to other OECD nations (EIU, January 2012, pp. 14, 17).

5 AFTER FUKUSHIMA: SOUTH KOREA AFFIRMS INCREASED RELIANCE ON NUCLEAR ENERGY

As noted in last year's volume, the current South Korean government has ambitious plans for the civilian use of nuclear energy, which it sees not only as necessary to lower the country's high dependence on energy imports[15] (and to tackle climate change), but also more broadly

---

[15] As a consequence of soaring oil prices, the value of the ROK's crude oil imports in 2011 for the first time passed the threshold of US$100 billion. According to gov-

as a 'new growth engine' for the ROK economy (see *Korea 2011: Politics, Economy and Society*, p. 37). South Korea is the world's fifth largest producer of nuclear energy, which accounts for 36 percent of the ROK's electric power output. How then did the government react to the nuclear catastrophe that occurred in neighbouring Japan on and after 11 March 2011? In late March, the government announced, after a nuclear safety meeting chaired by the prime minister, that all of the country's 21 nuclear reactors would undergo extensive safety checks within one month. (The reactors are concentrated in four plants located in South Jeolla, North Gyeongsang, and South Gyeongsang, which hosts two plants.) At the same time the government confirmed its nuclear energy policy 'while placing more emphasis on safety' (Yonhap, 28 March 2011). The ROK plans to finish five new reactors by 2014 and two more by 2017. A further 13 more reactors are planned to go online by 2030. By that date, nuclear energy is supposed to account for 59 percent of South Korea's electricity production (Yonhap, 24 December 2011).

Only two months after the Fukushima disaster, the ROK government had largely returned to business as usual in terms of nuclear policy. In mid-May, during a visit to South Korea's nuclear safety agency, President Lee confirmed the government's stance in this area, arguing that it would 'be moving backward to give up on the efficient and clean energy and Japan's nuclear accident should serve as a chance to make atomic power plants safer' (Yonhap, 17 May 2011). Lee also compared the risks of operating nuclear plants to that of flying aircraft, which had a low accident rate combined with a high fatality rate in such accidents. Still, should we not use aircraft because of that?, Lee asked rhetorically. The president also called on Japan and China to exchange information on nuclear safety as part of their trilateral co-operation. In late July, Korea Nuclear Fuel, a subsidiary of the national electricity company KEPCO announced that it planned to boost annual nuclear fuel production from 490 tonnes in 2011 to 820 tons by 2019 (Yonhap, 31 July 2011). And finally, late in the year, Korea Hydro and Nuclear Power Co. disclosed candidate sites in North Gyeongsang and in Gangwon province, where two plants with

---

ernment data released in early 2012, the import value of crude oil grew from US$78.7 billion in 2010 to US$108.7 billion in 2011, when the ROK imported 926 million barrels. In terms of value, crude oil accounted for over 19 percent of South Korea's imports in 2011. The ROK, which has no domestic oil resources, is the world's fifth largest buyer of crude oil (Yonhap news agency, 15 January 2012).

four reactors each are planned to be built. The company said that it would take the potential effects of tsunamis and earthquakes into account when designing the plants (Yonhap, 24 December 2011).

6 SOUTH KOREA'S ECONOMY IN 2011: THE BIG PICTURE

According to preliminary data, the ROK economy grew by 3.6 percent in 2011, driven mainly by another brisk export performance coupled with moderate growth in private consumption and facility investment. While such growth might be considered disappointing by South Koreans (and others) still used to the higher growth rates the country experienced in earlier years, it has to be noted that growth in 2011 was in tune with more recent growth rates (2009 and 2010 were exceptional; the setback and subsequent quick upswing in those years coming amidst and on the heels of a major crisis); that South Korea performed rather well in 2011 compared to other OECD nations; and that the ROK is slowly nearing mature-economy status, making high growth rates increasingly difficult to achieve. In sectoral terms, the manufacturing sector expanded by 7.2 percent in 2011, with general machinery, transport equipment and metal products doing particularly well, while the agricultural sector (including forestry and fishing) declined by 2 percent, mainly an effect of bad weather and an outburst of food-and-mouth disease. Construction was down by 4.6 percent amidst sluggish residential building activities, while the services sector grew moderately by 2.6 percent (*ROK Economic Bulletin*, April 2012, p. 44). Whereas many large companies continued to do well in 2011, the situation was much tougher for many small and medium enterprises struggling to meet costs and pay off loans.[16]

In 2011, exports constituted again the main driving force of the ROK economy. Exports of goods and (less importantly) services were equivalent to close to 58 percent of South Korea's gross national income (GNI) in 2011, marking a new all-time high in this regard. GNI per capita measured in dollar terms reached nearly US$22,500. Exports grew by 19 percent in 2011, while imports expanded by 23.3 percent. Taken together, South Korea's external trade in 2011 for the first time passed the US$1 trillion barrier. China was again by far the

---

[16] On this widening gulf see, for example, Christian Oliver and Song Jung-a, 'An Economy Divided', in: *Financial Times*, 30 May 2011, p. 7.

main destination for exports but also the biggest source of imports, with ROK exports to China reaching US$132.2 billion (+14.9 percent) and imports from the PRC amounting to US$86.4 billion (+20.8 percent) in 2011 (according to Korea International Trade Association data[17]). The US and Japan were the next most important export destinations (US$56.2 billion and US$39.7 billion, respectively) as well as, in reversed order, the next largest sources of imports (US$68.3 billion and US$44.6 billion, respectively). South Korea's top four export items in 2011 in terms of value were ships and related components (US$56.5 billion), petroleum products (US$51.6 billion), semiconductors (US$50.1 billion) and automobiles (US$45.3 billion), while import items were led by crude oil (US$100.8 billion), semiconductors (US$32.5 billion), natural gas (US$23.8 billion) and petroleum products (US$22.9 billion). Although the ROK's trade surplus declined to around US$30 billion in 2011, it was still substantial. The decline was not least due to the steep rise in energy prices, which drove up the value of such imports, in particular crude oil. Rising energy prices also contributed to higher inflation, especially producer prices, which went up significantly by 6.1 percent (see Table 1).

In spite of higher consumer inflation—and rising energy, food, housing and other prices were a concern for many South Koreans in 2011—private consumption grew by 2.3 percent, based on significant demand especially for durable and semi-durable goods. A main reason why private consumption picked up was undoubtedly the positive employment situation. The number of unemployed went down from 920,000 in 2010 to 855,000 in 2011 (see Table 1). However, the employment situation was not rosy for every group. For example, the youth unemployment rate (i.e. of those 15 to 29 years of age) remained well above average, reaching 6.8 percent in November 2011. Many new university graduates were having a hard time finding a job (see *Korea Herald*, 14 December 2011). In addition, South Korea notably has one of the highest rates of non-regular workers, i.e. people without a permanent work contract, among OECD countries. In August 2011, such non-regular workers accounted for 34.2 percent of the workforce or six million in total (EIU, December 2011, p. 13).

---

[17] Available at http://www.investkorea.org/InvestKoreaWar/work/eng/bo/conten... (accessed 12 June 2012).

Table 1   ROK basic economic data

	2007	2008	2009	2010	2011
GDP (billion won, at current prices)	975,013	1,026,452	1,065,037	1,173,275	1,237,128
GDP (billion US$)	1,049	931	834	1,015	1,116
GDP growth (%)	5.1	2.3	0.3	6.3	3.6
Per capita income (GNI base, in US$)	21,632	19,161	17,041	20,562	22,489
Exports (billion US$)	371.5	422.0	363.5	466.4	555.2
Imports (billion US$)	356.9	435.3	323.1	425.2	524.4
Trade balance (billion US$)	+14.6	-13.3	+40.4	+41.2	+30.8
Balance of payments (current account, billion US$)	+21.8	+3.2	+32.8	+29.4	+26.5
External debt position (billion US$, end of year)	333.4	317.4	345.7	359.4	398.4
International reserves (billion US$, end of year)	262.2	201.2	270.0	291.6	306.4
Inward foreign direct investment (bn US$, notification basis)	10.5	11.7	11.5	13.1	13.7
Consumer prices (%)	+2.5	+4.7	+2.8	+3.0	+4.0
Producer prices (%)	+1.4	+8.6	-0.2	+3.8	+6.1
Unemployed (in thousands)	783	769	889	920	855
Unemployment rate (%)	3.2	3.2	3.6	3.7	3.4

Note: Data for 2011 provisional.

Sources: Bank of Korea, *Monthly Statistical Bulletin*, 2012/4 and earlier editions; Bank of Korea, *Quarterly Bulletin*, March 2012; Ministry of Strategy and Finance, *Republic of Korea Economic Bulletin*, May 2012.

In terms of inward foreign direct investment, the ROK did relatively well in 2011 as relevant pledges grew by 4.6 percent year on year, reaching US$13.7 billion. Investment pledges by EU companies were up by 57.4 percent year on year, amounting to more than US$5 billion in 2011. US, Japanese and Chinese investors came next with official pledges of US$2.4 billion, US$2.3 billion and US$651 million, respectively (*Korea Herald*, 12 January 2012). Intensified conflict with North Korea in 2010 did not seem to have deterred many investors (though of course we cannot know for sure). Labour conflicts have always been an issue for foreign investors, though arguably less so in recent years. Still, South Korean unions are hardly docile. A two-month-long strike, the longest-ever bank strike in the ROK, took place in summer 2011 at Standard Chartered First Bank, the South Korean subsidiary of Standard Chartered. The UK-based bank had wanted to introduce performance-related pay schemes in its subsidiary and in the end, or so it appeared, prevailed in this regard. Other foreign companies might now be tempted to follow suit (EIU, September 2011, pp. 12–13).

7 Social Issues

It is well known that most South Koreans are hard-working and many thrive and excel in the country's competitive environment. Yet, for others the pressure is too high and some choose to opt out by committing suicide. In 2010 (more recent data are not yet available), South Korea had the highest suicide rate among OECD nations, with 31.2 such deaths per 100,000 people. (The OECD average stood at 11.3 per 100,000 people.) More than 40 people killed themselves each day in 2010, which represents a doubling of the suicide rate compared to ten years before and a five-fold increase since 1989. In fact, in 2010 suicide was the number one cause of death among South Koreans under 40 years of age (Yonhap, 8 September 2011). Among the people who committed suicide over the past ten years were a number of popular artists and athletes, as well as politicians and businesspeople such as former president Roh Moo-hyun, former Busan mayor Ahn Sang-Young, former South Jeolla governor Park Tae-young, and former Hyundai Asan chairman Chung Mong-hun.

While neighbouring Japan has also seen an alarming rise in the country's suicide rate, in South Korea the phenomenon occurred in the absence of a stagnating economy and related job losses, factors that have bedevilled Japan during the past two decades. For younger people, a stress factor includes the highly competitive education and examination system. To succeed in this system, 77 percent of all South Korean elementary to high school students spend on average 10.2 hours per week in cramming schools, which they attend after their usual school hours (*Neue Zürcher Zeitung*, 9 March 2011). While South Korean society's emphasis on education as a means to get ahead in life has paid out in macro terms, for some young Koreans the resultant pressure is more than they can bear. In 2009, 202 middle and high school students committed suicide. In the same year, the suicide rate among 15 to 24 year- olds stood at 15 per 100,000, compared to rates of ten in the United States, seven in China and five in the United Kingdom (*Economist*, 17 December 2011). While it is probably wrong to lay all the blame for the high suicide rate among young South Koreans on the country's competitive education and examination system, it certainly constitutes an important element in this regard. Observers also note that in some cases unemployment and bullying (offline and online) as well as Internet-co-ordinated suicide pacts play a role in the suicides of young South Koreans. Some measures have been taken by the national government and local authorities to prevent deaths such as installing emergency phones on bridges and barriers in subway stations, and setting up more suicide prevention systems.[18] Still, South Korean government and society will have to tackle the root causes of the high suicide rate in order to be able to turn the tide.

How to cope with unfavourable demographic developments constitutes a big challenge for many rich, poor and middle-income countries. The challenge is particularly onerous for South Korea, where the fertility rate has fallen from six children per woman some fifty years ago to around 1.2 in 2010, i.e. one of the lowest levels in the world. On the other hand, life expectancy, which stood at 52 years in 1960 and 58 years in 1970, had risen to on average 80 years by 2010 (77 years for men and 84 years for women). South Koreans who are today 35 years of age can expect to turn 100. As a consequence of these twin developments, the share of senior citizens aged 65 or above is estimated to double from 11 percent in 2010 to over 24 percent by 2030,

---

[18] See Lynn Herrmann, 'Suicide Rate in South Korea Doubles in Last Ten Years', in: *Digital Journal*, 5 September 2011. Online: http://www.digitaljournal.com/article/311163 (accessed 6 June 2012).

when South Korea will have one of the oldest societies in the world. Already by 2016, there are likely to be more senior citizens in the ROK than youngsters below the age of 14. These demographic developments arguably make for a bigger challenge to South Korea's society than a possible integration with the North (which, however, might slightly mitigate the South's demographic conundrum).

Current demographic developments raise tremendous tasks not only for government welfare and family-oriented policies but also for individual South Koreans. How well prepared are ROK citizens for this challenge? Not too well, according to a number of surveys. For example, a survey conducted in 2009 on behalf of the National Pension Service found that 'nearly seven out of every 10 people aged 50 or above had made no effective preparation for post-retirement life' (*Korea Herald*, 17 May 2011). Old-age poverty is a particular problem in the ROK. As noted by the *Economist*, '[i]n other rich countries, people between 66 and 75 are no more likely to be poor than the population as a whole. In Korea, they are three times as likely to be poor.'[19] Many of the over seven million 'baby boomers' in South Korea, i.e. people born after the Korean War between 1955 and 1963, find it especially difficult to put aside sufficient funds for their old age, when struggling already to pay their mortgages and to see their children through the expensive education system. Whereas in the olden days, elderly South Koreans could expect to live with their offspring, such constellations are becoming increasingly rare; today 'only 4.8 percent of the country's total households are extended family households having three generations or more as their members' (*Korea Times*, 26 January 2011). Small wonder then, perhaps, that some alarmist commentators refer to South Korea's unfavourable demographic development as a 'time bomb'. While the metaphor itself is not very apt, it might at least help to address demographic issues with a greater sense of urgency.

---

[19] 'South Korea's Economy: What Do You Do When You Reach the Top?', in: *The Economist*, 12 November 2011. Online: http://www.economist.com/node/21538104/print (accessed 16 November 2011).

NORTH KOREA IN 2011:
DOMESTIC DEVELOPMENTS AND THE ECONOMY

Rüdiger Frank

1 INTRODUCTION

This overview looks at domestic developments in the Democratic People's Republic of Korea (DPRK—North Korea) in 2011. Its structure follows the established practice of preceding volumes of *Korea: Politics, Economy and Society* and thus starts with a systematic analysis of the main regular events such as the joint New Year editorial and the annual session of the Supreme People's Assembly (SPA), based on official publications issued through the Korea Central News Agency (KCNA). The joint editorial, which is studied intensively in North Korea, provides insights into the strategic planning of the leadership, even though these are often obscured by repetitive and propagandistic phrases. The annual parliamentary session is the only regular official meeting of the top North Korean leadership that the public is informed about. Rare information on economic issues is provided, most importantly on the state budget. The parliamentary session is also a time for the announcement of personnel changes.

The overview will examine other outstanding events of the year, with a focus on the economy but also going beyond. The areas of interest common to all these analytical endeavours are leadership, ideology and general trends of development such as a 'neoconservative'[1] or 'neo-orthodox' trend the author has identified in North Korea in recent years. Against the background of the emergence of a new leadership in Pyongyang, such an assessment provides an important yardstick for developments in 2012 that will be discussed in next year's volume of this publication.

---

[1] See the author's overview articles on North Korea in *Korea Yearbook 2009: Politics, Economy and* Society, pp. 35–55, and *Korea 2010: Politics, Economy and Society*, pp. 29–53.

Kim Jong Il's death and the announcement of Kim Jong Un as successor on 19 December 2011 are discussed in more detail in a separate article in this volume and are therefore only briefly mentioned in this overview.

2 THE 2011 JOINT NEW YEAR EDITORIAL

2.1 Key topic: improvement of the people's standard of living

Since the death of Kim Il Sung, the most important regular programmatic publication of the year has been the joint New Year editorial. Starting in 1995, it is published each January simultaneously by the major media of the DPRK including the Party newspaper *Rodong Sinmun*. It is studied intensively in the country and is thus not a propaganda effort directed only at outside observers.

As in 2010, the key topic of the 2011 joint editorial was the 'improvement of the people's standard of living'. This theme was linked with a number of other goals and issues. As in the previous year, the connection between a further improvement of living standards and opening the gate towards a great and prosperous country (*kangsŏng taeguk*) in 2012 was emphasised. In 2010, the focus for related activities was both agriculture and light industry. The 2011 editorial highlighted only the latter as the 'major front', pointing to the already achieved goals of building up key industries and training the necessary human resources in the research and development (R&D) field that are now to serve as the foundations for leaping to the next level. We could also speculate that in January 2011, the food issue was no longer regarded as being as pressing as the year before, despite the pleas for international assistance made in 2010.[2]

A few noteworthy details could be observed in this regard. One is the repeated stress on consumer goods (*sobip'um*); they are explicitly mentioned eight times. Also stressed are the quality, diversity and competitiveness of these goods on the world market. This is hardly remarkable for a market economy. In the case of a state-socialist sys-

---

[2] Nonetheless, in March 2011, a food security assessment carried out by three UN humanitarian agencies working in the DPRK recommended the provision of large amounts of food to needy people. In July of the same year, the EU announced it would supply North Korea with food aid, and in August, USAID also undertook to donate food aid following severe floods. Russia was a further donor.

tem like the one in North Korea, however, a departure from the typical focus on producer goods, on mass production of a few standard items, and on quantity indicates a continuation of the shift to a new paradigm, or what we have called 'normalisation' in the past few years. North Korean comment about production 'on a modern, scientific basis' is reminiscent of East German rhetoric in the 1980s, when technological development was regarded as a cure-all for the ailing socialist economy. Computerised numerical control (CNC) equipment is duly mentioned in this connection, as it was in 2010.

The hint on international competitiveness adds to the overall impression of North Korea's becoming more 'normal' as it obviously aspires to a certain degree of export-led growth or at least acknowledges the need to earn hard currency. This is a belated fruit of the 2002 economic reforms and certainly also a result of continued Chinese efforts. The acknowledgement in the editorial of 'the people's diverse demands and tastes' could be read, with some optimism, as an expression of the development of a middle class.

Continuity can be discerned in the repetition of the 2010 emphasis on local or rural industries in connection with the production of consumer goods. This, too, is not to be taken for granted in a socialist system that would usually stress central planning and the major industries of the 'commanding heights'. The editorial adds some North Korean flavour by stressing production of 3 August consumer goods[3] and the need for import-substitution or, according to official North Korean language, production of materials 'on a Juche-oriented, domestic basis'.

2.2 Highlights of the editorial

2.2.1 Culture, technology and the environment

In addition to the central theme of improving the people's standard of living by stressing light industry, the editorial contained some other noteworthy details.

---

[3] The 3 August People's Consumer Goods Production Movement was based on guidance given by Kim Jong Il in 1984 at an exhibition of light industrial products. The idea was to identify and process unused resources, convert them into consumer goods, and then sell them in a way that appeared to be outside the centrally planned distribution channels (through special 3 August stores or markets).

The 2010 editorial had announced North Korea was an 'economic giant'.[4] In 2011, the country was also called a 'socialist cultural giant'.[5] This emphasis on culture shines through on a number of occasions, often related to the function of culture in giving people a break from their hard labour or in boosting their morale. In this connection, a passage on coal miners is interesting. North Korea holds large reserves of anthracite.[6] It is thus not surprising that in the editorial we find the usual passage stressing the contribution of coal mining to the country's economic success. However, the call for the whole country to 'inspire the coal miner's morale' is somewhat unusual and could be interpreted, with due caution, as the implicit reflection of a mood that needs such 'inspiration'.

Technology was another core issue. A scent of Great Leap emerges from calls to 'surpass in the shortest time the scientific and technical standards the world has reached', a goal voiced in connection with the by now already established buzz-word 'CNC technology'. The ambitious 'cutting edge' (*ch'oech'ŏmdan*) is another keyword that appears in connection with technological development. It is interesting to note that 'the enemy's blockade' in technology is mentioned, forcing the DPRK to develop key technologies on its own. Against this background, it sounds much less like a deliberate policy when the editorial stresses that 'the principle of self-reliance should be applied thoroughly'. The slogan 'looking out over the world while keeping their feet firmly planted on their own land', as quoted in the editorial, has been seen frequently on the ground in North Korea.

A new policy first noted in the report on the Cabinet's work in April 2010 was also reflected in the 2011 editorial. What was announced by the prime minister as a 'new "sports myth" (*ch'eyuk sinhwa*)', supported by the creation of a number of sports universities, found its expression in the appeal to make North Korea 'widely known as a football and sports power'.

Given the rapidly increasing number of cars on the streets of Pyongyang, and the fact that the country has much more substantial

---

[4] This is a somewhat odd translation in the English KCNA version; the Korean original, *kyŏngje kangguk*, simply means 'economically strong country'.

[5] The original term is *sahoejuŭi munhwa kangguk*, i.e. a 'country strong in socialist culture'.

[6] The estimated size of the deposit is around 11.7 billion tons, worth around US$760 billion. For a detailed discussion of the North Korean mineral reserves, see Edward Yoon (2011), 'Status and Future of the North Korean Minerals Sector', in: *Korean Journal of Defense Analysis*, 23 (2), June 2011, pp. 191–210.

worries, the call to make Pyongyang a 'pollution free city' needs to be taken with a grain of salt. Nonetheless, as it has on a few occasions in the past, North Korean propaganda does mention environmental issues.

2.2.2 *Political balance of power*

As for the political balance of power, if we may so term it, the nature of mentioning the Party is instructive. I have interpreted the 2010 party conference as a widely visible step to upgrade the role of the Korean Workers' Party (KWP) as the primary instrument of leadership in North Korea. This impression is not contradicted by the editorial.

Calls to 'raise the Party's leadership role in every way' make one wonder why the Party's leadership role is stressed so explicitly and strongly: should it not be taken for granted? I have previously expressed my scepticism vis-à-vis a dichotomist perspective on power in North Korea as being the object of fierce competition between the Party and the military. Rather, I understand the ongoing power struggle as a fight for supremacy among groups that transcend both organisations, such as families. I therefore tend to interpret calls such as the above as the expression of succession-related debates. Will the Party lead North Korea, headed by a *primus inter pares*; or does the country need a powerful dictator who relegates the Party to the position of being his mere transmission belt? With this in mind, phrases like 'invariably defend the centre of unity and leadership despite the passage of time' and 'the Party's leadership system should be established more thoroughly in politics, the military, the economy and all other sectors' sound much less hollow.

The military is mentioned only in third place, after the economy and the Party have been covered. Even here, the supremacy of the Party is explicitly stated: 'The People's Army should firmly carry forward the precious tradition of absolutely trusting and following the Party and the leader and defending them unto death.' Signs of potential issues inside the military might be hidden in passages that stress the need to 'improve the command and management of units', in particular 'by enforcing strict military discipline'.

After covering these domestic topics, the editorial shifted its focus to unification, which it called the most vital task, but as usual accused the South Korean government of having betrayed the wish of the Korean people.

The editorial ended with what became the central slogan for 2011: a call to rally around the Party Central Committee headed by Kim Jong Il ('General' in the English version, 'Great Comrade' in the Korean version), which continued the previous trend to put the Party in the centre.

2.3 Ideology

Unlike the 2009 and 2010 editorials, neither 'socialist principles' nor the 'socialist planned economy' are mentioned in the 2011 editorial. The term 'socialism' appears, of course, but in phrases like 'socialist economic management of our own style', which is an expression of North Korean *chuch'e* nationalism, not of the original Marxist-Leninist principle.

The frequency of the use of key ideological terms has remained stable compared to the 2010 editorial which, it will be recalled, marked a sharp drop in such language over 2009. In the 2011 version, *sŏn'gun* (songun) was used 14 times (2009: 26; 2010: 13), socialism/socialist 12 times (2009: 27; 2010: 11), and *chuch'e* (juche) appeared eight times (2009: 14; 2010: 7).

This trend was continued in an even more pronounced way throughout 2011, as Graph 1 illustrates. It shows the development of the use of these terms in *all* KCNA articles over the past years. In absolute terms, only 'socialism/socialist' showed an increase; '*chuch'e*' remained stable, and '*sŏn'gun*' even dropped. In relative terms, the use of all three terms fell significantly. 'Socialism' reached the level of the reform period around 2002; the other two terms are at historical lows.

Such simple quantitative analyses of complex matters should be interpreted very carefully. However, it would also be wrong to ignore them as they provide one of the few ways to look behind the curtain of North Korea's massive and obscure state propaganda. With relative safety, we can state that the year 2011 has seen no renewed emphasis on the Military First policy, and that the neoconservative turn observed for 2008/2009 seems to be nearing at least a break, if not an end.

Graph 1   Number of English KCNA articles with the terms 'songun', 'socialism' and 'juche' (1997–2011, weighted)[7]

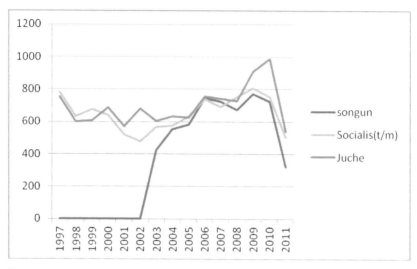

Source: Author's calculations based on www.kcna.co.jp.

2.4 *The leader(s)*

Like the 2009 editorial that followed what was thought to be a stroke on the part of the North Korean leader in August 2008, the 2011 editorial mentions Kim Jong Il's inexhaustible energy as exhibited through his on-the-spot guidances 'day and night, braving the biting cold and sultry weather, heavy rain and snowstorm'. Little is known about the actual number of such guidance trips; but it can be observed that the absolute number of related reports grew steadily from just 30 in 2001 to 346 in 2011. Displaying the results in weighted form seems to make limited sense in this case, as it is unlikely that the frequency of report-

---

[7] As the overall number of articles each year is different, the results were weighted by dividing the number of articles with the terms in question by the total number of that year's KCNA articles. We then multiplied the result by 4,000 and were thus able to restore a value on the y-axis that comes close to the original numeric dimension. For example: for the term *sŏn'gun*, 935 articles were counted in 2009, out of a total of 4,852 articles. The weighted value for *sŏn'gun* in 2009 is 935:4,852=0.1927; this result was multiplied by 4,000, yielding 771 (rounded), which is the numeric value used in the graph. This procedure was applied to all graphs analysing KCNA articles in this overview.

ing increases with the number of daily published KCNA articles. We thus include the absolute numbers in Graph 2.

Graph 2 Number of English KCNA articles with the terms 'on-the-spot guidance' and 'field guidance' (1997–2011, weighted and in absolute terms)

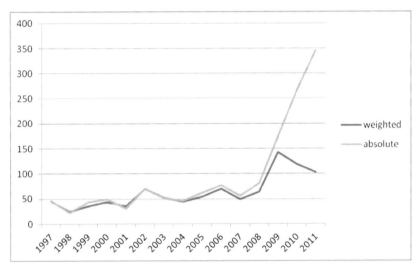

Source: Author's calculations based on www.kcna.co.jp.

A popular exercise in 'Pyongyangology' used to be looking at the titles used for Kim Jong Il.[8] In 2011, Kim Jong Il was mentioned ten times (in 2010: 19) in the English version of the editorial; in the Korean version, his name appears eight times (in 2010: 9). In Korean, he is addressed as 'Great Comrade' (*widaehan tongji*) or simply 'Great Kim Jong Il' four times, followed by 'Respected Comrade' (*kyongaehanŭn tongji*) two times. The latter is interesting because Kim Jong Un seems to have inherited that title during the first weeks of his life as the new leader of the DPRK. The English version differs markedly from the Korean version and from the editorial of 2010, when the title 'General' appeared only once. In the 2011 English version, he is called 'General' seven out of ten times. No other of the standard titles (General Secretary, Great Leader) is used.

---

[8] For obvious reasons, this will be undertaken for the last time in 2011. But there is no need to worry—it will certainly be continued for his son Kim Jong Un.

This seems confusing; a look at Graph 3 helps us to see the bigger picture beyond the confines of just one single document. Here, we find what has already become visible from Graph 1 (analysis of key ideological terms). The neoconservative turn that marked the end of the reform period seems to be over. The use of the Party title drops, the use of the worldly, management-oriented title 'Leader' increases. And despite the North's belligerent rhetoric (and our stereotypic images), the military titles still seem to play a minor role. Among the less frequently used titles for Kim Jong Un in 2011 was 'Sagacious General' (*yŏngmyŏnghan taejang*), while Kim Jong Il was reportedly called 'Dear Supreme Commander' in a North Korean TV programme aired on 8 January 2011.

Graph 3 Number of English KCNA articles with Kim Jong Il's titles (1997–2010, weighted)

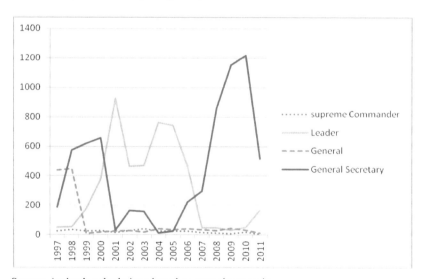

Source: Author's calculations based on www.kcna.co.jp.

3 THE ANNUAL PARLIAMENTARY SESSION

3.1 Overview

The fourth session of the 12th Supreme People's Assembly, the North Korean parliament, was held in Pyongyang on 7 April 2011.[9] Premier Choe Yong Rim (in 2010, Kim Yong Il) gave a report on the work of the cabinet (see below). As in 2010, Pak Su Gil, vice-premier and minister of finance, presented the report on the state budget. The third agenda item called 'organizational matter' concerned the shifting or replacement of personnel in government. Jon Pyong Ho was replaced by Pak To Chun as a member of the DPRK National Defence Commission 'due to the transfer to another post'. Ri Myong Su was appointed as minister of people's security, and Jang Pyong Gyu followed him as chairman of the SPA Legislation Committee. Ri Thae Nam was relieved of his post as vice-premier of the Cabinet 'for health reason'. Given the advanced age of the men in question, the reference to health issues might indeed be true.

3.2 Budget report

As each year, a report on the state's budget was presented during the parliamentary session. The presenter in 2011 was, for the second year in a row, Pak Su Gil. As usual since 2003, no absolute numbers were provided. In March 2002, the last time North Korea announced a budget in monetary terms, planned revenue for 2002 was around 22 billion won. The 2002 budget report was read by the same Mun Il Bong who was allegedly executed in 2011 in connection with the failed currency revaluation of late 2009.[10]

Despite their somewhat unorthodox structure and wording, these budgetary reports nonetheless represent the only available official information on the status of North Korea's economy. Considering that the state owns the economy, the state budget comes close to resem-

---

[9] The third session of the 12th SPA was held somewhat unusually on 7 June 2010. It appointed Choe Yong Rim, former Pyongyang Party chief, as the new prime minister and promoted Jang Sung Taek from member to vice-chairman of the National Defence Commission.

[10] Radio Golos Rossii (Radio Voice of Russia). Online: http://rus.ruvr.ru/2011/04/04/48406659.html (accessed 3 April 2012).

bling the North Korean GDP, minus the sectors that are treated separately including, as is widely suspected, a large part of the military economy.

A look at Graph 4, updated on the basis of the 2011 budget report, shows that after a recession following the economic reform period, the DPRK seems to be catching up—at least in terms of its own statistics. Growth has been moderate but steady. We also find that growth rates of planned expenditure (planned E) have been higher than those for planned revenue (planned R) since 2009. This is somewhat more expressive than the typically socialist announcements of achieved revenues (achieved R) having grown faster than planned (although the two curves seem to narrow towards the end). It implies that North Korea is either calculating with higher-than-expected income growth, or deliberately factors in some debt. The sources thereof are very limited. If the numbers below are to be trusted, then we can speculate about China providing loans to the North Korean state.

Graph 4 Economic growth in North Korea according to the DPRK budget (growth rates in %)

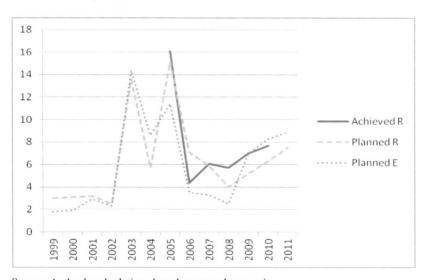

Source: Author's calculations based on www.kcna.co.jp.

According to the budget report, the plan for budgetary expenditure was carried out at 99.9 percent. The official growth rate of the North Korean economy in 2010 was 7.7 percent (in 2009 it was 7 percent), as this was the rate at which state budgetary revenue had grown compared to the previous year. At the core of the investment strategy for 2011 were, in accordance with the New Year joint editorial, the areas of light industry, agriculture, and science and technology.

The key data of the report are summarised in Table 1 below, which provides the data for the previous two years for comparison. Note the growing consistency of the structures of the annual reports.

Table 1   Comparison of state budgets 2009/2010/2011

	Plan for 2009	Achieved in 2009	*Plan for 2010*	Achieved in 2010	*Plan for 2011*
State budgetary revenue	*+5.2%*	101.7% *+7%*	*+6.3%*	*+7.7%*	*+7.5%*
Profits of state enterprises	*+5.8%*		*+7.7%*		*78.5%*
Profits of co-operative organisations	*+3.1%*		*+4.2%*		*+3.8%*
Fixed asset depreciation	*+6.1%*		*+2.5%*		*+1.4%*
Real estate rent	*+3.6%*		*+2%*		*+0.7%*
Social insurance	*+1.6%*		*+1.9%*		*+0.4%*
Local budgetary revenue		'over-fulfilled'			*16.1%*
State budgetary expenditure	*+7%*	99.8%	*+8.3%*	*+8.2%*	*+8.9%* *83.9%*
National defence	*15.8%*	*15.8%*	*15.8%*	15.8%	*15.8%*
Priority sectors of the national economy (metal, power, coal, railway)	*+8.7%*	'huge investment'	*+7.3%*	*+8.0%*	*+13.5%*
Development of science and technology	*+8%*	*+7.2%*	*+8.5%*	*+8.1%*	*+10.1%*
Agriculture	*+6.9%*	n.a.	*+9.4%*	*+9.4%*	*+9.0%*
Light industry	*+5.6%*		*+10.1%*	*+10.9%*	*+12.9%*
City managment/ capital construction	*+11.5%*		*+8.6%*	*+12.9%*	*+15.1%*
Popular policies			*+6.2%*	*+6.0%*	*n.a.*
Education	*+8.2%*				
Culture and arts	*+3.2%*				
Public health	*+8%*				
Sports	*+5.8%*				

Source: KCNA. See earlier editions of this publication for budget data before 2009.

3.3 *The work of the Cabinet*

Choe Yong Rim's report started with a somewhat startling announcement. He declared that the most important achievement gained in North Korea's economic development in 2010 was progress 'in putting the national economy on a Juche-basis' (*inminkyŏngjeŭi chuch'e-hwa*). Most North Korea experts would have assumed that this 'chuch'e-isation of the national economy' was long concluded, at least officially. Whether this was an acknowledgement of an incomplete process of import substitution, a side-blow against the Chinese on whom the North Korean economy depends heavily, or merely a reference to the steel industry (*chuch'e* steel was discussed in the previous year's volume) is unclear. In any case, structural changes in the metal industry were mentioned prominently in the prime minister's speech. As did the editorial, he stressed that successful developments in electricity, coal and metal production laid the foundation for the new focus on light industry and agriculture. Science and technology, especially the ubiquitous term CNC, were duly mentioned. But amidst the usual self-praise was the claim that North Korea had succeeded in nuclear fusion (*haekyunghap*), 'stunning the world'. No further substance was added. As in 2010, bio-technology was mentioned; however, space technology was omitted.

The outlook for 2011 reflected the tenor of the editorial. Light industry and the production of consumer goods were to be boosted to benefit the people. In the field of agriculture, stock breeding and fruit farming were particularly emphasised. Seafood production was also to be boosted. The latter was reflected in December when one of the first, widely publicised actions of Kim Jong Un was to provide fresh fish to the citizens of Pyongyang.

In electricity, after the construction of major and minor power stations, the new focus seemed to be on transmission. In transportation, railways received particular mention as an area of priority investment. In the metal industry, North Korea would focus on increasing the output of non-ferrous metals. In construction, a number of projects including 100,000 new apartments in Pyongyang were mentioned.

Towards the end of the report, the determination to diversity and increase foreign trade, in particular exports, was expressed. The reference to diversification is important: according to South Korean data, in 2010, North Korea conducted 83 percent of its trade with China, a sharp increase from 53 percent in 2005.[11] The fact that the defence industry was mentioned only last and in one sentence along with 'socialist cultural construction' is also noteworthy. Unlike 2010, neither the 'foolish sanctions' of the imperialists nor the 'new sports myth' were part of the prime minister's report.

4 Death of Kim Jong Il

The year 2011 was almost over when the announcement of the death of Kim Jong Il, who had ruled the country as chairman of the National Defence Commission, was made via the North Korean news agency on 19 December.

Kim Jong Il had de facto succeeded his father Kim Il Sung in 1994. Officially, he refrained from taking any new position until 1997, when he became secretary-general of the KWP. He had ruled the country in difficult times; the socialist block had collapsed, and so did North Korea's economic relations with its allies. Meanwhile, South Korea emerged ever stronger both economically and politically, as manifested by the establishment of diplomatic relations with Russia and China. The first years of Kim Jong Il's rule were overshadowed by a serious famine. Despite successes such as the first inter-Korean summit in June 2000 that led to the intensification of South-North tourism and the opening of the Kaesŏng Industrial Complex, the situation in North Korea remained tense.

Economic reforms that were started around 2000 and culminated in the measures of July 2002 did not produce the expected economic results. Plagued by inflation and mismanagement, and faced with an international environment after September 2001 that was less forthcoming towards a country which President George W. Bush in January 2002 branded as a member of the 'axis of evil', the state attempted to stop the reforms. This was a futile effort, as changes, in particular on the societal level, had been set in motion that seem to be largely irreversible.

The state then resorted to military strength, including the development of nuclear weapons, with two nuclear tests in 2006 and 2009. An

---

[11] Bloomberg, 'North Korean Dependence on China Trade Rises as Sanctions Worsen Isolation', 27 May 2011. Online: http://www.bloomberg.com/news/2011-05-27/north-korean-dependence-on-china-trade-rises-as-sanctions-worsen-isolation.html (accessed 3 April 2012).

escalation of tension with South Korea included the fatal shooting of a tourist in the Mt Kŭmgang resort in 2008, the sinking of the South Korean corvette *Cheonan* (*Ch'ŏnan*), and the shelling of Yeonpyeong (Yŏnp'yŏng) island in 2010.

This is what Kim Jong Un, the new leader of North Korea, has inherited. Clearly, he is taking on a difficult and complex task. We have yet to see how he will manage this situation, which new initiatives he can start, and how he will deal with old liabilities. In any case, his policies will have to consider what had been created and attempted in the past. The events and issues discussed in this overview are thus of great relevance for the changing of the guard in the DPRK.

5 OTHER EVENTS

5.1 *Trade and investment*

Among the most crucial problems facing the North Korean leadership is the economy. The food shortage rightly receives particularly large international attention. However, it is only the tip of the iceberg. As a typical socialist economy, under constant pressure through economic sanctions, North Korea also suffers from a permanent shortage of hard currency and hence a limited capability to import goods and services that are not domestically available. The country has for many years relatively successfully applied self-sufficiency, also known as import substitution, as a counter-strategy. However, with the deepening sophistication of its industrialised economy and growing demands on the consumer side, the limitations of this strategy become more obvious. Accordingly, efforts at expanding foreign trade and international cooperation are discernible, while at the same time the state makes sure that it remains in control of these activities. The events in this section are clear evidence of such a trend.

North Korea insists that 'it is a consistent policy of the DPRK Government to enhance economic cooperation with other countries, while beefing up its self-reliant national economy' (KCNA, 23 March 2012). While it would be difficult to characterise North Korea as an open economy, 2011 witnessed a number of positive attempts. In December 2011, investment-related laws were amended, 'in step with the nation's developing economy and international practices'. They included the DPRK Law and Regulations on Foreign Investment, laws on joint venture and joint collaboration, and the Law on Foreign-funded Businesses and Foreigners' Tax Payment. In 2011, in a related effort, the focus seemed to be mostly on the long-ailing 'Golden Triangle' in the northeast of the country, in particular on Rasŏn, newly created a special city in 2010.[12] The minimum wage at Rasŏn was set at US$80 by September 2011 (Yonhap, 08.09.2011), which is more that the US$63 paid at the Kaesŏng Industrial Complex. Obviously, North Korea reacted to the rising wages in China (around US$170) which make investment in the neighbouring country more cost-efficient.

Nevertheless, the southwestern zone of Kaesŏng is so far North Korea's real success story in terms of inward foreign direct investment (FDI). According to a Congressional Research Service report, as of the end of 2010, over 120 South Korean companies were employing over 47,000 North Korean workers, yielding US$323 million in output. Of the 120, 71 firms were producing clothing and textiles, four were making kitchen utensils, another four were manufacturing auto parts, and two were producing semiconductors.[13] Meanwhile, the US Treasury Department issued an ordinance imposing an import ban on goods produced in North Korea's special economic zones (the South Korean news agency Yonhap, 22 June 2011).

In May, the 14th Pyongyang Spring International Trade Fair opened at the Three-Revolution Exhibition Hall in Pyongyang. The first Rasŏn International Trade Fair was held from 22 to 25 August (KCNA, 2 August 2011). It was the first time North Korea had hosted a trade fair outside the capital. One day later, a seminar was held in Rasŏn city to attract foreign investment. Incentives for investors include a preferential tariff system and investments in infrastructure. In another attempt at fostering economic exchange, North Korea indicated that it was working on a double taxation avoidance agreement with China, after having already concluded such deals with more than ten other countries.

On 8 June 2011, a groundbreaking ceremony was held on the Hwanggŭmp'yŏng and Wihwa islands in the Amnok (Yalu) river separating the Chinese city of Dandong and the North Korean city of

---

[12] The revived fortunes of the Rasŏn special economic zone are discussed in Bernhard Seliger's article in this volume.

[13] See Dick Nanto and Mark Manyin (2011), 'The Kaesong North-South Korean Industrial Complex', Washington DC: Congressional Research Service, 17 March 2011. Online: www.crs.gov.

Sinŭiju. A memorandum of understanding to develop the islands into a special economic zone had been signed in December 2010. On 9 December 2011, KCNA reported that the presidium of the Supreme People's Assembly had adopted a law on the new economic zone, without providing further details.

Co-operation with Russia continued over the extension of the cross-border railway, which was tested in October 2011. It is supposed to link with the Trans-Siberian railway. Discussions between the two countries over a gas pipeline project culminated in September in an agreement to set up a joint working group. A newly emerged solution to the food shortage in North Korea also involves Moscow. Lacking arable land, North Koreans have reportedly declared an interest in utilising vacant land in Russia's sparsely populated Amur region. This could indeed be a win-win situation, as Russia is worried about an inflow of Chinese migrants.

5.2 *Economic development*

On 15 January 2011, KCNA announced the Cabinet's adoption of the 10-year state strategy plan for economic development (*kukka kyŏngje kaebal 10 kaenyŏn chŏllyak kyehoek*) and the establishment of the State General Bureau for Economic Development (*kukka kyŏngje kaebal ch'ŏngguk*). Responsibility for carrying out projects related to the 10-year plan was assigned to the Korea Taepung International Investment Group (*chosŏn taep'ung kukje t'uja kŭrup*). This was the official announcement, but the matter was not entirely new, and information on the plan and the Taep'ung Group's role appeared in the previous volume of this publication. Not too many details were provided beyond the fact that this is a strategic plan, and that its main emphasis will be on building infrastructure and developing agriculture and basic industries. With the exception of agriculture, this approach is reminiscent of a typical 'big push' developmental strategy along the lines laid out by Western economists in the 1950s. What is interesting is the claim to become one of the 'advanced countries' (*ap'sŏn nara*) by 2020, which can also be read as a rare acknowledgement that this status has not yet been achieved. Moreover, ambitions expressed in the KCNA article cited above include taking a 'strategic position in Northeast Asia and international economic relations'.

Meanwhile, the South Korean Bank of Korea (BoK) painted a bleak picture of North Korea's economy. In a report issued on 3 November 2011, it estimated that the North's economy shrank by 0.5 percent in 2010, after a contraction of 0.9 percent in 2009. This stands in marked contrast to the official North Korean data discussed above in the context of the state budget (Yonhap news agency, 10 November 2011). According to the BoK estimates, mining and manufacturing industries accounted for the major part of the North's overall industrial structure at 36.3 percent, followed by the service sector at 31 percent, the agricultural and fisheries industry at 20.8 percent, the construction sector at 8.0 percent, and electricity, gas and water supply divisions at 3.9 percent. North Korea's nominal gross national income amounted to US$26.5 billion in 2010. In a rare direct response to the BoK report, KCNA (10 November 2011) countered by stating that 'the Ryonha General Machinery Plant ... is leading the world in CNC technology and machine-building industry', that North Korea had succeeded in nuclear fusion, and that domestically developed light water reactors were going to be constructed soon.

At least for some North Koreans, things seem indeed to be getting better. In a forum held at the South Korean National Assembly, Lee In-ho, senior researcher at the Institute for National Security Strategy, stated that an estimated 500,000 North Koreans had cash assets worth more than US$100,000 (Yonhap, 7 October 2011). They included 50,000 high profile officials and their relatives living in the North, 100,000 long-term employees dispatched overseas, and those with connections with such countries as Japan, China and the United States. The number also included 200,000 migrant workers and their families in foreign countries. The latter figure is remarkable, as the EU, for example, has been keen on discouraging companies in its member countries from employing such North Koreans because of human rights considerations including harsh labour conditions and low pay.

5.3 *Mining and minerals*

The greatest source of hope for North Korea's economy, and one of the major differences in a comparison of the Korean case with Germany's, is the abundance of mineral resources in the country. It has also been the subject of frustration on the South Korean side, as China is very actively exploiting these resources that would otherwise contribute to the post-unification prosperity of Korea.

In 2011, North Korea appears to have developed a particular interest in so-called rare earth minerals including cerium and neodymium, which are used as a crucial element in semiconductors, cars, computers and other advanced technology areas. A KCNA report in September mentioned long-standing efforts to develop rare earths such as fluorocarbonic cerium, monazite, phosphor johnstrupite and pyrochlore. It stressed the domestic utility of related products and the need to prevent environmental pollution during the production process (see section on environment).

In July 2011, Yonhap quoted a *Choson Sinbo* report according to which about 20 million tons of rare earth minerals had been found in North Korea. The Seoul-based North Korea Resources Institute estimated that the North's rare earth resources were worth around US$10.4 trillion, up 39.3 percent from 2009 due to surging prices on the world market. In addition, the DPRK held coal deposits worth about US$3.5 trillion, gold worth roughly US$134 billion, silver worth US$790 billion, and uranium worth US$16 billion (Yonhap, 23 August 2011). As part of North Korea's efforts to facilitate the export of mineral resources, the east coast port of Tanch'ŏn in South Hamgyŏng province has been modernised.

5.4 Telecommunications

The case of the landmark 105-storey Ryugyŏng hotel in Pyongyang shows how closely connected business and political activities can be in North Korea. The outside cladding of the hotel, for two decades a widely visible disgrace and sign of economic failure, was completed well ahead of the April 2012 celebrations with the help of Orascom, the Egyptian telecommunications provider which, according to the *Financial Times* (8 May 2011), has leased the hotel for 100 years.[14] Orascom Telecom Holding and the North Korean Posts and Telecommunications Corporation had already formed a 75:25 joint venture called Cheo Technology, which since the end of 2008 has operated the North Korean mobile telephone network Koryolink. The network has reportedly been granted a monopoly for 25 years. The door-opener

---

[14] *Financial Times*, accessible online at www.ftd.de.

was a 2007 investment of US$117 million by Orascom Construction in the North Korean company Sangwŏn Cement.

As of 2011, the mobile telephone network covered 15 percent of DPRK territory and 94 percent of its population. Services are available in about 15 cities including the capital, over 80 small cities and on 22 main roads in North Korea. The growth rate has been impressive. By March 2011, the number of subscribers was 523,000; at the end of the year, the number reached one million. Owning a mobile phone is a costly luxury. Usual plans include 200 minutes plus 20 SMS per month, in addition to a one-time initial fee for the telephone and the SIM card, to be paid in hard currency. The total cost for acquiring a mobile telephone is said to be around US$350, although information varies. In any case, the fact that one million North Koreans can afford to spend such a huge amount in a country where the average wage is said to be less than US$50 per month raises a number of questions. The most obvious insight would be that, once the growth rate has slowed down, the number of subscribers would offer us a rough but important estimate of the actual size of North Korea's newly emerged middle class. However, along with anecdotal reports that South Korean 'choco pies' sell for US$1 apiece in North Korean markets, this could also serve as a call to re-think our estimates of the average North Korean's available income (or the quality of information about North Korea).

Further developments related to telecommunications in 2011 included the announcement by KCNA (27 January 2011) that the Information Center of Kim Il Sung University had developed a VOIP (internet) telephone exchange service system and that a separate mobile telephone network had been set up in the Rasŏn zone by the Thai Loxley Pacific Company. (Thai Loxley Pacific had earlier operated a mobile telephone system effective only within the zone.) The revolutions in Egypt, Tunisia and Libya have prompted some observers in the West to attach high hopes to the effects of mass communication on the stability of autocratic political systems. For North Korea, at this point it seems too far-fetched to expect similar developments. However, it is remarkable that the state has, despite the obvious risks involved, decided in favour of a massive expansion of the mobile telephone network. This could be related to simple profit motives, as the premium added on to hardware and services seems to be extraordinarily high. An optimist would regard it as a sign of pragmatism.[15]

5.5 Science and technology

The development and introduction of new technologies have been identified by the New Year editorial as among the strategic goals of North Korea. There are essentially two ways of doing so: by domestic R&D efforts, or through imports in the form of license acquisitions or FDI.

The former avenue includes the establishment of the Pyongyang University of Science and Technology (PUST; see previous volumes of this publication for more details) and the development of *chuch'e* steel. However, actual R&D output seems to be still low. In October 2011, Radio Free Asia reported that, according to the World Intellectual Property Organisation, North Korea had applied for only one international patent in the first ten months of that year (in 2010, it had applied for four; in 2009, for none; in 2008, for seven; and in 2007, for three). This is certainly not an expression of the intellectual capacity of North Korean scientists; rather, it can be interpreted as a result of the working conditions of researchers. One example is a report by University World News (30 June 2011),[16] on the closure of North Korean universities for up to ten months to send students for work on farms, in factories and in construction. Informal contacts suggest that some students have been taken out of class to engage in construction work. From earlier years, we have known that in autumn and spring, mass mobilisation to help in farm work takes place, and that a large part of students' time is spent on ideological training.

North Korea has also tried to reach out to the world. Smaller and larger measures on capacity-building included a tour by a 12-member North Korean delegation to California's Silicon Valley in April 2011, including a visit to Google. Whether as a result of this visit or as part of a new media strategy, in 2011, North Korea started exploring a switch from analogue to digital TV and significantly upgraded and expanded its internet presence. After opening accounts on Twitter,

---

[15] For a detailed discussion of North Korea's telecom and IT sectors, see Alexandre Mansourov (2011), 'North Korea on the Cusp of Digital Transformation', www.nautilus.org.

[16] University World News. Online: http://www.universityworldnews.com.

Facebook and YouTube, it introduced photo and video services on the new KCNA website. The Party newspaper *Rodong Sinmun* can now be accessed online, with PDFs of the print version available for download.[17] A new propaganda website Voice of Korea (*chosŏnŭi sori*) has also been opened.[18] But North Korea has also experienced the risks of such new ventures. In January 2011, the official website Uriminzokkiri ('by our nation itself', a key unification slogan) announced that it had been hacked. The site went offline on 8 January, the alleged birthday of Kim Jong Un.

5.6 *Tourism*

As part of its strategy to acquire much-needed hard currency, North Korea in 2011 continued to intensify its measures to boost income from international tourism. These included an improvement of access via air, and the development of tourist destinations.

A refurbishment of the passenger terminal has been under way at Pyongyang's Sunan international airport (facilitated by the erection of a temporary terminal). This was one of the infrastructure projects to mark the 100th birthday of Kim Il Sung in 2012; but it also improves the capacity for handling incoming and outgoing flights. According to Yonhap, from April 2011, Air Koryo, North Korea's national airline, replaced the previous charter flights by regular flights to the Malaysian capital Kuala Lumpur. Other destinations for regular Air Koryo flights include Bangkok as well as Beijing, Shenyang, Moscow, Khabarovsk and Vladivostok.

In June 2011, an attempt was made to bring international investors including those from South Korea into the Mt Kŭmgang resort by issuing a new law on investment in what now appears to be a special tourism zone with visa-free access, internet connection, and other facilities. The related monopoly of Hyundai Asan was in doubt after a South Korean tourist was killed in the resort in 2008 and was formally brought to an end by North Korea in April 2011. The new DPRK Law on the Special Zone for International Tours of Mt Kŭmgang, published by KCNA on 2 June 2011, replaces the earlier Law on Tourist Area in Mt Kŭmgang of 13 November 2002. As an alternative to

---

[17] *Rodong Sinmun*, accessible online at www.rodong.rep.kp.
[18] Voice of Korea, accessible online at www.vok.rep.kp.

South Korean visitors, North Korea seems to have identified the growing wealth and subsequent appetite for tourism of the Chinese neighbours. On 30 August 2011, tours were launched through a sea route from the Rasŏn economic zone to Mt Kŭmgang. The ship *Mangyongbong-92*, which gained prominence as a ferry between North Korea and Japan but had lain idle since the collapse of the bilateral relationship due to the abduction issue, was brought into the new tourism project. Since June 2011, Chinese are said to be allowed to enter the Rasŏn area with their own cars. In October 2011, Beijing-based Young Pioneer Tours announced five-day cruises at a cost of around US$1,300. According to Yonhap news agency, the number of Chinese tourists to North Korea reached 131,100 in 2010, an increase of 36.4 percent from 96,100 in 2009. In late September 2011, on the occasion of World Tourism Day, KCNA published a statement declaring North Korea's intention to further develop tourism. Related offices are said to exist in China, Malaysia and Germany.

5.7 *Environmental issues*

Against the background of the looming food crisis, exacerbated as ever by heavy rains and floods during June to August 2011, energy shortages and a tense international situation, environmental issues are among the less expected topics relating to North Korea. However, the year 2011 brought a number of developments in this regard.

On 26 July 2011, the North Korean Cabinet released a new Law on the Protection of the Environment (*hwangyŏng pohobŏp*) with 60 articles, replacing the previous one enacted in 1999. According to KCNA, the purpose of the law was to 'landscape the country, improve the people's health and provide them with better living and working conditions'. Regulations include environmental protection and the prevention of pollution. A few weeks later, KCNA (18 August 2011) reported a supplement to the law. It now includes, among others, regulations on the development and use of renewable energy including solar, wind and geothermal power; recycling; and the reduction of the use of fossil fuels. An explicit connection was established between related measures and stable economic growth.

In the past years, reforestation had been at the focus of North Korea's environmental policy. In 2011, specific measures included the decision to stop the sale of leaded gasoline by 2013 with help of the

United Nations Environmental Programme. In November, Voice of America reported that North Korea had submitted a plan for the reduction of methane gas emissions from its about 100 coal mines to the United Nations Framework Convention on Climate Change.

The earthquake and tsunami that struck Japan on 11 March 2011 caused anxiety in North Korea and seem to have prompted discussions between the North and the South in March and April on a joint study of potential volcanic activity from Mt Paektu, situated on the North Korean–China border. It is, however, far from clear if a proposed on-site survey of the mountain has taken place. In November, KCNA (23 November 2011) reported that the DPRK had adopted a law on the prevention of damage from earthquakes and volcanoes.

As it is often the case, we are left wondering about the actual background to regulations and measures. In addition to speculation about access to related subsidies, we can interpret them as another example showing that North Korea, despite its negative image, does care about its international reputation and is willing, to a limited extent, to participate in international co-operation.

5.8 *Traditionalism*

A continuing trend in 2011 was North Korea's rediscovery of ancient traditions, which for decades had been banned or ignored because of their allegedly reactionary or religious background. Only recently, tomb sweeping day (*ch'ŏngmyong*) had been re-introduced as a holiday. In 2011, KCNA reported celebrations to mark Buddha's birthday and the Korean thanksgiving (*chusŏk*). The latter is traditionally a day when Koreans pay respect to their ancestors. In North Korea, it was commemorated in 2011 by paying respect to the Kim family and revolutionary martyrs. This does not mean that private ceremonies are not being held. They have been allowed since 1972, and since 2003, *chusŏk* had been designated as a national holiday. These and other developments deserve our attention because of their ideological implications. They mark the ongoing trend to merge socialism ever closer with nationalism, a trend that can be interpreted as one of the reasons for the remarkable resilience of the North Korean system despite its poor economic performance and international isolation.

5.9 *Administrative and personnel changes*

Keeping track of developments regarding North Korea's administrative structure, and in particular of the changes in the top group of leaders has traditionally been one of the core fields of North Korean analysis. Because of the unsystematic nature of related announcements and the resulting need to use implicit means of analysis, such as listening to radio broadcasts that mention new leaders on the side, it should be stated that the below details are by no means complete; but they provide a certain impression of the related dynamics.

In January 2011, North Korea's Price Bureau, previously belonging to the State Planning Commission, was upgraded into a State Price Commission (KCNA, 13 January 2011). For a centrally planned economy, this is a key economic institution as it determines the relations in prices between single commodities. It is not clear to what extent the State Price Commission includes the outcome of demand-supply interaction in the markets in its calculations. In March, when reporting a meeting of commercial officials, KCNA (7 March 2011) named Ryang Ui Gyong as the chairman of the State Price Commission.

Another upgrading took place in April (KCNA, 17.04.2011), when the State Administration for Quality Management was renamed the State Commission for Quality Management, thus raising its status and implying a stronger focus on the production of quality goods as discussed above in connection with the New Year editorial.

Further personnel changes included the appointment of the 49-year-old son of the late foreign minister Paek Nam Sun as head of the Central Bank; the dismissal of Ju Sang Son, minister of the people's security of the National Defence Commission 'due to illness'; and the promotion of Ri Mu Yong, minister of chemical industry, to the rank of vice-premier. Again, we are mostly left to speculate about the background, which would include a power reshuffle and the promotion of strategic sectors.

6 CONCLUSION

Domestic developments in North Korea in the year 2011 again formed a mixed picture, although thanks to the absence of any major military clash or nuclear test, positive signs dominate. We may be particularly hopeful about the indications of an end to the return to orthodox pre-reform positions, as diagnosed in this publication since 2008. As in 2010, there are signs of a strong interest in international economic cooperation to resolve the country's deep-rooted problems in the food and energy sectors, including a further improvement in the related institutional and legal structure. There are also cautious signs of a slow economic recovery despite a less favourable assessment by the (South Korean) Bank of Korea.

However, all of the above considerations can easily become invalid. One major source of uncertainty—the unresolved succession problem—has disappeared. But it has been replaced by strong concerns about the stability and the future direction of the Kim Jong Un leadership. As this is a particularly complex topic, it will be covered separately in this volume.

RELATIONS BETWEEN THE TWO KOREAS IN 2011

Sabine Burghart

INTRODUCTION

In 2011, relations between the Republic of Korea (ROK—South Korea) and the Democratic People's Republic of Korea (DPRK—North Korea) did not significantly improve despite a few hopeful signs. The Lee Myung-bak administration continued to pursue its 'principled' policy towards the North (the phrase chosen by Lee to describe the policy), while showing some more flexibility, particularly in the area of social and cultural exchanges.[1] Undergoing a dynastic leadership transition and faced with internal power consolidation after Kim Jong Il's death, the DPRK announced that no policy changes were to be expected. Although no major incidents were reported, military drills and provocations continued on both sides of the Demilitarised Zone. South Korean media reported that the DPRK military fired artillery shells near the Northern Limit Line shortly before the 'Ulchi Freedom Guardian' ROK-US joint military drills started in August. The sinking of the *Cheonan* (*Ch'ŏnan*) and the shelling of Yeonpyong (Yŏnpy'ŏng) island in 2010 left the ROK military showing signs of nervousness, which led to their mistakenly shooting at a South Korean civilian aircraft[2] and random firing towards the North. Economic exchanges between the ROK and DPRK show a mixed picture: while production at the Kaesŏng Industrial Complex (KIC) has been increasing, other inter-Korean business projects have continued to face financial difficulties and bankruptcy as a consequence of the ROK's meas-

---

[1] To be precise, the ROK government speaks of a 'flexible approach to North Korea within a framework of resolute principles'. See Ministry of Unification. Online: http://eng.unikorea.go.kr/CmsWeb/viewPage.req?idx=PG0000000531#nohref (accessed 10 May 2012).

[2] The Asiana Airlines aircraft on its way to Inch'ŏn International Airport was mistakenly identified as a North Korean aeroplane by ROK marines.

ures announced on 24 May 2010 in the aftermath of the *Cheonan* sinking—the '5.24 measures' (5.24 *choch'i*).³

1 KIM JONG IL'S DEATH: A WINDOW OF OPPORTUNITY?

To some observers, the sudden though not unexpected death of Kim Jong Il opened a window of opportunity for a step towards rapprochement between the two Koreas. In South Korea, there was controversy about the appropriateness and the form of condolences expressed towards the DPRK. Sending an official delegation to the funeral was a highly political question that divided the main political forces, even more so with the upcoming election year ahead. On the one hand, conservatives were concerned that a high-ranking delegation to the North would be interpreted as a conciliatory gesture that could reduce voters' support; on the other, representatives of the democratic-progressive camp saw an opportunity to revitalise inter-Korean relations and suggested a visit by lawmakers to attend the DPRK leader's funeral. These hopes were disappointed after the ROK government made it clear that it would not allow officials to go to the North. In carefully chosen wording, Unification Minister Yu U-ik, speaking on behalf of the government, expressed sympathy with the North Korean people. Although no official government delegation was sent to the funeral, the ROK government authorised private visits by former first lady Yi Hŭi-ho and Hyundai Group chairwoman Hyŏn Chŏng-ŭn. According to a statement by the ministry of unification (MOU), these two visits were justified in return for the visits of North Korean officials to the funerals of former ROK President Kim Dae-jung and Hyundai Group chairman Chŏng Mong-hun. A survey conducted among 700 South Koreans showed that the majority was in favour of sending official condolences to the North: 49.6 percent in favour versus 31.4 percent of respondents opposing such an act.⁴

---

³ For a summary of these measures and their immediate effect, see the author's overview article on ‚Relations between the two Koreas in 2010' in: *Korea 2011: Politics, Economy and Society*, pp. 61 and 65.
⁴ *Korea Times*, 21 December 2011, p. 1.

2 A CHANGE IN THE ROK'S POLICY: PRINCIPLED FLEXIBILITY?

The ROK government has remained firm on its policy principles, but to some degree has softened its stance towards the DPRK. In an attempt to reduce the tensions that had reached a new level of escalation in 2010, both sides chose a more conciliatory tone at the beginning of the year. The DPRK's joint new year's editorial called for 'proactive promotion of dialogue and economic co-operation' (*taehwawa hyŏmnyŏk saŏp*) and the implementation of the two inter-Korean summit agreements but expressed strong criticism of the conservative political forces in the South.[5] Similarly, in his new year's address President Lee Myung-bak said that the door for dialogue was open, while stressing that the ROK military would 'strongly respond' to any provocative acts. However, the Lee administration has not moved away from its demand that the North apologise for the two deadly incidents in 2010, the sinking of the warship *Cheonan* and the shelling of Yonpyeong island. While the DPRK took responsibility for the latter, it has denied any involvement in the former. To the DPRK leadership the South's offer for dialogue that has been linked with this precondition seems therefore unacceptable. The ROK's approach towards the DPRK has also influenced the (lack of) progress in multilateral negotiations, particularly the stalled Six Party Talks.[6]

In what might be regarded as an attempt at a visible modification, though not re-orientation, in the ROK's policy towards the DPRK, the ministry of unification was given a 'facelift': in September 2011, Unification Minister Hyŏn In-t'aek—considered a hardliner by many observers—was replaced by Yu U-ik, a close aide of President Lee and former ROK ambassador to China. Yu stressed that the government's policy towards the North remained a principled approach while 'flexibility in non-political areas' would be increased. Wi Sŏng-rak, the ROK's chief negotiator on the DPRK's denuclearisation, was replaced by the deputy leader of the ROK delegation to the Six Party Talks, Yim Sŏng-nam. Through the channel of the Committee for the Peaceful Reunification of Korea the DPRK rejected the ROK government's proposed flexibility to improve inter-Korean relations.

---

[5] KCNA, 1 January 2011. Online: http://www.kcna.co.jp/index-k.htm (accessed 1 May 2011).
[6] See overview by James E. Hoare on the 'Foreign relations of the two Koreas in 2011' in this volume.

Although the 5.24 measures are still in place,[7] the ROK authorities approved several exchanges with the North in the social and cultural field: religious leaders, archaeologists, scientists and the South Korean conductor Chŏng Myŏng-hun were allowed visits to the North. In September, representatives of the Chogye order, the largest Buddhist sect, and religious leaders representing Buddhists, Catholics and Protestants held joint prayers and events in Pyongyang and other parts of the country. In November, a group of Protestant church leaders visited Pyongyang and met with their DPRK counterparts in the Korean Christian Federation (*chosŏn kŭrisŭdokyo yŏnmaeng*). There were also signs of the resumption of the stalled inter-Korean excavation project of the ruins of Manwŏldae in the city of Kaesŏng.[8] In mid-November, archaeologists of both Koreas were authorised by their respective governments to conduct a safety study at the site of the royal palace. Agreement was also reached for conducting a joint on-site survey of volcanic activity at Mt Paektu.

The DPRK proposed Red Cross talks to discuss pending humanitarian issues. Initially, the ROK government responded positively but linked the pursuit of these talks to the successful outcome of high-level defence talks that started at the beginning of 2011 but eventually ended without results. Former US President Jimmy Carter after his visit to the DPRK with the Elders in April conveyed the message that Kim Jong Il was prepared to hold a summit with Lee. The South declared that it would negotiate further on this proposal provided that the DPRK took responsibility for the *Cheonan* incident. Despite its emphasis on 'principles', the Lee administration showed some flexibility and apparently held a secret meeting in May with the DPRK. The North leaked this information and accused the South Korean delegation of having offered bribes for the arrangement of a summit meeting, a claim that was denied by the ROK government.

Prominent leaders of the conservative Grand National Party (GNP, now Saenuri Party), such as Park Geun-hye and Hong Chun-p'yo, in an attempt to distance themselves from the current administration

---

[7] These countermeasures led to the suspension of inter-Korean exchanges in the economic and social and cultural field (except for the KIC).

[8] *Yŏksa Pokwŏn Sinmun*, 'Kaesŏng Manwŏldae (Koryŏ hwanggungt'ŏ) nambuk kongdong palkulsaŏp sŭngin' [Joint South–North excavation project at Kaesŏng Manwŏldae (Koryŏ royal palace) agreed], 25 October 2011. Online: http://www.historynews.kr/sub_read.html?uid=686&section=sc3&section2= (accessed 12 January 2012).

opted for a more flexible approach in the ROK's policy towards the North. In the journal *Foreign Affairs*, Park advocated a new approach towards North Korea in what she called an 'alignment policy'. In her view, this 'trustpolitik' 'should be buttressed by public consensus and remain constant in the face of political transitions and unexpected domestic or international events'.[9] This policy would combine cooperation with the DPRK with tough measures in case of military provocations, while taking international factors, particularly the alliance with the US and relations with China, into account. It has to be seen what this concept will look like in reality. Hong, the first (former) GNP party leader ever to have visited the KIC, stressed that he would seek to change the current North Korea policy 'from strict reciprocity to flexible reciprocity'.[10] These proposals can be interpreted as an indirect critique of how the Lee administration deals with the North, but they also reflect intra-party power shifts.

3 A (W)HOLE OF INFORMATION?

The fact that the South Korean government and public learned about Kim Jong Il's death from DPRK broadcasts has called the ROK's intelligence capabilities into question. In the South, political parties criticised the National Intelligence Service (NIS) and the ministry of defence for having failed to provide exclusive and timely information about the DPRK leader's death. This issue was even more critical as President Lee had left the country for a summit meeting with the Japanese Prime Minister Noda that same day. Some observers spoke of a 'spying fiasco'[11] and claimed that human intelligence had been reduced for the sake of high-tech surveillance, including reconnaissance satellites. There were voices demanding the resignation of the NIS chief, Wŏn Se-hun, whose appointment in 2009 had already raised some questions over his inexperience in the field.

In recent years the Lee administration has been intensifying efforts to collect all available information about the DPRK. While cutting

---

[9] Park Geun-hye, 'A New Kind of Korea: Building Trust between Seoul and Pyongyang', in: *Foreign Affairs*, 90 (5) (September/October 2011), p. 15.
[10] *Hankyoreh*, 'GNP Chief Calls for Flexibility in S. Korea's Policy on N. Korea after Trip to Kaesong', 1 October 2011. Online: http://english.hani.co.kr/arti/english_edition/e_northkorea/498854.html (accessed 12 January 2012).
[11] *Korea Times*, 22 December 2011, p. 2.

funds for inter-Korean projects that would have allowed direct access to the North, the ROK government has established several information-gathering units and centres in the South. An 'army' of South Korean officials and researchers is 'digging' for data about anything related to the North, particularly names of DPRK officials and their positions in the party, state institutions, etc. Apart from efforts to expand this data base there are also plans to open a public information centre on North Korea in 2012. Access to information about the DPRK and North Korean materials (publications, movies, etc.) will be restricted to officials and will require pre-registration.

The National Security Law (NSL), which prohibits the possession and dissemination of North Korean propaganda, was defended by President Lee in an interview with US National Public Radio by pointing to the pure need for it.[12] The NSL has been criticised for its vague wording that allows a high degree of interpretation and leads to inconsistency in the standards applied by the ROK courts. According to a human rights advocate, 'the current standard set by the Supreme Court for determining what expression qualifies as a threat to national security appears low enough that the freedom of expression protected by Article 19 of the ICCPR [International Covenant on Civil and Political Rights] is threatened.'[13] Although the authority to block websites lies with the state-run Korean Communication Commission (KCC, *pangsong t'ongsin wiwŏnhoe*), recent cases show that proper legal procedures are not observed. For example, in December 2011, ROK police ordered the closure of two pro-North Korean blogs (*ollain k'ap'ae*) without prior approval from the KCC. The owners of the websites filed complaint at the National Human Rights Commission (NHRC, *kukka in'gwŏn wiwŏnhoe*), saying that this action would infringe their freedom of expression. The NHRC, a state-run institution, argued that although the closure of the websites was not legal it was not a violation of human rights. The NHRC's statement was not supported by all of its eleven members: three of them stressed that any restriction of the freedom of expression should be done through 'proper legal pro-

---

[12] *Chosun Ilbo*, 3 December 2011.
[13] Brush, Kaitlin, 'South Korea's National Security Law: Legitimate Measure or Threat to Freedom of Speech?', The Human Rights Brief, Center for Human Rights and Humanitarian Law, 11 March 2011. Online: http://hrbrief.org/2011/03/south-korea%E2%80%99s-national-security-law-legitimate-measure-or-threat-to-freedom-of-speech/ (accessed 8 December 2011).

ceedings', while others regarded the closing of the website as a 'matter of the web portal's self-regulatory decision'.[14]

The death of Kim Jong Il led to tightened surveillance of social networking service (SNS) posts and messages in South Korea. The KCC stressed that it was 'vigilant to stop false rumours surrounding Kim's death from spreading' and determined to control 'status updates and other material promoting the communist nation's political and social system'.[15] In 2011, more than sixty websites were classified as pro-North Korean and blocked by South Korean police. However, Internet users can bypass these blocks with special software that can be downloaded from the Internet. There were also reports of North Korean cyber attacks against ROK government institutions.

4 INTER-KOREAN ECONOMIC EXCHANGES: A MIXED PICTURE

As far as economic exchanges between the two Koreas are concerned, there is good and bad news: on the one hand, the KIC continues to grow in production value, output and the number of North Korean workers, although the total number of production plants has not increased. On the other, South Korean companies engaged in joint ventures in the DPRK are faced with huge financial losses due to the 5.24 measures that discourage direct trade with and investment in the North. As Table 1 shows, total trade decreased by 9 percent from US$1,912.3 million in 2010 to US$1,713.9 million in 2011. It seems

Table 1   Inter-Korean trade (2001–2011) (in US$ million)

Year	2001	2002	2003	2004	2005	2006	2007	2008	2009	2010	2011
KIC	-	-	-	41.7	176.7	298.8	440.7	808.4	940.6	1,442.9	1,697.6
Other trade	403.0	641.7	724.2	655.3	879.1	1,050.9	1,357.2	1,012.0	538.5	469.4	16.3
Total trade	403.0	641.7	724.2	697.0	1,055.8	1,349.7	1,797.9	1,820.4	1,679.1	1,912.3	1,713.9

Source: Ministry of Unification, January 2012.[16]

---

[14] *Korea Times*, 8 December 2011, p. 2.
[15] *Korea Times*, 'Pro-North SNS Messages under Tighter Monitoring', 21 December 2011, p. 4.
[16] Ministry of Unification, 'Nambuk kyoyu hyŏmnyŏk tonghyang' [Trends in South–North exchanges and co-operation], January 2012, p. 50.

that the KIC is more and more taking the place of all other forms of economic exchanges between the two Koreas: while the trade volume at the KIC increased by US$254.7 million compared to the previous year, trade outside the KIC decreased sharply from US$469.4 million in 2010 to US$16.3 million in 2011.

Although the number of South Korean staff at the KIC was reduced on account of security concerns in May 2010 to about 800 people (compared to 1,461 in 2008), the value of exports increased from US$39.7 million in 2007 to US$190 million at the end of 2011. This means that on average total production at the KIC amounts to US$30 million per month. In 2011, over 120 medium-sized companies were in production at the KIC with almost 50,000 North Korean workers, of whom the majority are women (72 percent) and high school graduates (81.8 percent).[17] According to data provided by the MOU, the potential for further expansion of the KIC is high, fuelled by the demand for an additional 20,000 workers. Monthly expenses per North Korean worker amount to US$110 comprising the minimum wage (currently US$63.80) paid to the DPRK authorities as well as contributions for social security and the social culture policy fee (*sahoe munhwa sich'aek kŭm*). The North Korean workers are 'paid' either in coupons or domestic currency, but also receive contributions in kind from the KIC factories such as free meals and snacks.

In November, South Korean newspapers reported on the 'choco pie dispute' (*ch'ok'o p'ai ssaum*) that had emerged at the KIC and which triggered calls for a unified 'choco pie policy'.[18] The (South Korean) choco pie, a cookie between two layers of marshmallow covered in chocolate, is said to be a famous snack among North Korean workers. However, unequal distribution of this cake—ranging from three to ten pieces per person depending on the factory—has led to discord among workers. Some managers proposed setting up a 'recommended standard', but so far, ROK companies have failed to agree on a uniform choco pie policy. There were reports that a certain amount of choco pies were smuggled out of the KIC and sold at local markets. The DPRK authorities demanded that the distribution of what could be perceived a 'symbol of capitalism' had to be curtailed.

---

[17] 9.5 percent of the KIC workers graduated from North Korean universities and 8.7 percent from technical schools. Yonhap News, 1 February 2012.

[18] *Joongang Ilbo*, 'Kansik 3-10 kae kongjangmada dalla ... ch'ok'o p'ai ssaum nan kaesŏng kongdan' [3–10 snacks depending on the factory ... choco pie dispute erupts at the Kaesong Industrial Complex], 21 November 2011.

The 'choco pie issue' was probably regarded as trivial by those South Korean companies that used to trade with the North outside of the KIC or hold joint ventures with DPRK enterprises. Most of them have needed to cope with huge financial losses since general trade with the DPRK was banned by the ROK government in May 2010. In an interview with Yonhap News, the CEO of Pyongyang Andong Hemp Textiles, a joint venture between the South Korean company Andong Hemp Textiles and the Saepyŏl General Trading Co., complained that South Korean businesses that had invested about US$179 million in Pyongyang and Nampo were 'on the brink of bankruptcy'.[19]

The MOU defended its policy by stressing that despite frozen inter-Korean relations both the number of workers and volume of exports were steadily increasing at the KIC. Recent statistics support this argument, but one may wonder if the creation of the joint economic zone would have been possible under President Lee's 'grand strategy' (*taebuk ch'ŏngch'aek*).[20] The KIC is the last remaining symbol of the Sunshine policy that has not only survived but to a certain extent has even flourished under the Lee administration. Nevertheless, there are concerns that the KIC could face a similar fate to the Mt Kŭmgang project, where the DPRK authorities froze the assets owned by South Korean businesses and the government. In that case, financial losses would be twice as much: ROK companies could lose about US$500 million, while public corporations that have invested in infrastructure, electricity and communication facilities would face financial losses of an estimated US$352 million.[21]

---

[19] *Korea Times*, 'S. Korean Firms Reeling from Inter-Korean Trade Ban', 6 March 2011. Online: http://www.koreatimes.co.kr/www/news/include/print.asp?newsIdx=82536 (accessed 13 February 2012).

[20] The strategy includes adherence to a 'consistent policy stance towards North Korea based on firm principles', 'focus on North Korean people' (ranging from efforts to improve the human rights situation in the DPRK to sending leaflets carrying information about the South to the DPRK), the reinforcement of reciprocity, and efforts to 'build a national consensus' in South Korea. Ministry of Unification, '2011 nyŏn t'ongilbu ŏmmu kyehoek' 2011 [Work plan of ministry of unification for the year 2011], 29 December 2010. Online: http://www.unikorea.go.kr/CmsWeb/viewPage.req?idx=PG0000000478 (accessed 6 May 2012).

[21] *Chosun Ilbo*, 24 August 2011.

5 MT KŬMGANG RESORT: LOST FOREVER?

There seems to be little hope that the stalemate over the Mt Kŭmgang resort will be resolved in the foreseeable future. Since July 2008, when a South Korean tourist entering a militarily restricted area was shot dead by a North Korean soldier, the tours have been put on hold by the South Korean government. Negotiations between the two Koreas to re-open the resort have ended without tangible results. After the DPRK authorities decided to seize a number of ROK assets worth US$448 million,[22] further measures were taken in 2011 to open the resort to international tour operators. The DPRK authorities declared the exclusive rights of Hyundai Asan no longer valid and the Presidium of the DPRK's Supreme People's Assembly issued a decree on the further development of Mt Kŭmgang. In May, the 'Law on Mount Kŭmgang Special Tourism Zone' (*kŭmgangsan kukche kwan'gwang t'ŭkku pŏp*) comprising six chapters was passed and a tour programme for international investors announced.[23] The ROK government denounced the new law as a violation of inter-Korean agreements and an infringement of South Korean property rights. It called for an international boycott of the Mt Kŭmgang resort and threatened to take diplomatic and legal measures against tour operators. According to media reports, several international operators showed interest in exploring this area. Since the ROK government shut its borders with the North, international tourists can only access the resort by ship from Rajin (in the DPRK) or Russian ports. There were rumours that the company Korea Pyongyang Trading USA, the Beijing Tourism Bureau and another international investor were in negotiations with the DPRK authorities to revitalise the resort. The South Korean democratic-progressive Democratic United Party (DUP), embracing the continuation of the engagement policy, announced that it would reopen the resort for South Korean tourists provided that it comes to power after the elections in 2012.

---

[22] *Chosun Ilbo*, 24 August 2011. Online: http://english.chosun.com/site/data/html_dir/2011/08/24/2011082401039.html (accessed 12 February 2012).

[23] The sections of the law include (1) Key principles of Mt Kŭmgang Special Tourism Zone, (2) Management of the special zone for international tourism, (3) Tourism and tour service, (4) Establishment, registration, and operation of enterprises, (5) Provision of conditions for business activities, and (6) Sanctions and settlement of disputes (KCNA, 'Law on Special Zone for International Tour of Mt Kumgang', 2 June 2011. Online: http://www.kcna.co.jp/item/2011/201106/news02/20110602-15ee.html (accessed 1 May 2012).

6 HUMANITARIAN AID FURTHER SCALED DOWN

After Lee Myung-bak took office large amounts of official aid were sharply reduced and private aid organisations took over the lead in delivering humanitarian aid to the DPRK. The ROK administration with rare exceptions rules out the delivery of rice and cement, which was part of the flood relief aid delivered in the summer of 2010. The government's objective is that pure humanitarian aid projects that benefit the most vulnerable groups are to be continued despite the political crisis. Since all private aid needs to be authorised by the government, South Korean NGOs' engagement in the North has further decreased since May 2010. Data published by the MOU show a sharp reduction in humanitarian assistance to the North in 2011.

Table 2   South Korean aid deliveries for DPRK (in US$ million)

Year	2001	2002	2003	2004	2005	2006	2007	2008	2009	2010	2011
ROK government aid	75.2	89.2	93.8	115.4	135.9	227.4	208.9	39.9	24.2	17.8	5.7
Private aid	60.2	45.8	63.9	132.5	76.7	70.8	95.7	64.7	28.6	17.5	11.7
Total	135.4	135.0	157.7	247.9	212.6	298.2	304.6	104.6	52.8	35.3	17.4

Source: Ministry of Unification, January 2012.[24]

After Lee took office, aid dropped by 80 percent to US$39.9 million compared to the situation under his liberal-progressive predecessor Roh Moo-hyun and has further decreased since then. In 2011, aid dropped by about 70 percent to a historically low level of US$5.7 million. Private aid also decreased by 35 percent compared to 2010. However, there were reports that some private aid from the South was delivered to the North without prior authorisation by the ROK authorities. For example, a South Korean Christian group provided 172 tons of flour worth US$91,700 through a Chinese aid group. These deliveries were managed through the Chinese border town of Dandong.[25]

---

[24] Ministry of Unification, 'Nambuk kyoyu hyŏmnyŏk donghyang' [Trends in inter-Korean exchanges and co-operation], January 2012, p. 111–12.
[25] Yonhap News, 'South Korean Christians Deliver Unauthorized Food Aid to North Korea', 18 May 2011. Online: http://english.yonhapnews.co.kr/northkorea/2011/05/18/22/0401000000AEN20110518009400315F.HTML (accessed 24 June 2011).

When providing aid to the North the Lee administration usually uses the channel of international aid organisations. This approach also allows delaying aid deliveries by withholding the necessary funding. For example, the delivery of vaccines for more than one million North Korean children was approved but withheld after the *Cheonan* incident. In November 2011, the ROK government requested the World Health Organisation to deliver the vaccines and medical aid worth US$6.94 million to the North. According to data published by the MOU, in 2011 the South Korean government provided primarily medical aid and baby food via the international aid agency the UN Children's Fund (UNICEF). At the end of 2011, the MOU announced that it would donate US$5.65 million to humanitarian projects operated (and monitored) by UNICEF. The Lee administration also gave US$2.3 million to a South Korean NGO foundation to build an emergency medical facility at the KIC.

In addition, private organisations supplied powdered milk, soya milk, medication, flour, and malaria prevention kits. In May, a delegation of the Buddhist Chogye order supplied 100,000 tablets of a medicine for treating intestinal parasites. Civic groups were authorised to deliver food and medical aid worth US$769,000 to the DPRK. In the second half of the year, the Korea NGO Council for Cooperation with North Korea (KNCCK, *taebuk hyŏmnyŏk min'gan tanch'e hyŏbŭihoe*), which comprises more than 50 aid groups, and the Join Together Society delivered several hundred tons of flour to selected institutions in the city of Sariwŏn. Later, access to these facilities was granted for a delegation to verify that the aid has reached its intended beneficiaries. KNCCK also donated food aid to North Korean children. In addition, the Unification Church donated 300 tons of flour to Chŏngju, the city where the founder of the Unification Church, Mun Sŏn-myŏng, was born. The ambassadors of the Peace Association conducted monitoring visits and were planning to send more food aid to the DPRK. The group sent another 300 tons of flour aid to the DPRK later in 2011. One can only guess if the sharp increase in aid deliveries towards the end of 2011 is related to the change in leadership at the MOU.

7 EMPOWERMENT OF ROK'S SECOND-CLASS CITIZENS

Although North Korean refugees account for about 0.05 percent of South Korea's population, the ROK government through its 'hope project' (hŭimang p'ŭrojekt'ŭ) has increased efforts to support the new citizens over integration into the capitalist society. The counselling Hana centres have been expanded to meet the needs of the 'new settlers'. The South Korean Red Cross has launched a mentoring programme and started to train specialised volunteers who will assist the refugees in their daily lives. In 2011, with the arrival of about 2,700 persons the number of defectors rose by 15 percent to 23,100.[26] With regard to the gender rate the trend of the last year continued: more than two-thirds are women and the majority of the refugees are in their twenties (27 percent) and thirties (32 percent). Seventy percent of the refugees graduated from middle or high school, and the number of student defectors is reported to have increased.

When it comes to the integration of the new citizens into the South Korean labour market, the ROK government's support programmes are regarded as insufficient. As a survey conducted by the North Korean Refugees Foundation (*pukhan it'aljumin chiwŏn chaedan*) among 4,028 new settlers in 2011 revealed, the majority of the interviewees face challenges on the labour market. Although the participation rate of this group is only slightly lower (56.5 percent against 61.0 percent) compared to the ROK-born peer group, refugees are more likely to end up in temporary employment or as day labourers. The unemployment rate is more than three times higher than among 'ordinary' South Koreans (12.1 percent versus 3.7 percent). In addition, 50.5 percent work more than 45 hours per week compared to 14.6 percent of their South Korean compatriots.[27] Observers and activists claim that most defectors are employed in precarious and often inappropriate work places that do not correspond with their professional background and experiences. Unlike migrant workers, North Korean defectors have no well-established network they can make use of in face of a 'lack of

---

[26] Ministry of Unification, 'Pukhan it'aljumin chŏngch'aek ch'oekŭn hyŏnhwang' [Current status of policy towards North Korean defectors]. Online: http://www.unikorea.go.kr/CmsWeb/viewPage.req?idx=PG0000000166 (accessed 10 May 2012).

[27] *Pukhan it'aljumin chiwŏn chaedan* [North Korean Refugees Foundation], '2011 pukhan it'aljumin saenghwal silt'ae chosa kich'o punsŏk pogosŏ' [2011 report: basic analysis of living conditions of North Korean refugees], Seoul, p. 68.

their own community'.[28] Since temporary workers or day labourers are not represented by South Korean labour unions, North Korean defectors have taken initiatives to protect their rights and fight discrimination. These efforts include the establishment of a Preparatory Committee for the Labour Union of North Korean defectors (*t'albukja nojo sŏllip chunbi wiwŏnhoe*). Once this labour union is approved by the ROK ministry of labour and employment, it is expected to become an important representative of this rather marginalised group and to contribute to the empowerment of those whom many perceive as the ROK's 'second-class citizens'.

In the event of a sudden collapse of the DPRK, the Korea Employment Federation (KEF) has predicted that up to 3.65 million North Koreans would flee to the South, an influx that would 'seriously disrupt' the South Korean labour market and cause other social problems.[29] In the view of the analysts, the new settlers are likely to take over positions held by foreign migrant workers in the future.

8 DEFENCE, PROVOCATIONS AND UNIFICATION

Military exercises and rhetorical provocations continued in 2011. In October, the South Korean government announced a reform of its defence system in order to strengthen the ROK military in the face of the threat from the DPRK.[30] On the first anniversary of the *Cheonan* sinking and the attack on Yeonpyeong island the ROK military held several military drills in the West Sea, in the vicinity of the maritime border. The DPRK threatened via its central communication channel (*chosŏn chungang t'ongsin*) that it would turn the Blue House into a 'sea of fire' (*ch'ŏngwadae pulbada*). The DPRK's Committee on National Peace and Unification warned that its 'soldiers would be merciless and wipe out the [South Korean] puppet warmongers'.[31]

---

[28] Kim Ki-Sŏng, chairman of the Preparatory Committee for the Labour Union of North Korean defectors, quoted in *Korea Times*, 1 December 2011, p. 1.

[29] KEF, 'Changes in Labour Market and Policy Priorities after Unification between South and North Korea'. Online: http://www.kefplaza.com/kef/kef_eng_intro_6_1.jsp?num=3029&pageNum=0 (accessed 1 April 2012).

[30] Speech from President Lee Myung-bak on the occasion of the 63rd Armed Forces Day, 3 October 2011.

[31] *Donga Ilbo*, 'Puk "ch'ŏngwadae pulbada mandŭlketta" wihyŏp' [North threatens to turn the Blue House into a sea of fire], 25 November 2011, p. 6.

In March 2011, the ROK ministry of defence published a 309-page *Cheonan* White Paper[32] in which the incident, investigation and findings as well as the 'honourable treatment of the victims' (*hŭisaengja ye'u mit posang*) and compensation to the victims' families were laid out in detail. The document also looked carefully into the Lee administration's initial response to the incident and its crisis management. The authors concluded that public trust was damaged by inappropriate communication which led to misunderstandings and doubts and nurtured conspiracy theories.

As the German experience has shown, unification can happen at any time, and ROK governments have been seeking advice and means to prepare for such an event.[33] Although a survey conducted by the Korean Broadcasting Service among 102 North Koreans visiting China came to a different conclusion,[34] in the view of many conservatives, unification is 'imminent'. Therefore, Unification Minister Yu has proposed creating a 'unification account', literally 'unification pot' (*t'ongil hang'ari*). If the South Korean parliament adopts this proposal the government would start raising some US$50 billion. Significant (and voluntary) contributions are expected from South Korean individuals and companies. In addition, taxpayers' money annually allotted for the already existing unification fund would be transferred to this account, according to the MOU's plans.

As part of its 'grand strategy' the Lee administration has been increasing efforts in the field of North Korean human rights. The NHRC has established two units, the North Korean Human Rights Violations Reporting Center and the Hall of North Korean Human Rights Violation Records. Whereas the former collects information and testimonies about human rights violations in the DPRK, the latter will be used as an archive of such reports. The ROK's offensive push for human rights in the DPRK also includes the unsolved issue of the estimated 100,000 persons kidnapped during the Korean War. Since March 2011 the South Korean government has been running a nationwide informa-

---

[32] Taehanmin'guk chŏngbu [Government of the Republic of Korea], 'Ch'ŏnanham p'igyŏk sagŏn paeksŏ' [White Paper on the Cheonan attack], 17 March 2011.

[33] The MOU also announced a plan to establish a 'Korea-Germany Senior Advisory Committee for Unification' (*han dok t'ongil wŏllo chamun wiwŏnhoe*). See Ministry of Unification, '2011 nyŏn t'ongilbu ŏmmu kyehoek' [Work plan of ministry of unification for the year 2011], 29 December 2010. Online: http://www.unikorea.go.kr/CmsWeb/viewPage.req?idx=PG0000000478 (accessed 6 May 2012).

[34] *Hankuk Ilbo*, 'Puk chumin chŏlban "t'ongil pulganŭng"' [Half of North Korean citizens (say) unification is impossible], 25 November 2011, p. 6.

tion campaign to encourage citizens to report abductions to the authorities. In August 2011, the Korean War Abductees Fact Finding Commission (*6-25 chŏnjaeng nappuk chinsang kyumyŏng wiwŏnhoe*) led by the prime minister said it could confirm 55 cases. In addition to the wartime abductees, ROK officials estimate that about 500 South Korean prisoners of war and a similar number of civilians who were abducted in the post-war period are still alive in the DPRK. In December 2011, a task force comprising officials of the MOU, the ministry of foreign affairs and trade, the police and the intelligence agency was set up to gather relevant information about the fate of these persons.

9 OUTLOOK

Despite some (half-hearted) efforts to re-start dialogue, the year 2011 brought little improvement in the stalemate in inter-Korean relations. The outcome of the 2012 parliamentary and, particularly, presidential elections in South Korea will set the direction for future policies towards the North. After the leadership transition in the DPRK most analysts do not expect any radical changes with regard to the North's South policy. However, the DPRK leadership is carefully watching domestic political developments in the South. Although the common aim of the two major political parties (Saenuri Party and DUP) is peace and stability on the Korean peninsula, their approaches in reaching this goal remain different. The conservatives are likely to adopt a more flexible approach towards South–North co-operation while continuing to advocate the enactment of North Korea-related human rights laws. The democratic-progressive parties have already announced that their 'North policy' would be formulated on the basis of two summit agreements reached in 2000 and 2007. This would mean the withdrawal of the 5.24 measures and the re-opening of the Mt Kŭmgang tourist resort. In the end, improved inter-Korea relations are also a precondition for the restarting of the Six Party Talks and stability in Northeast Asia. However, the decision of the South Korean voters and sincere steps towards rapprochement by the new leadership in the DPRK will be crucial.

FOREIGN RELATIONS OF THE TWO KOREAS IN 2011

James E. Hoare

INTRODUCTION

Until December, this was a year in which the Korean peninsula attracted relatively little international attention. The alarms and excursions that had marked inter-Korean relations in 2010 were not repeated, and there were no changes on the nuclear front. As a consequence, international media interest declined dramatically. Kim Jong Il's death changed all that, and the end of the year was marked by a strong focus on the Korean peninsula. Inevitably, most of the media frenzy concentrated on developments in the Democratic People's Republic of Korea (DPRK—North Korea). But since these clearly had consequences for the Republic of Korea (ROK—South Korea), and since most journalists and academics could not get much nearer to events in the DPRK than Seoul, the South Korean capital, there was naturally much speculation on what Kim's death meant for the ROK.

1 REPUBLIC OF KOREA

1.1 *Relations with the United States*

Relations with the United States remained good. The US continued to support the ROK position vis-à-vis the DPRK internationally after the events of 2010, particularly in the early part of the year.[1] In January, Obama raised the issue with the Chinese President Hu Jintao but the Chinese maintained their unwillingness to condemn the DPRK. Following the death of Kim Jong Il, the US made it clear that should

---

[1] The two incidents were the sinking of the ROK corvette, the *Cheonan* (*Chŏn'an*) in March and the shelling of the ROK's Yeonpyeong (Yŏnp'yŏng) island in November—for background, see Sabine Burghart, 'Relations between the two Koreas in 2010', in *Korea 2011: Politics, Economy and Society*, pp. 59–62.

there be any problems on the peninsula the US would be there to support the ROK. Further signs of the closeness of the relationship included the conclusion of an agreement in August for the exchange of diplomatic officers between the State Department and the ROK's ministry of foreign affairs and trade. While such exchanges may not in practice mean a great deal, it was a much appreciated symbolic gesture of the closeness of the relationship. Also symbolic, but probably more substantive, was the appointment of Sung Kim as US ambassador, the first time a Korean-American has held the post. Kim was born in Seoul but grew up in the US. Before his appointment as ambassador to Seoul, he had served as the US representative to the Six Party Talks on the DPRK nuclear issue, with the personal rank of ambassador. For some months, his nomination to Seoul was held up by Senator Jon Kyl, a Republican from Arizona. Kyl apparently had no objection to Kim per se, but objected to the administration's failure, as he saw it, to pursue a tough line with the DPRK. Eventually the objection was withdrawn, and Sung Kim presented his credentials on 3 November. The two countries agreed to look at the question of whether the ROK should be permitted to engage in reprocessing of some types of spent nuclear fuel. They also continued talks, begun in 2010, on the revision of their joint nuclear co-operation agreement, which covers civilian nuclear development and which is due to expire in 2014. Talks also continued on the ROK request for more leeway over missile development. Some ROK lawmakers and right-wing commentators called on the US to re-establish a nuclear presence on the peninsula as a deterrent to the DPRK and, less explicitly, to China, but there was no official ROK support for the idea and the US made it clear that it did not intend to do so.

For President Lee Myung-bak, there were two highlights in the relationship with the US. The first was the passing of the Free Trade Agreement (FTA), which was both a trade and a foreign policy triumph, even if rather belated. Originally signed in 2007,[2] the FTA had been strongly contested in both countries right to the end. Its US ratification in early October cleared the way for the second highlight, Lee's five-day state visit to the US later the same month. Lee has visited the US several times as president and there is a good relationship between him and US President Obama, but this, the first ROK state

---

[2] See James E. Hoare, 'Foreign Relations of the Two Koreas', in *Korea Yearbook 2008: Politics, Economics and Society*, p. 59.

visit since the late President Kim Dae-jung went in 2001, was something special. Obama provided a good programme for Lee, who celebrated the 60-years' ROK-US alliance in an address to both Houses of Congress. The Pentagon also cosseted Lee. He was admitted to the Think Tank secure conference room and was briefed by Secretary of Defence Leon Panetta. The ROK ratification of the FTA came in November. Despite the formal measures, however, sniping at the agreement continued in both countries, and the battle may not yet be completely over, especially since 2012 is a presidential election year in both countries.

All was not entirely smooth in the relationship. Following the rape of a Korean teenager by a US soldier in October, Kurt Campbell, US Assistant Secretary of State for East Asia, made a formal apology and some troops were placed under a temporary curfew. Although the number of such sexual crimes was slightly less than in previous years, the ROK government said that it would seek a further revision of the ROK–US Status of Forces Agreement, last revised in 2001, which many Koreans perceive as biased towards the US.[3] Joint investigations began over possible dumping of toxic chemicals at former US bases. Protests at the decision to build a naval base on Cheju Island also took on an anti-American tone, even though the ROK says that the base is solely for the use of the ROK navy. Protestors claimed that it was really a US outpost against China, and would drag the ROK into the growing tension between China and the US.

1.2 Relations with China

The heady days of the 1990s that saw ROK–China rapprochement are now long past. China is one of the ROK's major trading partners, with the balance in the ROK's favour. Figures for two-way trade in 2011 show ROK exports to China at US$162.7 billion and imports at $82.9 billion. This makes the country the ROK's third largest trade partner and it is also the ROK's third largest investment destination. The amount was somewhat short of the $250 billion hoped for, but is still an impressive figure. There are plans for it to reach $300 billion by

---

[3] A good explanation of the ROK–US Status of Forces Agreement and what it means in practice was put out on Facebook by US Forces Taegu in November 2011: 'The SOFA and you', USAG Daegu, Tuesday, 1 November 2011. Online: http://www.facebook.com/note.php?note_id=255678571149389 (accessed 11 June 2012).

2015. This was one of the themes discussed during Chinese Vice-Premier Li Keqian's visit to the ROK in October, at which a six-point plan for increasing economic co-operation was agreed. Discussions on a free trade agreement with China, Japan and the ROK are under way, but worries have already arisen over issues such as the quality of Chinese foodstuffs, and there are fears of the possible consequences of market opening. China appears to have joined the countries exporting labour to the ROK; in June it was reported that the country's first 120 government-brokered migrant workers had been sent to South Korea.

Members of the Chinese-Korean community, however, are no longer as welcome as they once were. Concerned at the way relations seemed to have soured, the ROK ministry of foreign affairs and trade (MOFAT) established two teams of China experts and language specialists in January to strengthen diplomacy. One will report on Chinese political, economic and foreign affairs, while the other will look at public sentiment in China. MOFAT's think tank, the Institute of Foreign Affairs and National Security, launched a 'Centre of China Affairs', to collate ROK research on China.

Chinese and ROK leaders and officials meet in a variety of contexts, some multilateral, others bilateral, and they engage in a strategic dialogue. There were foreign minister-level visits in the early spring, and the ROK prime minister went to China in April. Defence strategy talks were held in July, and the fourth such 'high level strategy dialogue' took place in Seoul in December. Other signs of co-operation included a joint environmental study of the Yellow Sea (West Sea to Korea), which is an important fishing and maritime area for both countries. But ROK concern at China's long-term intentions shows no sign of abating.

Behind much ROK concern is the relationship between China and the DPRK. The role of China on the Korean peninsula is a long and complicated one, made more intense by the divisions imposed in the 1940s and by the Korean War. Koreans want a benevolent China but the existence of two Koreas, both now with diplomatic links to China but with very different agendas, makes that difficult to achieve. The ROK, like the US, looks to China to act as a restraint on the DPRK, especially over nuclear and missile matters. The Chinese have to some extent fulfilled such a role, brokering the Six Party Talks on the nuclear issue since 2003, and maintaining the pressure on the DPRK to return to such talks. But while the Chinese might not like what the DPRK does, and may even express public condemnation as it did in

2010 over the shelling of Yeonpyeong island,[4] it has so far refused to increase the country's isolation and what it sees as the risk of conflict by imposing effective sanctions. Concern over the continued and growing Chinese economic involvement with the DPRK also remains strong, even if this is a direct consequence of the tougher policy towards the DPRK that has marked Lee Myung-bak's approach since 2008. One new twist has been the growing number of Chinese tourists visiting the DPRK, replacing the ROK tourists that used to come until 2008. Tourist facilities that were originally developed with South Korean tourists in mind, and often by South Korean companies, are now being used by Chinese. The takeover of the Mt Kŭmgang resort, built with money from the Hyundai group, was particularly galling.[5]

Another regular cause of tension between the two countries is over fishing in the Yellow Sea. There may be co-operation on the broad question of the environment, but when it comes down to the competing claims of fishing fleets, co-operation tends to be in short supply. Every year there are clashes between Chinese and ROK fishing boats. The Chinese vessels, ranging wider afield as stocks in Chinese waters run down, are supposed to be licensed, but the ROK newspaper *Hankyoreh* at the end of 2011 said that only about 2,000 of the 10,000 Chinese vessels that operate in ROK waters have permits and even they engage in illegal fishing methods. The result is regular clashes, which often involve coastguard vessels as well. ROK coastguard vessels have become increasingly heavily armed to meet the threat, but even so the number of Chinese vessels seized while fishing illegally has been only between 370 and 550 a year since 2005, and there are occasional fatalities.[6] A run-in between the ROK coastguard and Chinese fishing boats in December left one coastguard dead, stabbed by the captain of a Chinese trawler, who was subsequently put on trial. The incident led to protests at the Chinese embassy in Seoul.

Then, to add to ROK worries about the role that China might play on the peninsula, came the death of Kim Jong Il and the succession of

---

[4] See James E. Hoare, 'Foreign Relations of the Two Koreas in 2010', in: *Korea 2011: Politics, Economy and Society*, pp. 75–76.

[5] The issue of Chinese tourism to the DPRK is also looked at in Rüdiger Frank's overview of domestic and economic developments in the DPRK in 2011 in this volume.

[6] *Hankyoreh*, 13 December 2011. Online: http://english.hani.co.kr/arti/english_edition/e_national/509932.html (accessed 28 May 2012).

Kim Jong Un. It provided an uncertain start for 2012, which is to be a 'Visit Korea' year in China.

1.3 Relations with Japan

As with China, history hangs heavy over ROK–Japan relations. In theory, the two countries should be well able to get along together. Both are long-term allies of the US, both are democracies, they have complementary economies, and they share common concerns about the DPRK and about China. Despite rhetoric, to some extent this does work. At the beginning of the year, there were reports in Japan about closer military co-operation as a result of the security tensions of 2010. But although the rumours of such co-operation regularly resurfaced, there was no development of the idea.

The March Tōhoku earthquake and tsunami seemed to offer some hope of a better relationship. The ROK reaction was immediate, with an ROK rescue team the first to arrive on the spot to give assistance. As well as the government, private organisations and ordinary people from the Salvation Army to the former 'comfort women'[7] contributed to relief funds. Within three weeks, some $46 million had been collected for Japanese relief. There were references to a 'paradigmatic shift in the Korean mindset'[8] and a new era in relations. It was not to be. On 30 March, the Japanese ministry of education issued its review of middle-school history textbooks that firmly asserted Japan's claim to Tokto, the group of islands in the East Sea/Sea of Japan, that are known as Takeshima in Japan.[9] This did not stop ROK aid, but it began to drop away.

Tōhoku had other consequences and raised other issues. There is still a very close economic relationship between the two countries, and the setback for Japan proved beneficial for the ROK in reducing its trade deficit, although this still remained high. Total trade was $1080.2 billion, with ROK exports to Japan being $397.1 billion, and

---

[7] 'Comfort women' is the term for women from Korea and other places who were forcibly recruited as military prostitutes after 1937. They have mounted a protest outside the Japanese embassy in Seoul for some years.

[8] Unnamed 'Japanese specialist' quoted in Cheol Hee Park, 'Post-Earthquake Japan-Korea Ties', in: *The Diplomat*, 18 April 2011. Online: http://the-diplomat.com/a-new-japan/2011/04/18/post-earthquake-japan-korea-ties/ (accessed 28 May 2012).

[9] For background, see James E. Hoare, 'Foreign Relations of the Two Koreas' in *Korea Yearbook 2008: Politics, Economy and Society*, p. 62, note 5b.

imports $683 billion. The earthquake and its consequences raised other issues that have perhaps still not been fully addressed. The ROK is very dependent on nuclear power for the production of electricity and its nuclear power stations, like those of Japan, are often in coastal regions. Although not as prone as Japan to earthquakes, the ROK is by no means exempt from them or from tsunamis. No doubt this was one reason why the two countries and China concluded an agreement on sharing disaster information at the end of November. The ROK and Japan also agreed to work together on obtaining Liquid Petroleum Gas (LPG)—Japan is the world's number one importer of LPG and the ROK number two.

But the historic tensions would not go away. Tokto continued to crop up regularly during the course of the year, as one side or the other pushed its claim. In July, following a Korean Air decision to fly over Tokto, the Japanese foreign ministry instructed its diplomats not to use Korean Air. This was pure symbolism on both sides. Flying over Tokto takes aircraft off normal flying routes, while Japanese diplomats are expected to fly Japanese airlines whenever possible. The ROK later announced plans to develop the islands as a tourist resort, to further Japanese protests. More serious was the ruling by the Seoul Constitutional Court at the beginning of September that the failure by the ROK government to seek individual compensation for the Korean 'comfort women' was unconstitutional. The ROK government had no choice but to take up the issue with the Japanese government. The latter's response was as usual that all such questions had been settled by the 1965 treaty normalising relations and there was nothing further to be done. Time may soon solve the issue. When ROK President Lee Myung-bak visited Tokyo in December, he noted that 16 former comfort women had died in 2011, which leaves only 63 still alive. This did not move the Japanese. One positive development in the history wars was the Japanese decision to return over 1,000 volumes of Korean archive material seized during the colonial period (1910–45). The ROK–Japan FTA negotiations remained stalled, as they have been since 2004.

If bilateral relations did not change much, there were signs of increased trilateral co-operation between the ROK, Japan and China at all levels from head of government downwards. Ministers from the three countries met to consider a variety of issues, including the environment, culture, nuclear safety and trade. ROK President Lee, Chinese Premier Wen Jibao and Japanese Premier Kan Nato held the fourth trilateral summit in Tokyo in May. They also visited the Fukushima disaster area. Other meetings included a summit in Bali in November in the margins of the ASEAN plus three meeting. Security co-operation and a free trade agreement figured high on the agenda.

1.4 *Other relations*

President Lee pursued his resource diplomacy travels, with visits to the Middle East, Africa and Central Asia. He also visited Germany, Denmark and France. Like Japan, France agreed in the course of the year to return Korean archival material looted by French forces in 1866. Formally, this was a long loan but it seems unlikely that the documents will ever return to France. The ROK and Israel concluded a deal in September for the purchase of Israeli missiles. During the Indian president's visit to the ROK in July, the two sides signed an agreement on nuclear co-operation. A free trade agreement with Peru, originally suggested in 2005, was signed in March and came into force in August. The ROK expects improved sales of cars, electronic goods and pharmaceuticals, while Peru's main exports will be raw materials and foodstuffs. Beef, rice, garlic and onions are excluded. Products from the Kaesŏng Industrial Zone will be treated as being of ROK origin. The possibility of a Malaysian FTA was also raised in the course of an April visit by the Malaysian prime minister. Relations with Russia remained static. The possibility of a gas pipeline from Russia to the ROK, which would pass through the DPRK, may have receded in the wake of the security incidents of 2010. The ROK view was that there would be little progress until the nuclear issue was settled, although it, like the DPRK, signed a preliminary agreement with Russia's Gazprom. The BBC reported in July that the barriers on Scotch whisky, Britain's top export to the ROK, had been lifted under the terms of the European Union–ROK free trade agreement. In September, the ROK newspaper, *Joongang Daily,* reported that an unnamed ROK official had said that if Britain continued to accept 'Sea of Japan' as the term for the waters between Japan and the Korean peninsula, the ROK might start using 'Malvinas' instead of the Falkland islands.¹⁰ This momentous threat to the remains of the British empire does not seem to have gone any further.

2 PEOPLE'S DEMOCRATIC REPUBLIC OF KOREA

2.1 *The Six Party Talks and relations with the United States*

The nuclear issue made little progress in the early part of the year. Kim Jong Il regularly told visitors that the DPRK was ready to return to the Six Party Talks (SPT), suspended since 2009. DPRK officials and the media made the same point. Chinese leaders echoed such statements, but there seemed no question of a unilateral North Korean denuclearisation. The DPRK was prepared to talk about managing its programme, not abandoning it. The SPT apparatus remained formally in existence. The other members, who regularly met and discussed the matter, included a new US representative, Clifford Hart, who took over after the appointment of Sung Kim as US ambassador to the ROK (see above). The five were somewhat divided. The DPRK position struck no chord with the ROK, the US or Japan, all of whom demanded full denuclearisation. The ROK made it clear that it was not just the DPRK's plutonium-related programme that should end, but also the uranium enrichment programme revealed in 2010.¹¹ On the other hand, Russian and Chinese officials indicated that they thought some form of acceptance of the DPRK's nuclear programme might be required. Rumours that the DPRK would conduct another nuclear test surfaced from time to time but proved unfounded.

From July, however, the picture appeared to improve. US and DPRK officials met in the margins of the ASEAN Regional Forum meeting in Bali in July; the contacts were described as constructive. Following the meeting, US Secretary of State Hillary Clinton announced that the DPRK's Vice-Foreign Minister Kim Kye Gwan would be allowed to visit the US and to meet with officials. He duly visited at the end of July and met with the US chief negotiator Stephen Bosworth and others. Kim said that the talks had been 'very construc-

---

¹⁰ *Joongang Daily*, 20 September 2011. Online: http://koreajoongangdaily.joinsmsn.com/news/article/html/688/2941688.html (accessed 11 June 2012).

¹¹ For background on the enrichment programme, see *Arms Control Today*, December 2010. Online: http://www.armscontrol.org/act/2010_12/NorthKorea (accessed 11 June 2012).

tive and businesslike'. Nothing happened publically for a time but in October, talks began in Geneva. There were reports that there had been some progress, with the DPRK agreeing to move towards denuclearisation, including a freeze on the uranium enrichment programme, in return for food aid. These talks marked the end of Bosworth's role as US special representative for North Korean policy, a post that he had held on a part-time basis since 2009. His successor, Ambassador Glyn T. Davies, former ambassador to the International Atomic Energy Agency (IAEA), was appointed on 20 October. In mid-December, US press reports said that the DPRK was ready to suspend nuclear and ballistic missile testing, readmit IAEA inspectors, and resume the ROK–DPRK dialogue. No formal agreement had been reached by the time of Kim Jong Il's death in December, however, which immediately put everything on hold.

The other major theme in US debates about the DPRK was the question of whether or not to supply food aid. In 2010, the DPRK had appealed for such aid, citing a series of natural disasters as the major reason for the food shortfall. These claims aroused scepticism. Some argued that there was no real food problem and that the DPRK was attempting to stockpile food so that it could make special allowances in 2012, the centenary of Kim Il Sung's birth, and the year in which the DPRK was supposed to reach the goal of becoming a 'strong and prosperous country'. In March, the United Nations organised a Rapid Assessment Mission made up of staff from its agencies concerned with food aid. This group visited 40 counties in nine of the 11 provinces, including 20 where no international assistance is currently being provided. Their report supported the DPRK claims. Heavy rain in August and September 2010 and a cold and prolonged winter had damaged crops. As in the ROK, foot and mouth disease began in autumn 2010 and spread rapidly. The effect on food production was far more sever in the DPRK than in the ROK. The DPRK is dependent on cattle for ploughing, and diseased cattle cannot plough. The report noted that the Public Distribution System was in theory functioning, but that at best it delivered only part of the allocated supplies and often dried up altogether. People were then thrown back on private plots, markets, or private barter trade. In more remote provinces, the group found serious food shortfalls, with consequent stunting, wasting and malnutrition. In general, people suffered from chronic undernourishment. Although recent appeals had produced much less than was required, the report concluded that some 297,000 metric tonnes of food aid was needed to help the most vulnerable.

The UN reported no stockpiling of food but the accusations continued. There were claims that the DPRK needs were exaggerated, and that much food aid was diverted to the military. During the following months, other investigations took place. The Elders, a group established by Nelson Mandela, sent former US President Jimmy Carter accompanied by other senior former political figures in April. Despite the eminence of the group, Carter and his colleagues were not seen by Kim Jong Il in Pyongyang or by President Lee in Seoul. They too stressed the urgent need for food aid, but their report was met by claims in both the ROK and the US that they had been taken in by the North Koreans. In May, the US special envoy for North Korean human rights, Robert R. King, led a food assessment team, the first time the DPRK had accepted a visit from King or his predecessor. The team concluded that, while there was no overall food shortage, certain areas were in difficulties. They also said that any food aid should be of a quality that would discourage diversion to the military. King also secured the release of yet another US citizen, Jun Young-su, who had been arrested in November 2010. According to an announcement in April 2011, he was being indicted for engaging in unauthorised religious activity as well as for illegally entering the DPRK.

US food aid was linked to progress on other matters, and it fell short of what the UN team thought was needed, but it did begin to flow. The US aid agency, USAID, gave $950,000 worth of assistance in August, mostly provided through funds from private donors. This led to a DPRK offer to resume the programme of searching for the remains of US service personnel missing in action (MIA) since the Korean War. The programme began in the wake of the 1990s nuclear crisis, and was unilaterally suspended by the US in May 2005. Talks on restarting the programme began in October and seemed to make good progress.[12]

Other positive signs included a private visit by DPRK economic officials to the US in March–April to study US industry. Associated Press (AP), which already had a branch of APTN, its television and picture news service, in North Korea began negotiating to set up a

---

[12] For background to the MIA programme, see C. Kenneth Quinones, 'The US-DPRK 1994 Agreed Framework and the US Army's Return to North Korea', in *Korea Yearbook 2008: Politics, Economy and Society*, pp. 199–229.

press office in Pyongyang. The director of the DPRK's Korean Central News Agency signed an agreement in the US in June that paved the way for a planned opening at the end of the year, and an AP delegation went to the DPRK in December. However, the formal opening ceremony was postponed because of Kim Jong Il's death, but APTN was able to supply pictures of the public mourning and funeral procession.

These developments did not stop the US from keeping up pressure on the DPRK. President Obama signed the 'Continuation of the National Emergency With Respect to North Korea' in June, a measure introduced by his predecessor in 2008. Sanctions were tightened, with an increase in the number of DPRK banks and trading companies barred from trading. Some DPRK ships were deterred from completing their journeys. The US military continued to maintain that the DPRK was a major threat to the US. Unlike President Clinton in 1994 when Kim Il Sung died, President Obama sent no formal message of condolences on the death of Kim Jong Il. There were reports that former President Carter had done so.

2.2 Relations with China

The DPRK's main international partner remained the People's Republic of China. This was particularly marked in trade. Figures from ROK sources showed that the Chinese share of DPRK trade was some 87 percent of $4.2 billion, up from 48.5 percent in 2004. Coal and steel were the main DPRK exports, while the country imported fuel and machinery. The increasing Chinese involvement in the DPRK economy was evident. Chinese goods flooded the shops and the markets. Chinese tour groups flocked to visit a country they said reminded them of their own past, replacing the former ROK tourists. China's Jilin province ran a special tourist train to the DPRK in October. At the end of August, the *Mangyongbong*-92, a DPRK-built ferry that used to ply the Wonsan–Niigata route until banned by the Japanese in 2006, began sailing as a rather stripped-down cruise liner from Rasŏn in the northeast of the country to Mt Kŭmgang. Most of the passengers were Chinese, but there were also a number of Western journalists. Much scathing comment about conditions on board found its way into the media, with particular emphasis on the multi-occupancy cabins where most foreign journalists seem to have been put.[13] There were reports that Chinese companies had been offered the use of the ROK-constructed tourist facilities on Mt Kŭmgang, unused since 2008, on a 15-year lease. The Chinese were also major suppliers of aid. Putting aside the unhappy memories of the Shinŭiju Special Administrative Region,[14] an agreement was signed in June setting up a joint economic zone on two islands in the Yalu river estuary. Agreements relating to the Rasŏn special economic zone included one on the supply of electricity to the zone, signed in June. June also saw a ground-breaking ceremony for a new and much needed road between Rasŏn and the Chinese city of Hunchun. The growing trade and aid led to much hand-wringing in the ROK, as well as to international speculation and claims that China was ready to turn the DPRK into a Chinese province. There was no evidence that this was China's intention, or that it was the Chinese government that was pushing the mainly small- and medium-sized companies that conducted the bulk of the trade.

Kim Jong Il made two 'unofficial' visits to China, in May and August. On the latter occasion he was returning from Russia. He met with senior Chinese leaders, including President Hu Jintao and there were the usual pledges of mutual friendship. It was widely believed that the chief purpose of the visits was to obtain China's endorsement of the succession arrangements. As usual, there were frequent exchanges between the two countries at ministerial and other levels, including the respective ruling parties; the latter contacts, and those between the military forces in the two countries are probably the most important. The visits included one by the Chinese minister of public security, who signed an agreement on co-operation with his DPRK

---

[13] Rose Parker, 'The Least Luxurious Cruise in the World: North Korea Launches its First Liner (Where Cabins are Shared and the Ship is Rusty)', in: Mail Online, 1 September 2011. Online: http://www.dailymail.co.uk/news/article-2032602/North-Korea-launches-cruise-liner.html. A brochure about the ship can be seen at https://docs.google.com/a/soas.ac.uk/file/d/0B8IwVGFnT05NOGY1ODA5YmUtZmUxMy00ZmM3LWE2YTQtNmFiYmE2YmRiNzJj/edit?hl=en_US&pli=1. (Both accessed 29 May 2012).

[14] Established in 2002 at Shinŭiju opposite the Chinese city of Dandong on the Yalu river. In an apparent imitation of Hong Kong, the zone was to be a visa-free enclave with its own self-government and chief executive. There was no sign that the DPRK had consulted the Chinese on the project. Yang Bin, a Dutch Chinese, was appointed chief executive, but before he could take up his post, he was arrested in China and imprisoned on tax evasion charges. The project has languished ever since, although it has not formally been abandoned.

counterpart. This may relate in part to the handling of DPRK defectors/refugees in China. In early August, two Chinese naval vessels from the Chinese Northern Fleet visited Wonsan to mark the 50th anniversary of the 1961 Sino–DPRK Treaty of Friendship; there were also earlier ceremonies to mark the event.

There was no sign that the Chinese had been given any more notice than anybody else about Kim Jong Il's death, but Chinese leaders were the first to offer condolences and to welcome Kim Jong Un as successor. All the senior state and party leaders visited the DPRK embassy in Beijing on 20 or 21 December, and the Chinese media gave full coverage to events in the DPRK over the following ten days. There were also unconfirmed reports that China's ambassador in Pyongyang had been the only foreigner to attend the funeral. The death and succession appear to have prompted much discussion in Chinese think tanks and academic circles, which some confused with official Chinese policies.

2.3 *Relations with Russia*

Relations with Russia were more active. Vice-Foreign Minister Aleksei Borodavkin was in the DPRK in March, discussing economic cooperation in a number of fields, including railways, the gas pipeline and power transmission. Kim Jong Il went to eastern Russia in August and met President Dimitry Medvedev at Ulan-Ude in Siberia. On both occasions, the DPRK said it was willing to return to the nuclear talks. The most substantive discussions, however, seem to have been on the subject of a gas pipeline from Russia to the ROK. Preliminary agreements were signed with Gazprom, the Russian gas exporting company, and the two Koreas in September. Russia supplied several tranches of food aid to the DPRK during the year and also apparently wrote off much of the DPRK debt owed to the former Soviet Union. On the news of the death of Kim Jong Il, the Russian foreign minister said that '[w]e have friendly relations with North Korea. We hope that this loss that the Korean people have suffered will not have a negative impact on the development of our relations',[15] which was perhaps a bit less fulsome than might have been expected.

---

[15] BBC, 19 December 2011: 'Kim Jong-il Death: World Reaction in Quotes'. Online: http://www.bbc.co.uk/news/world-asia-16239940 (accessed 29 May 2012).

2.4 Relations with Japan

At the beginning of the year, the Japanese Foreign Minister Maehara Seiji said that Japan was willing to have talks with the DPRK. This suggestion seemed to be linked to the apparently more conciliatory statements that appeared from both the ROK and the DPRK at New Year. Nothing came of the idea, which quickly disappeared from view. Japan continued to insist that the DPRK should address the issue of Japanese citizens abducted by the DPRK, while for most of the year, the DPRK sniped at Japan over the same issues as the ROK: Tokto, textbooks, and comfort women. Two Japanese visitors were arrested in the Rasŏn special economic zone on drugs' charges in March.

A more positive development, which, however, failed to lead anywhere, was the DPRK reaction to the Tōhoku disaster. There was extensive media coverage, a comparative rarity for an event outside the DPRK. The DPRK Red Cross sent a message of condolence and followed this up with a donation of US$100,000. This was somewhat dwarfed by the US$500,000 that Kim Jong Il was said to have sent to help Koreans in Japan. Later, the DPRK expressed concern at radioactivity that apparently originated in the disaster area reaching the Korean peninsula.

2.5 Other relations

Developments in the Middle East were clearly known to senior officials and those who had dealings with foreigners, even if the DPRK media was generally quiet on the subject, although there was condemnation of the air attacks on Libya. DPRK workers in Libya were apparently told not to come home. As they had done when Saddam Hussein fell, officials greeted the news of the death of Libyan leader Muammar Gaddafi by noting that it was a mistake for Libya to give up its nuclear weapons' option.[16] The European Union announced in July that it would supply food aid worth some US$14.5 million, with

---

[16] Comment to the author by a senior DPRK official, Pyongyang, October 2010; see also Rüdiger Frank, 'Libyan Lessons for North Korea: A Case of Déjà Vu', in: *38 North*, 03/2011, U.S–Korea Institute at the School of Advanced International Studies, Johns Hopkins University. Online: http://38north.org/2011/03/libyan-lessons-for-north-korea/ (accessed 20 January 2012).

strict monitoring conditions. In October, Valerie Amos, EU undersecretary and emergency relief co-ordinator, visited the DPRK and reported that the food situation was worsening. A delegation from the ministry of foreign affairs of France visited in July. It was later announced that France would establish a cultural co-ordination bureau in Seoul from October. Its offices, like those of the German, Swedish and British embassies, would be situated in the former German Democratic Republic embassy in Pyongyang. A Dutch citizen, Willem van der Bijl, a stamp dealer from Utrecht, who had been a frequent visitor to the DPRK and whose main interest was philately, was detained in August, apparently for taking photographs that were deemed to show the country in a poor light. He was released after two weeks, but this, coupled with other stories about resident foreigners including diplomats being detained for short periods, indicated a tougher line from the authorities about possible 'insults' to the country. Choe Thae Bok, the speaker of the DPRK parliament, the Supreme People's Assembly, visited Britain in March, at the invitation of the UK–DPRK All-Party Parliamentary Group.

KORUS, KOREU AND BEYOND: SOUTH KOREA'S FREE TRADE DRIVE[1]

Patrick Flamm and Patrick Köllner

Summary

On 15 March 2012 the KORUS Free Trade Agreement between South Korea and the United States entered into force. With this agreement, and the comparable one with the European Union (KOREU), already effective since July 2011, South Korea's export-oriented economy has come to enjoy almost unlimited access to the world's two biggest economic areas. Together, these areas constitute more than 50 percent of the world's current GDP. One of the effects of the recent global financial and economic crisis, as well as the deadlock in the Doha trade negotiation round on multilateral trade liberalisation, has been to make numerous East Asian and Pacific states, among them South Korea, focus on an expansive, above all bilaterally oriented free trade policy. In South Korea, the last two free trade agreements crown this development. The country's trade strategy now aims at a diversification and further expansion of its free trade policy.

- The most recent agreements with the EU, India and the United States signal an upgrading of the free trade policy approach previously pursued by South Korea. Compared to initial agreements with Chile or Singapore, for example, these comprehensive and far-reaching accords are of a whole new quality.
- In the next free trade projects with such state associations or states as the Gulf Cooperation Council or Australia, South Korea will increasingly focus on issues such as resources, energy and food security.
- The conclusion of free trade agreements also follows a political agenda, by strengthening the alliance with the United States or establishing strategic ties beyond East Asia.

---

[1] This paper forms part of a series of publications emanating from a project entitled 'South Korea as an Emerging Power in International Politics', which was carried out at the GIGA German Institute of Global and Area Studies between mid-2011 and early 2012. Financial support from the Korea Foundation is gratefully acknowledged. An earlier German-language version of this paper was published as *GIGA Focus Asien* 12/2011.

- KORUS and KOREU pose an economic policy challenge for Japan in particular. It is possible now that further free trade agreements will follow in the East Asian and Pacific region.

1 EXPORT DEPENDENCE AND INCREASING REGIONAL COMPETITION

The Free Trade Agreement (FTA) between the Republic of Korea (ROK—South Korea) and the United States (KORUS) finally, after five years of negotiations and a fiercely contested ratification in the South Korean parliament in late November 2011, came into effect on 15 March 2012 (*Korea Times* 2012). Back in July 2011, a similar FTA between South Korea and the European Union (KOREU) had been implemented. KORUS and KOREU constitute the biggest free trade agreements since 1994 when the North American Free Trade Agreement (NAFTA: US, Canada and Mexico) entered into force. With the EU, the US and the previously established FTA with the Association of Southeast Asian Nations (ASEAN), South Korea now has access to a free trade territory that constitutes more than 60 percent of the world's Gross Domestic Product (GDP). So far, no other Asian state has succeeded in concluding FTAs of such a magnitude. President Lee Myung-bak proudly stated in an address to the Korean public: 'Even though our land is small and even though it is divided into the South and North, it can be said that approximately 61 percent of the world has become our economic territory in terms of the GDP' (Cheong Wa Dae 2011). South Korea currently has five more FTAs and is negotiating several more with other states or state associations (see Table 1).

Hence, one can speak of a pronounced 'free trade offensive' on the part of South Korea. There are diverse motivations behind this free trade drive. The ROK started its bilateral free trade offensive comparably late, only after the 1997 Asian financial crisis (called the IMF crisis in South Korea) had laid bare the high interdependence of the East Asian economies, and the states in the region had begun to concern themselves increasingly with economic co-operation and co-ordination. In the following years, about 50 new bilateral and regional trade agreements were concluded, more than in any other region worldwide in that period. Observers speak in this context of a domino effect (Ravenhill 2008), because no one state wanted to lose its comparative advantages in the region's close-meshed production network.

Table 1 Overview of South Korea's FTAs

Free Trade Agreements in effect: • Korea–Chile   • Korea–Singapore   • Korea–EFTA   • Korea–ASEAN   • Korea–India   • Korea–Peru   • Korea–EU   • Korea–US
Free Trade Agreements under negotiation: • Korea–Canada   • Korea–Mexico   • Korea–Gulf Cooperation Council   • Korea–Australia   • Korea–New Zealand   • Korea–Colombia   • Korea–Turkey
Planned Free Trade Agreements: • Korea–Japan   • Korea–China   • Korea–China–Japan   • Korea–MERCOSUR   • Korea–Russia   • Korea–Israel   • Korea–Vietnam   • Korea–Mongolia   • Korea–South African Customs Union   • Korea–Central America   • Korea–Indonesia   • Korea–Malaysia

Source: MOFAT 2011, updated by the authors.

The result was a barely separable web of bilateral trade agreements that has been described as a 'cup of noodles', as the Asian variant of Jagdish Bhagwati's famous notion of the 'spaghetti bowl' of trade relations.

Amidst the deadlock in the Doha trade negotiation round on multilateral trade liberalisation and the recent global economic crisis, South Korea too focused on bilateral trade arrangements. The country tries not to fall behind its regional competitors and, on the basis of these trade initiatives, hopes to bolster Korea's export-based economic growth as well as to provide more jobs and to gain access to new sales and resource markets.

South Korea's export model is particularly vulnerable to the increasing competition in the region. A big share of its exports—approximately 40 percent—is made up of finished products, and technology-intensive parts and components constitute only a small percentage of exports. In Taiwan or Japan, in contrast, such intermediate goods amount for almost 75 percent of their respective exports. This makes Korean exported goods more price sensitive and increasingly prone to competition from China or Southeast Asia (Erixon and Lee 2010). Accordingly, the South Korean government endeavours to develop its domestic export industry structurally: a free trade setting resulting in higher competition and pressure to innovate is thought to provide the appropriate framework to achieve this aim. President Lee assessed the situation in his TV address on the occasion of the ratification of the KORUS by the US Congress in October 2011 as follows: 'The path we need to take is absolutely clear. With a lack of natural resources and a limited domestic market, we cannot sustain growth without exporting. This is why free trade agreements are important for Korea' (Cheong Wa Dae 2011). In 2010 the export of goods and services accounted for 54 percent of South Korea's Gross National Product (Bank of Korea 2011). Among OECD nations, South Korea exhibits the highest (and still growing) dependence on exports (see Table 2).

Table 2   South Korea's dependence on exports

	Exports and imports in terms of GNI* (%)	Exports of goods and services only (%)	Imports of goods and services only (%)
1975	65.0	27.6	37.4
1985	70.3	34.5	35.8
1995	59.3	29.9	30.1
2005	78.6	40.6	38.0
2006	80.9	41.2	39.7
2007	85.9	43.8	42.1
2008	110.7	55.1	55.6
2009	98.8	51.5	47.3
2010**	105.3	54.0	51.2

*   Gross National Income.
** Preliminary data.
Source: Bank of Korea 2011: 143.

2 SOUTH KOREA'S FREE TRADE AGREEMENTS

The ROK's free trade strategy was enshrined in the 2003 FTA Roadmap. A 'necessary trading network' is regarded as fundamental for securing the ROK's mainly export-based economic growth. Moreover, driven by FTAs and thus enhanced competition, the Korean economy is supposed to become more efficient and more attractive for foreign direct investment. An initial free trade agreement with Chile, which was eager to sign such an agreement with South Korea, led the way. Because of its rather marginal economic relevance, this agreement was largely seen as a trial run to gain experience for further, more important agreements (Sohn 2001: 7).

The FTA with Chile was followed by several agreements with smaller nations and regional associations such as ASEAN, Singapore, the European Free Trade Association (EFTA: Iceland, Liechtenstein, Norway and Switzerland) and most recently Peru. These agreements are free trade agreements in the original sense of the word, built around the elimination of tariffs and barriers restricting mutual trade and free access to markets. In most cases the parties defined exceptions for sensitive areas such as fishery and agricultural products, or they agreed on transitional periods for several years. Thailand, for example, did not sign the FTA between South Korea and ASEAN because the agricultural sector was not included in the treaty. Nonetheless, these agreements do not cover many issues that are not already addressed within the framework of the World Trade Organisation (WTO). This indicates the symbolic character of the agreements or rather, their role as test-pieces. Critics chide this policy for being too much focused on quantity instead of real content (Cheong and Cho 2009). Only the agreements with the European Union and the US and the agreement with India (Comprehensive Economic Partnership Agreement—CEPA), which has been in effect since 2010 (see Rai 2010), further address sensitive key issues with respect to services or investments, the WTO-plus topics.

3 ECONOMIC EXPECTATIONS AND CONCERNS

The United States is South Korea's second or third largest trading partner (after China and in some years Japan) with a trading volume of US$100 billion in 2011 (US Census Bureau 2012). In 2010, almost 12 percent of Korean exports were destined for the US and around 10 percent of all imported products arrived from the US (Bank of Korea 2011). At the same time the US is the second largest investor in Korea after the EU. Three years after the enactment of the KORUS FTA, almost 95 percent of consumer and industrial goods will be traded basically barrier free. Furthermore, the agreement does not stipulate exceptions for sensitive areas such as agriculture and the automobile and textile industries, although the two parties agreed on transitional periods. As a consequence of KORUS, South Korea hopes to boost its GDP by close to 6 percent over the next ten years, to create 350,000 new jobs and to lift the trade surplus vis-à-vis the US by US$4.6 billion (MOFAT 2010: 124; *Korea Times* 2012). The picture is different with respect to KOREU. From July 2011, when the agreement entered into force, 80 percent of the tariffs for Korean exports were eliminated immediately and in return around 70 percent of the tariff barriers for European exports were removed. After five years, 98 percent of all tariffs will be eliminated (BMWi 2011). Arguably, the free trade agreement with the EU has already shown some results. Between July and October 2011 alone, Korean automobile exports to the EU increased by 91 percent in comparison to the same period the year before (*Joongang Ilbo* 2011a). At the same time the EU export of automobiles, motor vehicle components and luxury goods increased significantly, contributing to a considerable trade surplus for the EU. It is, however, still too early for a detailed assessment of the agreement's impact.

Both agreements, KORUS and KOREU, represent high points in South Korea's bilateral trade diplomacy for several reasons. First, South Korea is the first and so far only Asian nation that has successfully concluded trade agreements with these two economic world powers. Second, these agreements include liberalisation measures in traditionally sensitive areas such as agriculture and fisheries. And third, for the first time extensive and wide-ranging liberalisation commitments in terms of WTO-plus issues were agreed upon. Both trade agreements include provisions regarding environmental protection standards and labour regulations as well as intellectual property rights. The Federation of Korean Industries believes that the KORUS agreement will positively influence the development of the ROK's service sector and will lead to the firm establishment of international standards in accounting or labour law in South Korea (Kang 2006). Both India and South Korea are also hopeful that the above-mentioned

CEPA agreement will drive growth in their respective service sectors. This would be particularly important to the Korean service sector, which has many small and medium-sized enterprises, few of which are internationally competitive.

The new quality of these comprehensive and deep-going liberalisation packages, however, has also produced strong reservations both in the US and in South Korea. Objections from the US car industry and labour unions led to renegotiations of the already initialled FTA, with the consequence that US President Barack Obama finally had to see through a compensation programme for employees, enterprises and farmers negatively affected by international trade. In the EU as well, reservations were expressed especially by the Italian car industry, which feared competition from Hyundai and Kia in the European automobile market. In South Korea, KORUS provoked intense, even violent confrontation in parliament. Besides economic concerns regarding the negative consequences of food imports for farmers, the opposition fundamentally objected to the Investor-State Dispute Settlement (ISD) clause in the treaty, fearing that the clause would unfairly benefit foreign enterprises in cases against the Korean government heard in international courts and that the ROK would be at a disadvantage. There was also anxiety that the agreement would contribute to a hollowing-out of social policy provisions in the ROK (*Joongang Ilbo* 2011b). According to the opposition, nothing less than the economic and social self-determination of South Korea was at stake. Overall, one can conclude that objections against the KORUS agreement were motivated more by political than economic concerns, not least in view of the upcoming parliamentary election in April 2012. For the fragmented opposition with the Democratic United Party at its core, fighting the KORUS agreement certainly served as an integrating campaign issue.

The free trade agreement with the EU proved conspicuously less controversial among the Korean public than the KORUS agreement. These different attitudes cannot be explained without reference to the more or less latent anti-Americanism in South Korean society. In 2008, the candlelight protests, with one million people demonstrating against President Lee Myung-bak's liberalisation of the import of US beef, attracted international attention. Just a year earlier, Lee, the business- and US-friendly candidate of the conservative Grand National Party (the predecessor of today's Saenuri or New Frontier Party), had been elected president by a large margin. During his campaign he had championed a 'global free trade network' which was also to connect the ROK to partners that had not been mentioned in the FTA Roadmap of 2003. In the new administration's 'global Korea' national security strategy, the new diversification strategy for free trade agreements was officially enshrined.

The strategy foresaw that in a second step, after concluding FTAs with big economic powers such as the US and the EU, agreements with important neighbouring economies such as China and Japan as well as additional key markets such as Canada or Australia were to be pursued (Cheong Wa Dae 2009). Further free trade agreements are planned with Russia, the Gulf Cooperation Council (GCC), Japan, Turkey, New Zealand and Colombia, which indicates a widened focus on issues such as resource or food security. Countries particularly rich in resources such as South Africa, the GCC states or Canada are seen as important and promising partners, whereas Australia and New Zealand are seen more as strategic food producers guaranteeing free access to food in times of a growing world population. Envisaged agreements with Turkey or with MERCOSUR are also of great interest in gaining better access to their respective domestic markets and to the Middle East and South America at large.

4 POLITICAL DIMENSIONS OF THE TRADE AGREEMENTS

Besides purely economic motives, at least with respect to the KORUS agreement political considerations also played a role. In view of the growing challenges emanating from China and North Korea, the ROK has for a number of years been keen on fostering its alliance with the United States. Isolationist voices in the US clamouring for reductions in US forces in Asia and Europe have been heard with concern by South Korean security strategists. Already under the previous president Roh Moo-hyun (2003–08), who had initially started the KORUS negotiations with the US, a decisive argument in favour of the agreement was its potentially positive impact on the US–ROK security alliance. Current and potential other leadership transitions in a number of East Asian and Pacific nations such as North Korea, China and the United States make a strong alliance between South Korea and the US all the more advisable.

The mere conclusion of the KORUS as well as of the KOREU agreement can be regarded as a big success for South Korean diplomacy. The country managed to negotiate on equal terms with the two biggest economic powers in the world and achieved substantial success in pursuing its interests. This is even more remarkable when one considers the formerly existing patron–client relationship between the US and the ROK. The transformation of the bilateral relationship and the deepening of US–South Korean ties by means of the FTA had been especially emphasised by proponents of the agreement including Korean business elites (Kim 2011).

The conclusion of the two FTAs with the US and the EU can also be seen as a further successful step in improving the prestige and image of South Korea and its industry products worldwide. It is a declared goal of the South Korean government to heighten the global recognition and visibility of South Korea and Korean enterprises and to transform the traditional 'discount' brand value of Korean products and Korea as a whole into a 'Korea premium' (Schmuck 2011: 103; Bark 2012). Finally, in symbolic terms the recently concluded free trade agreements can also be seen as an indicator for the international recognition of South Korea's rapid and successful development, which has transformed the country in two generations from a basket-case economy in Asia to one of the most dynamic OECD economies. International acceptance of this proud historical narrative through equal partnerships with world economic powers will certainly go down well with South Korea's status-sensitive public and elites.

5 Outlook

In macro-economic terms, the FTAs with the US and the EU might well live up to expectations: trade in goods and services with both partners is bound to increase. However, it may well turn out that there will not only be winners. Small and medium-sized enterprises in South Korea are likely to be especially affected by more severe competition. If the free trade drive is not be cushioned by substantial social, agricultural and industrial support measures, an unknown number of companies and individuals might well face negative consequences, which in turn could in the medium term erode the legitimacy of the prevailing paradigm of a free trade-based export strategy.[2]

---

[2] In fact, to cushion the expected impact of the KORUS agreement, the South Korean government plans to increase public spending on the agricultural sector by 22

The planned next round of South Korea's free trade initiatives is directed at the two important trade partners and neighbours, China and Japan, with which a trilateral trade agreement is sought in addition to bilateral ones. At the East Asia Summit in Bali in November 2011, the three countries' heads of state and government agreed upon starting formal negotiations for such a tripartite accord in 2012.[3] Besides problems regarding the sensitive agricultural and fishery sectors, expert-level talks have in the past stalled a few times over recurring political controversies. It remains to be seen whether the intensified negotiations concerning a larger free trade area in Pacific Asia (the Trans-Pacific Partnership, TPP), in which the Japanese government has recently shown eagerness to participate, will also provide momentum for a tripartite free trade pact.[4] Certainly, government and business circles in Japan were surprised at the relatively quick conclusion of the KOREU FTA and are now trying, against opposition from the agrarian lobby within and outside of the ruling Democratic Party of Japan, to catch up in free trade projects in order to stimulate the stagnating Japanese economy. But China also faces increased pressure to move ahead in terms of free trade initiatives in light of recent TPP-related developments (*Economist* 2011a). Compared to the free trade projects involving Japan and China, South Korea's FTA negotiations with smaller but strategically important trade partners such as Australia or the GCC are politically and economically far less delicate and are most likely to be easier to realise. In any case, South Korea's successful free trade drive has already contributed to new momentum on free trade initiatives in East Asia and the Asia-Pacific as a whole.

---

trillion won (around US$19 billion), of which more than a quarter had already been spent between 2008 and 2011 (*Joongang Ilbo* 2011c).

[3] As a precursor to a trilateral FTA, an accord on investment protection and liberalisation was to be signed by China, Japan and the ROK in May 2012 (*Nikkei Weekly* 2012).

[4] The TPP currently has only four smaller members: Brunei, Chile, New Zealand and Singapore. However the US, Australia, Malaysia, Peru and Vietnam have already applied for membership. At the 2011 Asia-Pacific Economic Cooperation summit in Hawaii, Japan, Canada and Mexico also announced that they wanted to start negotiations with a view to joining the initiative (*Economist* 2011b).

References

Bank of Korea (2011), *Monthly Statistical Bulletin*, April 2011, Seoul: BOK
Bark, Taeho (2012), 'Korea as a Global Free Trade Hub', in: *Republic of Korea Economic Bulletin* 34 (3), March 2012, pp. 42–43
Bundesministerium für Wirtschaft (BMWi) (2011), 'Schlaglichter der Wirtschaftspolitik', Monatsbericht Juli 2011 [Highlights of economic policy, monthly report July 2011], 1 July 2011. Online: www.bmwi.de/BMWi/Navigation/Aussenwirtschaft/handelspolitik-eu-wto.did=422026.html?view=renderPrint (accessed 21 November 2011)
Cheong Inkyo and Cho Jungran (2009), 'The Impact of Free Trade Agreements (FTAs) on Business in the Republic of Korea', ADBI Working Paper Series, Working Paper no. 156. Online: http://www.adbi.org/files/2009.10.15.wp156.impact.fta.business.korea.pdf (accessed 21 November 2011)
Cheong Wa Dae (2009), Global Korea: National Security Strategy 2009. Online: http://english.president.go.kr/government/golbalkorea/globalkorea.php (accessed 21 November 2011) [Cheong Wa Dae: the Blue House, official residence of the president of the ROK]
Cheong Wa Dae (2011), 'Through the KOR US FTA, the Bilateral Alliance is Ushering in a New Chapter', televised speech of President Lee Myung-bak, 17 October 2011. Online: http://english.president.go.kr/pre_activity/speeches/speeches_view.php?uno=5830&board_no=E03&search_key=&search_value=&search_cate_code=&cur_page_no=1≥ (accessed 21 November 2011)
Economist (2011a), 'Free-Trade Agreements: Opening up the Pacific', 12 November 2011. Online: http://www.economist.com/blogs/banyan/2011/11/free-trade-agree ... (accessed 16 November 2011)
Economist (2011b), 'Asia-Pacific Trade Initiatives: Dreams and Realities', 12 November 2011. Online: http://www.economist.com/node/21538214/print (accessed 16 November 2011)
Erixon, Fredrik and Lee Ho-suk (2010), 'Securing Korea's Prosperity in the Next Century: An Analysis of the Korea-EU Free Trade Agreement', ECIPE Occasional Paper, no. 5/2010
Joongang Ilbo (2011a), 'FTAs Boosted Auto Exports', 14 November 2011. Online: http://koreajoongangdaily.joinsmsn.com/news/article/article.aspx?aid=2944079&cloc=joongangdaily|home|newslist2 (accessed 21 November 2011)
Joongang Ilbo (2011b), 'ISD Clause Presents More Work for FTA Negotiators', 1 November 2011. Online: http://koreajoongangdaily.joinsmsn.com/news/article/article.aspx?aid=2943524&cloc=rss%7Cnews%7Cjoongangdaily (accessed 21 November 2011)
Joongang Ilbo (2011c), 'Farmers Already Getting FTA Budget', 25 November 2011. Online: http://koreajoongangdaily.joinsmsn.com/news/article/article.aspx?aid=2944664&cloc=joongangdaily|ho me|newslist1 (accessed 25 November 2011)
Kang, Shin-ho (2006), 'Korea-U.S: FTA Should Be Used as a Springboard for Take-Off Toward Advanced Country', in: *FKI Newsletter*, CEO Message, 2006-03
Kim, Chi-wook (2011), 'South Korea's Business Sectors and Transformation of ROKUS Alliance: A Case Study of KORUS FTA', EAI Security Initiative Working Paper, no. 16. Online: http://www.eai.or.kr/data/bbs/eng_report/201105261443 16.pdf (accessed 20 November 2011)
Korea Times (2012), 'Amid Brouhaha, KORUS FT Goes into Effect', 13 March 2012, p. 1

MOFAT (Ministry of Foreign Affairs and Trade) (2010), Diplomatic White Paper 2010, Seoul: MOFAT
MOFAT (Ministry of Foreign Affairs and Trade) (2011), 'FTA Status of Korea'. Online: http://www.mofat.go.kr/english/econtrade/fta/issues/index2.jsp (accessed 21 November 2011)
Nikkei Weekly (2012), 'Japan, China, South Korea Poised to Sign Investment Pact', 26 March 2012, p. 2
Rai, Durgesh K. (2010), 'South Korea's Economic Relations with India: Trends, Patterns and Prospects' in: Rüdiger Frank, James E. Hoare, Patrick Köllner and Susan Pares (eds), *Korea 2010: Politics, Economy and Society*, Leiden and Boston: Brill, pp. 189–215
Ravenhill, John (2008), 'The Move to Preferential Trade on the Western Pacific Rim: Some Initial Conclusions', in: *Australian Journal of International Affairs* 62 (2), pp. 129–50
Schmuck, Alena (2011), 'Nation Branding in South Korea: A Modern Continuation of the Developmental State?' in: Rüdiger Frank, James E. Hoare, Patrick Köllner and Susan Pares (eds), *Korea 2011: Politics, Economy and Society*, Leiden and Boston: Brill, pp. 91–117
Sohn, Chan-hyun (2001), 'Korea's FTA Developments: Experiences and Perspectives with Chile. Japan and the U.S. Regional Trading Arrangements: Stocktake and Next Steps', paper presented at the Trade Policy Forum, Bangkok, 12–13 June 2001
US Census Bureau (2012), 'Trade in Goods with Korea, South'. Online: http://www.census.gov/foreign-trade/balance/c5800.html (accessed 25 April 2012)

NORTH KOREA AFTER KIM JONG IL: THE KIM JONG UN ERA AND ITS CHALLENGES[1]

Rüdiger Frank

1 INTRODUCTION

On 19 December 2011, the official news agency of the Democratic People's Republic of Korea (DPRK—North Korea) announced the death of Kim Jong Il, who had been only the second leader since the foundation of his country in 1948: 'He suffered an advanced acute myocardial infarction, complicated with a serious heart shock, on train on December 17, Juche 100 (2011) for a great mental and physical strain caused by his uninterrupted field guidance tour for the building of a thriving nation' (KCNA, 19 December 2011).[2] His death as such did not come as a great surprise; he was 68 years old and from 2008 obviously suffered from serious health problems. But after his recovery from these, not only the West but also North Korea itself seemed to have expected him to live a few years longer. The most visible evidence of this was that, unlike his father, he had not announced a successor or made any explicit arrangements on power succession, although at least since his illness in 2008 and in particular since September 2010, signs had emerged that his third son, Kim Jong Un, was being prepared for such a function.

It was thus the Korean Workers Party (KWP, or simply the Party)[3] that took on the role as kingmaker. The official announcement of 19

---

[1] This is a revised and supplemented version of Rüdiger Frank (2012), 'North Korea after Kim Jong Il: The Kim Jong Un Era and its Challenges', in: *The Asia-Pacific Journal*, 10 (issue 2, no. 2), 9 January 2012.

[2] KCNA stands for Korea Central News Agency, the official news agency of the DPRK. Unless indicated otherwise, all direct quotations in English are taken from the English-language website of KCNA at www.kcna.co.jp. Other options include www.kcna.kp or www.rodong.rep.kp. The latter includes PDFs of the print version of the newspaper *Rodong Sinmun*.

[3] The North Korean media in their English versions apply the term Workers' Party of Korea (WPK). In other sources, 'Korean Workers' Party' (KWP) is used, which corresponds more closely with the Korean original *chosŏn rodong tang*.

December was signed first by the Central Committee and the Central Military Commission of the KWP. The key statement in this announcement read: 'Standing in the van of the Korean revolution at present is Kim Jong Un, great successor to the revolutionary cause of Juche and outstanding leader of our party, army and people' (KCNA, 19 December 2011).

The remaining few days of the year 2011 became a time of bustling activity marking this transition. This article seeks to provide a structured analysis of these events and discusses the insights they might provide into the future course of North Korea. The dynamics of time mean that many of my observations have later been supplemented or replaced, and some conclusions have become challenged by later events. But I have decided to present this short-term analysis precisely because of the rare insights into the often inconsistent policies of making a new myth and leadership that the chaos and turbulence of these few days in late December 2011 offer. In 2012 and thereafter, the edges will be smoothened and North Korea might again become what it used to be: an at least superficially monolithic system with no disruptions, no open discussions, and the appearance of continuity. Or it will embark on a path of dynamic changes that, one must hope, will be peaceful. In any case, we need to understand better where these future events will come from.

Not least, we need to develop an understanding of the new leader Kim Jong Un. His first moves tell us something about his personality, which plays a significant role in a dictatorship, about his leadership style, and his policy priorities. Readers will be able to compare the terminology, slogans and issues that were prevalent in late 2011 with the current state of affairs and draw their conclusions from detecting what has been discontinued, maintained or expanded.

The paper starts with an overview of actual events after 19 December and then turns to a number of key questions: Does Kim Jong Un have the power, and will he keep it? How is Kim Jong Un's legitimacy being built? Do the Party and the military compete for power in North Korea? How will China behave? What will happen to North Korea's nuclear programme? Finally, with a view into the future we ask: What will Kim Jong Un's policies be?

2 FROM DEATH TO FUNERAL: EVENTS BETWEEN 19 AND 31 DECEMBER 2011

To illustrate the beginning of the development of ideas and official versions of the past and the future regarding the death of Kim Jong Il and in particular the role and position of Kim Jong Un, this section draws heavily on official coverage by the Korea Central News Agency published on the internet.[4] Disclaimers about the validity of that source are not necessary here, because subjectivity is exactly what is looked for. We proceed with a chronological highlighting of developments; a thematically focused analysis follows in the next sections.

Reporting started with the above mentioned KCNA article announcing the death of Kim Jong Il and simultaneously declaring Kim Jong Un the 'successor to the revolutionary cause of chuch'e'. On the same day, a few technicalities were announced, such as a mourning period (from 17 to 29 December), a period for the reception of mourners (20 to 27 December), a farewell-bidding ceremony in Pyongyang on 28 December, and a national memorial service to be held on 29 December. A funeral committee comprising 231 persons was announced. The official reason for Kim Jong Il's death was fatigue. North Koreans were informed that he had worked himself to death for his nation, travelling tirelessly around the whole country to give on-the-spot guidance, eating frugal meals and accepting all kinds of discomfort to care for his people as a good father would do.

The campaign to establish Kim Jong Un was quickly under way. Along with reports about mourning people, there were passages quoting individuals who said: 'We will overcome sorrow and display fresh strength and courage to tide over the present difficulties and work harder for the great and fresh victory of the Juche revolution, true to the leadership of Kim Jong Un' (KCNA, 19 December 2011). This coincided with the deification of Kim Jong Il, something he—unlike his father Kim Il Sung—had avoided during his lifetime. Two slogans stood out: 'Kim Jong Il will always live' and 'Leader Kim Jong Il will always be with us' (KCNA, 19 December 2011). The latter is precisely the slogan that was chosen to commemorate Kim Il Sung; during visits in 2004 and 2005, the author estimated that about 50 percent of all slogans read: 'The Great Leader Kim Il Sung will always be with us'. In general, many at least superficial similarities to the events

---

[4] See footnote 2.

of 1994 have been discernible, when Kim Il Sung died. A major difference that has been widely noted was the speed with which the successor took over power officially; it took Kim Jong Il three years to officially assume the top leadership posts in the Party, the state and the military.

But in December 2011, the connection between the deceased and the new leader was established rapidly and explicitly, as if not to leave any room for doubt. Since the late 1990s, Kim Jong Il had been presented as being identical to his father Kim Il Sung. Now it was Kim Jong Un who was portrayed in such a way: 'He is another great person produced by Korea who is identical to Kim Jong Il ... Kim Jong Il passed away to our sorrow before seeing the victory in the drive for building a thriving nation, his great desire, but we are under respected Kim Jong Un identical to him. Kim Jong Un's leadership provides a sure guarantee for successfully carrying forward the revolutionary cause of Juche through generations, the cause which was started by the President and led by Kim Jong Il to victory' (KCNA, 19 December 2011).

The message from China arrived quickly, with a subtle flavour: 'We are convinced that the Korean people will overcome sorrow and display strength under the leadership of Kim Jong Un, united close around the WPK, true to the behests of Kim Jong Il, and make uninterrupted advances to build a thriving socialist nation and achieve lasting peace on the Korean Peninsula' (KCNA, 19 December 2011). The message was an explicit recognition of Kim Jong Un by the country's most important ally and partner in economic, military and diplomatic affairs, but carried the suggestion that the Party should form the centre of society. The Russian message, sent by President Medvedev, was more subdued, expressing hopes for good co-operation between the two countries and peoples.

One day later a pattern was already emerging in KCNA reporting. Four points stood out: (1) The various feats of Kim Jong Il were now praised in a rather structured way, stressing his roles as a father of the Korean people, a fighter for national reunification and independence, a defender of justice and socialism, a hero, and the great developer of *chuch'e*. (2) Kim Jong Un was praised as the successor, emphasising how closely he resembled his father and how precisely he would be following his policies. (3) The whole society was displayed as being covered in grief, and countless examples of individual and collective mourning were presented to readers. (4) Added to this was the international dimension, quoting in great detail messages of condolences from friendly individuals and countries, including Cuba's Raul Castro, the governor of the Amur region, the heir apparent of Qatar, and from pro-North Korean Japanese.

In particular, Kim Jong Un was portrayed in various functions. On one hand, he was shown as a son who had lost his father and who was respectfully mourning his death. As of mid-2012, we can say that this trend of displaying him in a more human fashion has been continued. He was also, however, portrayed as the leader around whom people could gather in such difficult times and seek for protection and consolation. This is an image we know from artistic depictions of Kim Jong Il after Kim Il Sung's death. Later, expressions of loyalty to Kim Jong Un aimed at cementing his role as the new leader.

From 21 December, the above was supplemented by familiar reporting of the mysterious behaviour of animals, birds in particular, to show that even nature was shocked and in grief; and by feelings of guilt for having failed the leader. In particular, the absence of any Kim Jong Il statue was loudly lamented by a number of individuals from among the 'ordinary' people. At the same time, this absence was also portrayed as yet another expression of Kim Jong Il's modesty, in particular as he was said to have opposed the erection of statues to his honour. The theme of an ascetic, selfless lifestyle was repeated in various forms: 'Kim Chun Sil, 31, a woman work-team chief of the Kaesong Textile Mill, said: We produce a lot of cloth every day, but we failed to make him a new dress with good cloth. This makes us feel compunction' (KCNA, 21 December 2011).

We also find expressions of a 'now more than ever' attitude: 'Ko Yong Sim, 24, female weaver of the Tetron rayon fabrics shop at the Pyongyang Textile Mill, told a reporter as follows: ... Weaving as much cloth as they can so as to produce more goods, this is the noble mental world and fighting spirit of the Korean working class determined to improve the standard of people's living as desired by Kim Jong Il.' A Kim Jong Un-oriented variation of this theme is here: 'All the officials and workers of the complex are pledging themselves to be loyal to Kim Jong Un ... by overcoming today's sorrow and displaying courage so as to bring about a leap forward in the production of modern machines' (KCNA, 21 December 2011).

For the first time on 21 December there was also mention of 'smiling Kim Jong Il'. This later became a standard verbal and visual image, adding to the above mentioned characteristics in the process of weaving and finalising the myth around Kim Jong Un's father. A total of 42 KCNA articles during the last ten days of December 2011 carried the term 'smiling Kim Jong Il'.[5]

The image of Kim Jong Un seemed to undergo a transformation in these few days in December. From being in the beginning little more than a name, he became increasingly human and featured prominently as a mourner and as the big hope for Koreans. The emphasis seemed to switch from his personal loss towards filial piety and his function of comforting the other mourners. It was their grief, or the people's suffering, that touched him to tears: 'There were tears in the eyes of Kim Jong Un as he was looking at servicepersons and people weeping bitterly and calling Kim Jong Il in chocking [sic] voices' (KCNA, 23 December 2011.

On the same day, what might be called the 'fish-episode' in North Korean propaganda started and lasted until 26 December. Kim Jong Il had paid particular attention to fish and visited farms and seafood stores four times in 2011 as part of his guidance programme. One day before his death, Kim Jong Il had reportedly ordered his officials to make sure that fresh fish was provided to the citizens of Pyongyang. Reporters and interviewees were touched to tears to learn that despite his great loss, Kim Jong Un spared the time to make sure this promise of his father was fulfilled. Echoing Brian Myers' observations,[6] KCNA made it clear that all Koreans should feel shame at having bestowed upon them such unmerited benevolent love and care on the part of their new parental leader. This care was supplemented on 24 December by the provision of hot drinks to mourners who were spending hours in the cold to pay their respect to the numerous statues and mosaic murals: 'Yesterday Kim Jong Un made sure that fresh fishes [sic] were supplied to every family in Pyongyang in reflection of Kim Jong Il's warm love for people and today he took a special step for meeting people's interests and providing the best conveniences to them on a top-priority basis under any circumstances' (KCNA, 24 December 2011).

---

[5] On a side note, the term initially used (*usŭsinŭn kimjŏngil*) bears a striking similarity to 'smiling Jesus' (*usŭsinŭn yesunim*), which is popular among (South) Korean Christians. For whatever reason, North Korean media keep using the English term but seem to have switched to '*t'aeyangsang*' in Korean.

[6] Brian Myers (2010), *The Cleanest Race: How North Koreans See Themselves and Why It Matters*, New York: Melville House Publishing.

On 24 December, in addition, there appeared for the first time the slogan: 'Let us defend with our very lives the Party Central Committee headed by respected Comrade Kim Jong Un!'. This slogan, which implies a certain leadership role by the Party, was used with the name of Kim Jong Il until October 1998. Then it disappeared from KCNA articles until a sudden re-emergence in late September 2010, during the KWP conference at which Kim Jong Un was first introduced to the public and given his first official titles and functions.

A new topic emerging on 25 December and later developing strongly was the alleged disrespect shown by the country's enemies and South Korea in particular over the death of Kim Jong Il. This would develop in 2012 into a massive campaign against the South Korean president in particular. Accusing South Korean authorities of preventing mourners from entering North Korea across the Demilitarised Zone via Kaesŏng or by air, KCNA stressed that '[t]he south Korean puppet authorities' unethical acts bereft of elementary etiquette and compatriotism have touched off unanimous outrage and wrath among Koreans and all other people of the world' (KCNA, 25 December 2011).

The ceremony of bidding farewell to Kim Jong Il took centre stage in KCNA reporting on 28 December. A very detailed and emotional description of the route that the motorcade with Kim Jong Il's hearse took through Pyongyang was followed by a sentence of consolation: 'During his lifetime Kim Jong Il, wishing a bright future of the country being confident of the steady continuity to the Juche cause, said: As there is General Kim Jong Un, the future of the country and the nation is in safe hands.' The mourning ended with a pledge that included all three leaders: 'We will accomplish the cause of building a thriving socialist nation, the behest of Kim Jong Il, like disciples of President Kim Il Sung, remaining loyal to the leadership of Kim Jong Un' (KCNA, 28 December 2011). Later in 2012, this concept would be developed further.

During the memorial service on 29 December, it was Kim Yong Nam[7] who gave the main address, repeating what had by now become solidified as the central theme: grief over the loss of Kim Jong Il, praise of his many achievements, and a positive outlook on the future

---

[7] Kim Yong Nam (Kim Yŏng-nam, born in 1928) has been chairman of the Presidium of the Supreme People's Assembly, the DPRK's parliament, since 1998. In that function, he operates as the de facto head of state, mostly for ceremonial purposes such as accepting the credentials of ambassadors, etc.

thanks to the new leader Kim Jong Un, who would continue the revolutionary path and loving care of his father. In a comment, KCNA stressed the revolutionary bloodline of Mt Paektu[8] and the fact that Kim Jong Un had accompanied Kim Jong Il on his military guidance tours.

As soon as the memorial service was over, the beginning of a new process could be observed—the elevation of Kim Jong Il and his merger with Kim Il Sung. At the same time, Kim Jong Un took over the now liberated posts, starting with the announcement of his assumption of the position of 'supreme commandership of the Korean People's Army at the behest of leader Kim Jong Il on Oct. 8 Juche 100 (2011).' Nobody bothered to explain why such a major transfer of powers had not been made public earlier; this was an obvious attempt at implying that Kim Jong Il himself had declared Kim Jong Un as his successor. We can only speculate about the reasons: a simple ceremonial act, or an expression of insecurity about the stability of the new leader's legitimacy? Why did the KWP on the same day stress that '[s]tanding at the helm of the Korean revolution is Kim Jong Un, the only successor [*yuilhan hugyeja*] of Kim Jong Il'—as if there were an alternative? The word 'only' or 'sole' reappeared when the Party pledged to 'hold Kim Jong Un in high esteem as the only centre [*yuil chungsim*] of unity, cohesion and leadership of the WPK, devotedly defend him politically and ideologically.'

The following sections will seek to provide a more analytical perspective on some key questions that arose in the context of Kim Jong Il's death and succession by Kim Jong Un.

3 DOES KIM JONG UN HAVE THE POWER, AND WILL HE KEEP IT?

Common sense is a bit at a loss here. He is the son of Kim Jong Il, but only the third son. North Korea is not a monarchy, but nevertheless a third-generation succession has taken place. Kim Jong Un has been announced as the successor and assigned a leading role, but he is very young and inexperienced. In face of this list of contradictory statements, it is better to turn to a more structured analysis.

---

[8] This is a reference to the Kim family; Kim Il Sung had fought in the area as a guerilla, and his son Kim Jong Il was allegedly born there in 1942. Inter alia, 'Mt Paektu' thus stands symbolically for anti-Japanese Korean nationalism.

Gregory Henderson's study of Korean politics suggests that the emergence of alternative centres of power is relatively unlikely.[9] Rather, various individuals and groups can be expected to compete for control of the centre, which is formed by or around Kim Jong Un. At his young age and with only a short grooming period, he will have to rely on others to maintain and expand his power. Before Kim Jong Il's death, Karoly Fendler, a veteran Hungarian diplomat with decades of experience in North Korea and many insights, in a private conversation with the author suggested a triumvirate: Kim Jong Il and his son responsible for army and ideology, Kim Yong Nam for protocol, and Premier Choe Yong Rim for the economy. This makes sense in many ways: hardly any ruler can rule alone. Later developments imply that indeed, individuals like Choe Ryong Hae[10] have taken on a relatively prominent role in the media in addition to leader Kim Jong Un. So Kim Jong Un will share power, but the system also needs him as a single leader. Brian Myers argues that Koreans, like others, seem to have a certain preference for a parental leader and, most importantly, that the state as such shows no signs of undergoing a legitimacy crisis.[11] Along the same line, Cheong Seong-chang argues that instead of a collective leadership, we will see the emergence of another single-person leadership system under Kim Jong Un.[12]

My own assessment is slightly different. It is true: now that the power vacuum left after the death of Kim Jong Il has been so quickly and massively filled with Kim Jong Un, he will be the man in the spotlight. But at least for the next few years, he will not have the capacity to control the country without having to rely heavily on support from powerful individuals. This, however, is risky. I agree with Andrei Lankov who expects a power struggle in North Korea, one level below Kim Jong Un: 'we might soon witness advisors and officials

---

[9] Gregory Henderson (1968), *Korea: The Politics of the Vortex*, Cambridge MA: Harvard University Press.

[10] Choe Ryong Hae is vice-chairman of the Party's Central Military Commission and secretary of the Central Committee of the KWP. In the first months of 2012, he seems to have acquired a particularly important position in the North Korean power hierarchy.

[11] Brian R. Myers (2011), 'North Korea's State-Loyalty Advantage', in: *Journal of International Affairs*, 65 (1), Fall/Winter 2011, pp. 115–29.

[12] Chŏng Sŏng Chang (2012), '2012nyŏn pukhan chŏngse chŏnmang' [View of the situation in North Korea in 2012], in: *Chŏngsewa Chŏngch'aek*, 2012 (1). Online: http://www.sejong.org/pub_ci/PUB_CI_DATA/k2012-01_6.PDF.

jockeying for power behind the throne and their struggle may become quite violent'.[13]

In fact, I believe that the hasty efforts at elevating Kim Jong Il posthumously to the same status as his father Kim Il Sung might come too late. They are the only choice the leadership thought it had after the sudden death of its top man, but it is only the second best option. Kim Jong Il knew very well why he avoided a real take-over during his lifetime. His legitimacy was built almost exclusively on being the sole prophet of his towering father Kim Il Sung. As such, he was accepted and untouchable. Kim Jong Il had very good reasons not to erect any statues of himself, and not to give his name to streets, plazas and so forth.

The country of Kim Il Sung: this is what most North Koreans, as defectors confirm, subscribe to with little hesitation. Kim Il Sung had liberated the country from the Japanese and won a shining victory against American aggression in the Korean War. This is what people were told, this is what they believed, this is what in their view granted Kim Il Sung every right to govern the country that he single-handedly had created and protected. Not least, he had his old guard of loyal followers around him. Parts of this old guard were alive and in control in 1994. But time took its toll. Their places have meanwhile been taken by the next, much better educated generation that grew up under more regular conditions. Now even the third generation is ready. Can these career-oriented children of apparatchiks replicate the Kapsan faction's unconditional, grim personal loyalty? Or is their primary concern the preservation of the system that has formed them and that they benefit from? Both forms of loyalty can have the same result, i.e. support of the leader. But the latter form is open to alternatives.

For two decades from the mid-1970s, Kim Jong Il was promoted as the only person in the world who could fully grasp the wisdom of Kim Il Sung, who joined him on his numerous journeys through the country, who learned from him, who assisted him, and who then humbly continued his work. Kim Jong Il's position after 1994 was weaker than that of his father, but he could convincingly claim to be the only logical choice for the continuation of a path and leadership that was largely undisputed and beyond any doubt. And he could count on the old guard to support him.

---

[13] Andrei Lankov (2012), 'It's not all change in Pyongyang', in: *Asia Times*, 5 January 2012. Online: http://www.atimes.com/atimes/Korea/NA05Dg01.html.

It is clear that the same degree of legitimacy simply cannot be passed on to Kim Jong Un. Kim Jong Il did not fight against Japan, but he was at least (officially) born on Mt Paektu. Kim Jong Il for a long time in his career was a moon, not a sun. He shone because Kim Il Sung was shining on him, and he reflected his light. This was part of the 'text', as Brian Myers calls it. But how can a moon illuminate the next generation as brightly as a sun could?

The trouble is that even dictators need legitimacy. The logical choice would have been to enshrine the two eternal leaders, father Kim Il Sung and son Kim Jong Il, forever and create a system that would claim to fulfil their combined legacy in the most perfect way. This would require a collective of trustees with a *primus inter pares* at their helm, very much like China's Central Committee and the Party's General Secretary, or the Catholic Church and the Pope, Lenin and Stalin—religion and history know many relatively successful cases where after only one successor, a new collective mode of leadership was chosen.

However, Kim Jong Il's untimely death means that a back-up plan is now being implemented, hastily, massively, too quickly. Suddenly we hear about Kim Jong Il country, about the need to erect statues to his honour, about Kim Jong Un being Kim Jong Il, about Kim Jong Un being the supreme leader of the Party, the state, and the military. But will this be enough? The North Korean population does not consist of mindless robots. They are well educated, and they are tough. The elite have acquired self-confidence and power in the last years. They know their country has problems. They desperately want a solution. And so far they have little reason to think that Kim Jong Un is the right man for the job. They will of course obey and show respect, but will their belief in the new leader be as genuine as it used to be?

4 How is Kim Jong Un's legitimacy being built?

Any leader, in any political system, needs legitimacy to maintain their claim to power. Max Weber's suggested use of the claim to legitimacy as the sole criterion for classifying various types of rule was not incidental.[14] It would be outright naive to expect that all it takes in North

---

[14] Max Weber (1972), *Wirtschaft und Gesellschaft*, Tübingen: Mohr Siebeck, p. 122.

Korea is an article in *Rodong Sinmun*, and everyone will stop asking questions and just follow the new top man.

Legitimacy in autocratic systems is a tricky issue. It is hard to acquire, and it lacks a mechanism of permanent renewal (such as elections in democracies). Merkel associates North Korea with the communist-totalitarian subtype, not with a monarchy.[15] Bursens and Sinardet show that there are two interrelated sides to legitimacy. In addition to the expected outcomes, an important source of legitimacy seems to be that the decision-making process, including the selection of the leadership, should follow approved rules.[16] My own research confirms that legitimacy in North Korea is based on performance, and that this includes a certain compliance with rules and formalities. This is why Kim Jong Un was still addressed with the title of vice-chairman of the Party's Central Military Commission despite having been announced as the great successor. This is why the eldest son Kim Jong Nam was so obviously unqualified for the post: he does not behave in a way that would be regarded as sufficiently dignified.

As indicated above, Kim Il Sung based his claim to power on his feats including the liberation of Korea from the Japanese, and the victory in a war fought to defend Korea against an invasion by the United States. As so often, what matters is not the actual truth of such claims, but their perception by the target group, i.e. the North Korean population. Kim Jong Il, too, had to earn the right to rule. He was given a number of tasks to prove that he was capable. These included most prominently work in the film studios and the development of the *chuch'e* ideology as the country's guiding principle. He went through a rather long period of training and grooming before he was designated as successor at the sixth Party congress in 1980. Ever after, he was portrayed as a tireless worker on behalf of the people.

But what about Kim Jong Un? He has had little time to accomplish any major feat, or claim to have done so, although there are unproven rumours that he was involved in a number of military operations vis-à-vis South Korea. He might have been groomed internally since 2008,

---

[15] Wolfgang Merkel (1999), *Systemtransformation*, Opladen, Germany: Leske+ Budrich, pp. 25–28.

[16] Peter Bursens and Dave Sinardet (2007), 'Democratic Legitimacy in Multilevel Political Systems: The European Union and Belgium in Comparative Perspective', paper presented at the European Union Studies Association 11th Biennial International Conference, Los Angeles, 23–25 May 2007. Online: http://www.euce.org/eusa2009/papers/bursens_11H.pdf.

and officially since the KWP conference in September 2010. This gave him little more than a year. We could thus in the days after the announcement of Kim Jong Il's death observe a massive, multi-layered strategy to build at least a provisional legitimacy for Kim Jong Un. I agree with Ken Gause's assessment that 'the regime appears to have launched a blitz campaign to portray him as the legitimate successor to his father, removing any doubt within the mind of the public and elite alike over who is in charge'.[17]

It started with the inclusion of him as the 'great successor' in the official obituary. The very moment North Koreans learned that Kim Jong Il was dead, they were also told who was going to be his heir. (Note that Kim Jong Un was not announced in that position during Kim Jong Il's lifetime; it was the Party that acted as kingmaker.[18] Even the introduction of Kim Jong Un to the public was done in the context of a Party conference.[19]) Then, a sense of guilt was instilled in the people. The very circumstances of Kim Jong Il's demise on the way to another on-the-spot guidance suggested that he had worked himself to death for the people. Even Associated Press conveyed the appropriate reaction, being told that '[w]e lost the great Kim Jong Il because we did not do our work well. How can we have a rest?'[20] This theme—which is Korean, not specifically North Korean—was repeated a number of times in KCNA and *Rodong Sinmun* reporting, as shown above. Particularly striking was the regret expressed by citizens at having failed to erect a statue of Kim Jong Il during his lifetime. As expected, Kim Jong Un took up this task very soon. In any case, he was soon portrayed in the media as a leader who personally took care of the physical needs of his citizens, like food or hot drinks. These minor details have a strong symbolic power and promise: Kim Jong Un will take care of the consumer economy.

Over the next days, Kim Jong Un was assigned various titles and functions. The latter included: successor to the revolutionary cause of

---

[17] Ken Gause (2012), 'Kim Chong-un and Pyongyang's Signaling Campaign', 3 January 2012. Online: http://blog.keia.org/.

[18] Rüdiger Frank (2011), 'The Party as the Kingmaker: The Death of Kim Jong Il and its Consequences for North Korea', in: *38 North*, 12/2011, U.S.–Korea Institute at the School of Advanced International Studies, Johns Hopkins University. Online: http://38north.org/2011/12/rfrank12211.

[19] Rüdiger Frank (2010), 'A Puzzle in Pyongyang', in: *Foreign Policy*, 8 October 2010. Online: http://www.foreignpolicy.com/articles/2010/10/08/a_puzzle_in_pyongyang.

[20] *The Guardian*, 1 January 2012, 'Nkorea's Kim Visits Tank Division on New Year's'. Online: http://www.guardian.co.uk/world/feedarticle/10019703.

Juche (*chuch'e hyŏngmyŏng wiŏbŭi kyesŭngja*), standing at the helm of the Korean revolution, the head (*suban*) of the KWP Central Committee, the Great Sun of the 21st Century (*21segiŭi t'aeyang*), reputable leader of our Party, state and army (*uri tanggwa kukka, kundaeŭi yŏngmyŏnghan ryŏngdoja*), supreme leader (*ch'oego ryŏngdoja*) of Party, state and army, and supreme commander of the Korean People's Army. This last role was reported to have been awarded on 8 October 2011, well before Kim Jong Il's death. However, the only formal title he held (until April 2012), one that was repeated constantly, was that of vice-chairman of the KWP Central Military Commission (*chŏsonrodongtang chung'angkunsawiwŏnhoe puwiwŏnjang*). By early January 2012, the title 'Dear Respected Comrade Kim Jong Un' (*kyŏngaehanŭn kimjŏngŭndongji*) has become a standard form of address.[21]

A look at the frequency of KCNA reporting about Kim Jong Il and Kim Jong Un reveals that the departure of the leader was unexpected for the North Korean propaganda machine. With the exception of July, the average monthly number of articles carrying Kim Jong Un's name was less than ten until November 2011, as opposed to over 300 for Kim Jong Il. The total number of such appearances in 2011 until November was 141 for Kim Jong Un and 3,471 for Kim Jong Il. This suggests that the campaign to promote Kim Jong Un was not at all in full swing.

5 DO THE PARTY AND THE MILITARY COMPETE FOR POWER IN NORTH KOREA?

This is one of the most commonly made assumptions about power in North Korea: that the military and the Party compete. Our minds seem to have a general inclination towards simple dichotomies: good and evil, black and white, civilians and military, yin and yang, sweet and sour, man and woman, and so forth. This predisposition seems to be

---

[21] In April 2012, Kim Jong Un became first chairman of the National Defence Commission (NDC) and first secretary of the Korean Workers' Party and thus formally the leader of the military and the Party. These were newly created positions, as his late father Kim Jong Il maintained his titles of chairman and general secretary. For a more detailed discussion, please refer to the (forthcoming) 2013 edition of *Korea: Politics, Economy, and Society*.

responsible for a great deal of the popularity of the 'military versus Party' theory. To put it bluntly: I disagree, and for manifold reasons.

To begin with, it is hard to imagine that a reasonable dictator would allow the military to become a political force in his country. He will use the military as a tool, he will stress military values such as hierarchy, obedience to orders, and self-sacrifice. All socialist societies that we have known used militant language (the economic front, shock brigade, fresh advance, speed-battle, struggle, etc.). They all had large militaries, huge defence budgets (alas, that is what eventually broke the backs of their economies), para-military training, a preference for uniforms, mass rallies and marches. Take the Soviet Union: Leonid Brezhnev often wore a military uniform and was surrounded by generals. Each year, the Red Square in Moscow hosted military parades of a scale that easily let anything seen in Pyongyang pale in comparison. Tanks, artillery, gigantic missiles and goose-stepping soldiers passed by an embalmed Lenin. Still, few observers would have characterised the Soviet Union as a country ruled *by* the military. Ruled *through* the military, maybe; but not in the form of a military dictatorship.

North Korea is admittedly an extreme case. Part of our perception problem is that since 1991, it is the only such system remaining. Many of those who today watch parades on Kim Il Sung square have no memory of any similar instance and easily think that nothing like this has existed on earth before. That would be wrong. What is observed might be extreme and North Koreanised, but in principle, it is not unique.

Most seasoned observers of North Korea agree that the country is ruled by something that can be called a theocracy. It consists of a few families, including that of Kim Il Sung and of those fifty comrades who entered the country with him in late 1945. This top elite whose right to power is explained in ideological terms has had seven decades to settle in. It has assumed control of all positions of power, be it the Party, the military, the security organs, the state, or the parliament. They have intermarried, have produced offspring and have expanded. Theirs is not a singular case. In medieval Europe, it was common to intermarry within the aristocracy, to have at least one son who became a knight, and another a cleric. In North Korea, it is the same families that control the Party *and* the military. If there is any rivalry, and we have no reason to believe that there is none, it will be between the families, not between the institutions. It will be army units against army units, Party leaders against Party leaders, ministries against ministries: not army against Party.

Another fact that seems hard to grasp for Westerners is that the glue that has held North Korea together so far is not direct repression, but ideology. Repression is systemic, and it is omnipresent. But it is not the only and probably not even the most powerful element of regime stability. It is no coincidence that Kim Jong Il identified ideological weakness as the reason for the collapse of socialism in Europe.[22] And indeed, North Korea is particularly strong in this respect. It has successfully merged anti-Japanese and anti-American nationalism, the fear of again losing independence, a crude type of Leninism, xenophobia and traditional familism into one. For the ordinary North Korean, the leader and socialism are the same as national independence and the nation. The latter are beyond any doubt, and so automatically are the former. And the owner of ideology is the Party. For reasons that are subject to speculation, the Party was pushed into the background for a while, but not by the military. Rather, it was the leader himself who after having solidified his position decided to put a check on this powerful institution.

My interpretation in 2003 of the Military First policy was not that of a radical turn towards militarism; how much more militaristic could North Korea become, anyway? Rather, I suggested seeing it as the ideological component of a market-oriented economic reform drive that the Party obviously opposed.[23] A strong signal regarding power in North Korea was sent through the very funeral held on 28 December. On the basis of our stereotypical knowledge, what would we expect? Kim Jong Il, Great General, the man of the Military First era, would get a military ceremony with soldiers carrying his coffin, or would it be mounted on a gun carriage or even a tank? Well, none of that happened, as we know. The whole ceremony was largely civilian, apart from the military salute. Most important, however, is the flag that covered his coffin. It was not the national flag, but the banner of Mother Party. How much more do we need to understand where power resides in North Korea?

---

[22] Kim Jong Il (1995), 'Giving Priority to Ideological Work is Essential for Accomplishing Socialism'. Online: http://www.korea-dpr.com/lib/101.pdf.

[23] Rüdiger Frank (2003), 'The End of Socialism and a Wedding Gift for the Groom? The True Meaning of the Military First Policy', NAPSNET Special Report and DPRK Briefing Book (Transition), 11 December 2003. Online: http://www.nautilus.org/publications/books/dprkbb/transition/Ruediger_Socialism.html.

The Party controls the governmental institutions including economic and foreign policy, and it controls the military. This, too, is not at all an exception. It was the rule in socialist countries from the time of Lenin that the Party hierarchy was superior to the military hierarchy. Despite the obvious militarism and the iron-fisted rule, North Korea is not a military dictatorship; rather, it is an extreme case of a state-socialist autocracy in a constant state of emergency and under quasi-martial law.

6 How will China behave?

China is often portrayed in Western media as North Korea's only ally. This is hard to deny but it is only one side of the coin. History knows very few cases where the relationship between a gigantic and a small neighbour has been positive from the perspective of both sides. The two countries have a long tradition of close co-operation, but also of tensions and mistrust. In the 16th century, China was Korea's ally but only sent troops after Toyotomi Hideyoshi had occupied half of the peninsula. Elder brother China failed as Korea's protector in the late 19th century, which led to colonisation by Japan. China came to the rescue of North Korea in the Korean War, but was not entirely free of selfish concerns, and it stayed until the late 1950s. A coup against Kim Il Sung during a trip to Europe in 1956 was led by pro-Soviet and pro-Chinese Koreans. During the Cultural Revolution, Chinese Red Guards heavily criticised Kim Il Sung and his leadership style, and even tried to trigger a similar movement in North Korea. There were territorial conflicts involving, among other sites, the sacred Mt Paektu. China's claim that the ancient kingdom of Koguryŏ was actually Chinese prompted outrage in both Koreas. The reforms in the neighbouring country are met in the DPRK with a mix of fascination and suspicion, and China's obvious hyper-presence in today's North Korean economy worries many Koreans.

Given the DPRK's nationalist ideology and its fear of external interference, China looks like more the biggest threat than the best friend. The country's massive economic dependence on China only supports that feeling of malaise. The South Korean Yonhap news agency reported on 29 December 2011 that in the first ten months of that year, China's trade with North Korea jumped 73.5 percent year-on-year to reach a new record high of US$4.67 billion.[24] In particular, China increased its imports of anthracite coal, alloy and non-alloy steel from North Korea by a whopping 124.8 percent. The DPRK's trade reliance on China jumped from 25 percent in 1999 to 83 percent in 2011. Its next largest trading partner in 2010 was Russia, with a mere 2.6 percent of the total.[25] When the author first visited North Korea in 1991, most foreign-made goods, if there were any, came from Japan. By contrast, in 2010, the whole country seemed to be flooded with Chinese goods of all types, from textiles to cars, repair shops, and restaurants. The Pyongyang International Trade Fair, which I visited in October of that year, was dominated by Chinese firms selling computers, home appliances, trucks and all other kinds of products.

However, mutual suspicion prevails. Officially, all is friendship, just as it was between the Soviet Union and its satellite states. (If you have a chance, ask a Hungarian or a Czech how they really felt about their Big Brother. 'Die Freunde' (the friends) was used in an openly ironic way when referring to Russians in East Germany.) In 2010, the mass spectacle Arirang contained a full act on North Korea-China friendship (*chochung ch'insŏn*) alone. There, too, the North Koreans could not refrain from issuing a side blow by showing a slogan from the Cultural Revolution: 'If there were no Communist Party, there would be no New China'. This can be interpreted as indirectly accusing China of having betrayed what Mao had fought for.

Be it true friendship or a rational alliance: in the context of its regional and global strategy, China is primarily interested in a stable North Korea. A collapse would place China in a complicated situation. If it sent in troops, angry reactions would be triggered worldwide and, in an instant, all of the past decade's painstaking attempts at portraying the giant's rise as peaceful would be discredited. But if it just watched the existing order disintegrate, Korea would quickly be reunified under South Korean leadership. That would mean an expansion of the US zone of influence right up to China's northeastern border—a strategic disaster. Not least, the thus proven inability to save a client state would drastically reduce China's chances of convincing any other country to trade protection by the US against protection by it, and set back dreams of becoming a regional superpower. It was there-

---

[24] See www.yonhapnews.co.kr.
[25] KOTRA (2011), *2010 Pukhanŭi taewoemuyŏgŭi tonghyang* [Trends in North Korean trade 2010], KOTRA charyo 11-033, Seoul: KOTRA.

fore little of a surprise that China was quick to express support for the new leadership in North Korea.

We can expect a continuation of the policy of the past years: invitations to the leader and high-level North Korean officials; tours of Shenyang, Beijing and Shanghai; the building of personal networks with the North Korean elite; and patience. Only if the DPRK is seen as going too far, for example, in the nuclear question, will China interfere—but as quietly as possible. Meanwhile, new economic zones will be built, old ones rejuvenated. It seems that the allegedly communist Chinese trust the transformatory power of the market more than the capitalist West does. The world is an ironic place.

7 WHAT WILL HAPPEN TO NORTH KOREA'S NUCLEAR PROGRAMME?

Common sense suggests that a change in policy would require a change in conditions. However, we have no reason to believe that any of the rationales for the nuclear programme's existence has changed. The DPRK uses its nuclear weapons as a means of deterrence according to the same logic as was applied during the Cold War between East and West. The programme is one of the few major achievements that Kim Jong Il was able to present to his people, and Kim Jong Un will not be stupid enough to shed it as long as he builds his legitimacy on the legacy of his father. Most importantly, the nuclear programme keeps the neighbours worried and the world interested. This attention translates into diplomatic and economic gains that are desperately needed. The case of Libya and the death of Gaddafi have been interpreted by North Korea as the long-term result of giving up the Weapons of Mass Destruction programme. Last but not least, this is about the only way North Korea can provide some counterbalance to the massive weight of China.

Alas, the biggest danger stemming from the North Korean nuclear programme might not be its military use. As the events in Japan in March 2011 have shown, even in rich and technologically highly developed economies accidents cannot be excluded. We can only hope that maintenance work in the DPRK is done properly, and that the nuclear facilities do not become affected by any natural or man-made disaster.

8 WHAT WILL KIM JONG UN'S POLICIES BE?

Obviously, very little aside from 'continuity' can be said at this point. It is also easy to see that Kim Jong Un must find a way to resolve his country's economic shortages. From the study of socialist systems done by Janos Kornai[26] and others, we know that such shortages are chronic and systemic. In other words, it requires a change of the system rather than mere coping measures. True, North Korea was able to survive for a long time on a muddle-through strategy. But this does not change the fact that the country's economy is malfunctioning. The Chinese example is the obvious solution, but will Kim Jong Un be willing, able and allowed to follow it?

For the time being, a number of indicators suggest that the economic well-being of his people is one of his top priorities. Remember that his introduction as successor on 19 December was soon supplemented by the 'fish episode' recounted above. That was followed by reports on the provision of hot water for mourners. On 3 January 2012, Kim Jong Un was quoted in the news with a number of remarks on the production and allocation of consumer goods that echoed those of his father during a similar occasion in July 2011.[27] In other words, this emphasis on consumer goods is relatively recent and is being upheld by Kim Jong Un. An emphasis on light industry and agriculture, i.e. consumer goods, is reflected in a new buzzword that emerged in close connection with the succession: 'flames of Hamnam' (*hamnamŭi pulgil*). It was first mentioned in *Rodong Sinmun* on 26 October and refers to an on-the-spot guidance by Kim Jong Il in October 2011. The 2012 New Year joint editorial confirmed this policy. This reference to economic policies, the improvement of living standards, the production of consumer goods and the satisfaction of the citizens' material needs is no coincidence.

North Korea is changing rapidly, self-confidence and individualism are growing, and a middle class has emerged. The old leadership initiated this process and then struggled to find a way to deal with the resulting phenomena. The new leadership has the task of continuing this search for a way to move forward, to accommodate the demands of its

---

[26] Janos Kornai (1992), *The Socialist System: The Political Economy of Communism*. Princeton NJ: Princeton University Press.

[27] *Rodong Sinmun*, 4 January 2012, 'Che 3 ch'a p'yŏngyangche 1 paekhwachŏm sangp'umchŏnsinhoe kaemak' [3rd Pyongyang Department Store No. 1 goods exhibition held], p. 3.

citizens. All this must be done without being self-destructive. This is clearly not an easy task.

THE CONCEPT OF MIDDLE POWER
AND THE CASE OF THE ROK: A REVIEW

Dong-min Shin[1]

ABSTRACT

In recent years, the ROK has often been named as a middle power (MP) state, and the concept of middle power is seen as a way of assisting the country to position itself satisfactorily in regional and global affairs. However, the concept still remains open to varying interpretations among International Relations (IR) academics as well as in the ROK policy field. Against this backdrop, this paper outlines the development of established MP perspectives, examines how ROK governments have used the concept, and explores the applicability of existing MP perspectives to the ROK through examining the ROK's political context and features. As a conclusion, this paper argues that, in order to be an analytical tool for ROK foreign affairs, the concept of middle power should consider such realist factors as security and power relationships with big neighbours as its main determinants.

Key words: middle power, conceptual review, ROK's foreign policy, realism

1 INTRODUCTION

In recent years, the Republic of Korea (ROK) has often been called a middle power state in both political and academic circles. Within the ROK, the country's foreign minister, Kim Sung-hwan, in his inaugural address in October 2010 proposed new diplomatic initiatives which the ROK needed to promote itself as a middle power. On the international academic scene, the US political scientist Joseph Nye has written that the ROK has become an important middle-ranking power in global affairs (Nye 2009). Such views on the ROK's current international status and its corresponding roles on the global stage might be

---

[1] The author would like to thank Dr Alessio Patalano and Dr Ramon Pacheco-Pardo of King's College London for their comments on this article. All translations of Korean texts in the article are the author's.

held to reflect its advancing national capabilities, as evidenced in the rapid growth of national and individual gross domestic product (GDP) (see *The Economist*, 12 November 2011), in its military strength (discussed in SIPRI 2011 and IISS 2010) and in the country's hosting of the Group of 20 Seoul Summit in 2010 and of the second Nuclear Security Summit in March 2012. In this respect, President Lee Myung-bak often claims that the ROK has become a middle power under its foreign policy slogan, 'Global Korea'.[2]

Yet the concept of middle power may be said to lack clear definition. It supports multiple meanings in multiple areas such as politics, economics and even culture without a commonly agreed conceptual ground.[3] Its application to the ROK is equally lacking in clarity. For the author this uncertainty is compounded by the absence of any security dimension in particular from the various middle power perspectives already established. An important question for the ROK is to position itself satisfactorily in regional as well as global affairs. Its need to deal with powerful neighbours and allies over security issues has determined courses of action in its foreign policy.

Against these observations, this article aims to investigate whether the existing discourses on the concept of middle power both in the field of foreign policy and among IR academics are appropriate for discussing the ROK's foreign affairs. To this end, the paper proposes to study the development of established middle power perspectives among IR academics; to review how ROK governments have used the concept of middle power; and to explore the applicability of existing middle power perspectives to the ROK through examining the political context and features of the ROK. As a conclusion, the paper proposes academic clues necessary to establish a concept of middle power that might address the foreign and security policies of the ROK and of other countries in similar international political conditions.

---

[2] Carl Ungerer sees President Lee's vision for a 'Global Korea' as aiming to transform the ROK into a respected middle power country with sufficient clout to effect change on the global stage (Ungerer and Smith 2010).

[3] Neufeld says that 'no fixed meaning is attached to the term, MP. "MP" will be approached as an essentially "contested concept", whose definitional content in any given context is a product of effort by societal agent' (Neufeld 1995: 12).

2 ACADEMIC DISCOURSES ON THE CONCEPT OF MIDDLE POWER

2.1 *Early development*

It was in the final stages of World War II that the concept of middle power received serious discussion. At its centre were Canada and Australia, two countries that had contributed to the Allies in terms of their economies and military effort and which subsequently tried to find ways of enhancing their influence after the end of the war.[4] On its side, Canada attempted to distinguish itself from such minor allies as Brazil or Mexico and to persuade the great powers to accept an increased role and influence for Canada in the process of establishing a new world order (Foreign Affairs and International Trade Canada 2011). In this respect, in 1944, at the early stage of the establishment of the United Nations (UN), Canadian Prime Minister Mackenzie King argued that all countries besides the great powers should be able to express their views in a new international organisation. Suggesting the concept of 'Middlepowerhood', he insisted that middle power countries should co-operate with each other in order to secure their influence and find their responsibilities in international society (Holbraad 1984: 57–67). Since then, the role of Canadian academics in facilitating middle power research has been considerable. In addition to Carsten Holbraad (1984), Andrew Cooper and others have discussed the features of middle power with a case study of the Cairns group of the Uruguay Round and the contribution of Canada and Australia to the Gulf War (Cooper et al. 1993), and Adam Chapnick (1999) has categorised trends in middle power studies. With this accumulated research, middle power has become a trademark to describe Canadian foreign policy (Hurst 2007).

The notion of middle power is also a popular diplomatic term in Australia, where the concept has likewise been actively discussed since the end of World War II. In the 1940s, the Australian Minister for External Affairs Herbert Evatt adopted a more independent approach to middle power to secure his country's national interest in a new world order (Holbraad 1984; Ungerer 2007). The changing nature of cold war rivalry during the 1960s–1970s led to stagnation in re-

---

[4] Shin Soon-ok says that the term middle power was coined by politicians and foreign policy practitioners from aspirant countries such as Canada and Australia in the post-war era (Shin 2009: 3).

search, but the concept was highlighted again in the beginning of the post-cold war era. During his tenure of office (1988–96), Foreign Minister Gareth Evans stated that as an active middle power country, Australia had distinctive foreign policy schemes, such as coalition-building with other like-minded countries. Australian academics have also contributed to broadening understanding of middle power.[5]

2.2 Trends in existing research

In light of its early development, what meaning does middle power have in the discipline of IR? Which countries can be called middle powers? There has been little agreement on what constitutes its features (Cooper et al. 1993: 17). The largely accepted approaches to the subject are classified into three perspectives: functional, behavioural and hierarchical (Chapnick 1999; Kim Chi-wook 2009). The functional perspective argues that a country that is able to influence certain areas and functions in international affairs is considered as a middle power. This perspective assumes that not every country has an equal right in every area and that subsequently each country should have a voice in areas where it is a major power (Foreign Affairs and International Trade Canada 2011). For example, in 1942, the Canadian diplomat Hume Wrong emphasised that international society should respect Canada's role as a middle power in three functional criteria, those of extent of involvement, interest, and ability. In this way, great powers and weak states also can be defined under the functionalistic approach. According to Chapnick, great powers are those countries able to make an effect in all fields of international relations without restriction and weak states are those that cannot do so (Chapnick 1999: 74).

Turning to the behavioural perspective, a remark of Laura Neack's demonstrates well its theoretical essence: 'MP theory was developed by statesmen, who hoped to describe the status, international role, and foreign policy behaviour of their states' (Neack et al. 1995: 224). Cooper et al. (1993: 19) argue that the essence of middle power diplomatic activity is best captured by what type of diplomatic behaviour countries do or can display in common. In other words, the behav-

---

[5] The major lists of MP studies in Australia are: Hill 1986; Higgott and Cooper 1990; Ping 2005; Ungerer 2007.

ioural perspective takes a view that a country would be a middle power if it played certain roles considered as those of a middle power or if it identified itself as such. Cooper and his colleagues propose that pursuing multilateral solutions to international problems, preferring compromise positions in international disputes and embracing notions of good international citizenship constitute behaviour typical of a middle power. Carl Ungerer also cites a preference for working through multilateral processes, a commitment to promoting international legal norms and a pro-active use of diplomatic measures as the typical middle power behaviour (Ungerer 2007: 539).

The third approach is the hierarchical perspective. This approach ranks and categorises states by applying standards relating to their capabilities. Accordingly, countries with capabilities recognised as being medium-sized are grouped as middle powers between great and weak powers, so to speak. Kim Chi-wook notes that the hierarchical perspective tends to use statistical indices for categorising countries (Kim 2009: 19). Thus Holbraad ranks states according to Gross National Product (GNP), population and offensive military capabilities and concluded there was a group of middle powers in each region such as East Asia and the Middle East (Holbraad 1984: 78). Kim Chi-wook suggests a new standard constituted by six realism-based indicators (size of territory, GDP, the volume of trade and foreign currency reserves, population, and number of soldiers) and two liberalism-based indicators (participation rate in international institutions and in diplomatic networks). He classifies countries into four groups of powers (great, middle, middle-small, weak). According to his analysis, the ROK has been a military power since 1995 along with Turkey and Mexico.

2.3 *Limitations of existing research*

The existing middle power perspectives contribute to the development of the theory and practice of IR through providing a third category of state beyond the dichotomy of great powers and weak states. Normally IR theories have focused on great powers and weak countries and have not paid much attention to middle power as a level of analysis. Research on the roles and relationships of weak states used to view a middle power as a type of weak power (Kim Chi-wook 2009:

9–10).[6] However, actual international politics seem to work in a different manner. Among those countries not considered as great powers, some can change the behaviour of great powers but others fail even to defend their own position against the latters' pressure. For example, during War World II, some small countries such as Turkey and Spain kept themselves from being entrapped in all-out war between the Allies and the Axis powers, while others, such as Norway and Poland, found themselves used as battlefields between them.[7] In other words, the dichotomy between great powers and weak states leads to an oversimplified explanation of international politics. In this respect, the middle power perspectives offer an opportunity for IR academics to come close to the reality.

The author finds that existing perspectives have several theoretical weaknesses. Among them is the possibility of fluctuations in a country's stature as a middle power. In the case of the functionalistic perspective, if the political weight of certain functions in IR changes in time, today's middle power can be tomorrow's weak state. This perspective, furthermore, can allow for segmentation in a country's international status. A country that has built up its economic base can be a middle power in functional economic areas, while remaining as a weak state in its military functions. The weakness in the behavioural perspective is that it does not suggest objective criteria for defining the concept of middle power, because whether a country is a middle power or not is dependent on the country proclaiming itself as such. Furthermore, there are few common patterns in how a group of middle powers behaves because the types of states, the categories of power that they possess, and the arenas within which they operate are all so varied (Shin Soon-ok 2009: 7). In this respect, the hierarchical perspective seems to be more objective because it uses quantitative indicators to categorise countries. However, an analyst's biases may intervene in the process of selecting indicators and middle powers. For example, one researcher may focus on the volume of military expendi-

---

[6] For example, Waltz categorises states into great powers and secondary states. The others are not counted. In other words, according to his theory, middle power and weak powers are at the same level of unit and are all objects of change in IR amidst structural factors such as the number of great powers and their polarities (Waltz 1979: 131).

[7] Fox compares the positioning of neutral countries such as Turkey, Norway, Sweden and Spain between the Axis powers and the Allies during World War II and the consequences for them (Fox 1959).

ture as a standard for selection, but another may prefer the manpower of a country's regular army.

Furthermore, existing perspectives on middle power cover aspects and issues of IR that in the author's opinion are limited. 'Realist' issues such as survival, security and conflict are not considered as decisive factors in defining the concept of middle power by the functionalistic and behavioural perspectives. The motive of the functionalistic perspective was to find ways for countries such as Canada to increase their influence within given international order shaped by the great powers.[8] Meanwhile, assuming a high chance of building co-operation among states, the behavioural perspectives inclined to the liberalist trends of IR (Shin Soon-ok 2009: 3–6; Kim Chi-wook 2009: 17).[9] In fact, the rise of behavioural perspectives was in parallel with changes in international politics in a direction that forms the focus of such trends. Cooper and his colleagues, who led the behavioural middle power research, suggested the end of the cold war, deepening globalisation and interdependence among countries, and the increased salience of economic, environmental and human rights issues on the agenda of international politics as their research background (Cooper et al. 1993: 13). Consequently, the typical behaviour of middle powers as identified by the behavioural perspective is not relevant to the realism issues of IR.[10]

As a third point, the author suggests that the level of analysis of existing middle power perspectives remains at that of the individual state. Although functional, behavioural and hierarchical perspectives approach the notion of middle power in different ways, they all assume that the main determinants of such power are individual state-

---

[8] For example, although Canada attempted to secure its influence in the negotiations to establish the UN, it did not oppose a veto for the great powers in the UN Security Council. As an alternative, it insisted that non-Security Council members should have the right to attend Council sessions when the use of their military forces was under discussion (Foreign Affairs and International Trade Canada 2011).

[9] There are many ways to define liberalism in IR. For example, according to Moravcsik, republican liberalism holds that democracies tends to be more pacific, commercial liberalism asserts that economic interdependence creates incentives for peace and co-operation, and regulatory liberalism contends that international institutions promote international accommodation. On the basis of Moravcsik's view, liberalism in this paper means a perspective of IR which puts the higher possibility on co-operation among states rather than on conflict, with a focus on economic interdependence among countries, and roles in international institutions (Moravcsik 1992: 1).

[10] Cooper and others suggest catalyst (triggering diplomatic initiatives), facilitator (forming collaborative activities) and manger (building institutions) as typical roles for middle power (Cooper et al 1993: 24–25).

level factors: a country's performance in certain functional areas, its behaviour and capabilities calculated in a quantitative way. In other words, the established middle power perspectives presuppose that whether a country is a middle power or not is decided by itself. However, it is questionable that defining middle power in the political arena without a consideration of interaction with other political entities is appropriate. As the term 'international relations' demonstrates, relations among states are embedded in the theory and practice of international politics.[11] A country's political actions and reactions cannot be established without the existence of other countries. In this respect, Kim Sang-bae points out that the existing literature on middle power concentrates only on state-level attributes without taking into account a country's relationship patterns (Kim 2011: 5–7).

3 THE KOREAN CONTEXT

3.1 *The middle power discourse within ROK governments*

It is unclear when the ROK government first began to call itself a middle power (*chunggyŏnguk*).[12] The administrations of Roh Tae-woo (1988–93), Kim Young-sam (1993–98) and Kim Dae-jung (1998–2003) used the term in their presidential and ministerial addresses. Although the expression had not appeared in the past, it may be said that traditionally the perception of a political situation related to the notion of a middle power had existed within Korea. Towards the end of the 19th century, when the country entered the Western-dominated international political system, some intellectuals from the time of the late Chosŏn dynasty perceived themselves as occupying a 'middle'

---

[11] Hans Morgenthau suggests that the autonomy of the political sphere is based on its attention to power, which he defines as 'anything that establishes and maintains the control of man over man'. This last phrase, 'man over man', suggests that power, in IR terms, conveys a relationship among actors. In other words, according to Morgenthau's view on the concept of power, without the existence of other entities and of the interactions between them the concept cannot be established, and subsequently it is hard for IR to exist as a distinctive area of social phenomena (Morgenthau et al. 2005: 186; 30–31).

[12] Similar terms, such as '*chungjinguk*', '*chungsoguk*', or medium power, have also been used in the contexts where the term 'middle power' has been noted.

country with respect to geopolitical position and international status.[13] Subsequently, early ROK governments shared that sentiment.

Considering the contexts in which the governments of the ROK have deployed the concept of middle power or similar terms with respect to their foreign affairs, the concept of the ROK as a middle power seems to have three meanings. Firstly, these governments have used middle power as a term to acknowledge the ROK's international status. Each government has referred to the notion of middle power in a declaratory manner in order to demonstrate the state's advances and achievements in diverse fields. For example, President Roh Tae-woo claimed that the ROK had successfully jumped from being one of the poorest countries in the world to a *chungjinguk* with a per capita GNP of over US$5,500 (Roh 1991).[14] The current president, Lee Myung-bak, also often uses the concept in this context. For example, he commented in his 34th radio address:

> There are two groups of states in the world. The first are rule-makers and the second are rule-followers. The ROK is the sole country in the world, which has been successfully transforming its role from a rule-follower to a rule-maker ...The ROK, once one of the poorest countries in the world, now has become a middle power (Lee 2010).

In the same context, the then vice-foreign minister Shin Kak-soo said that the year 2010 was the time when the ROK successfully consolidated its middle power status in the international community. In that year, the ROK hosted the G20 Summit as the first non-Western country to do so, and became the first former recipient of development assistance to join the Development Assistance Committee of the Organisation for Economic Co-operation and Development (Shin 2010).

Secondly, ROK governments have used the concept of middle power as a tool to compare the country with other state categories. They have utilised middle power as a term implying or making clear

---

[13] For example, Yu Kil-chun, a reformist and politician of the period, authored an article entitled 'Chungnipron' [Strategy for neutrality] in 1885. In this article, he argued that Chosŏn, which was at the centre of the struggle for power among large neighbours, should find ways to be a neutral country in Northeast Asia similar to Belgium in Western Europe and Bulgaria in the Balkan peninsula, in order to preserve its survival (Kang 1973).

[14] Although President Roh Tae-woo did not use the term 'chunggyŏnguk', the context in which he used the term 'chungjinguk' seems to have a similar meaning to that of 'chunggyŏnguk'. The term 'chungjinguk' also appeared during the Park Chung-hee government (1961–79), when it was mostly used in contexts that represented the ROK's economic status situated in the middle of the world economic order, in other words, between developed and developing countries.

that the ROK's status is different from that of great and weak powers. President Roh Moo-hyun's address at the 60th Session of the UN General Assembly in 2005 demonstrated well the usage of the expression in this context. He said:

> The new world order of the 21st century should be defined by all nations, be they a great, small, or middle power, coexisting under shared interests to achieve collective prosperity ... It is when great powers work further to embed a higher cause of peace and common prosperity in global order that the tension between 'power' and 'higher cause' can be defused (Roh 2005).

The Roh Moo-hyun government suggested middle power as a notion to counter that of 'weak-state realism', which it perceived as having been the Korean people's dominating mentality for a long time (Ch'amyŏchŏngbu kukchŏngunyŏng paeksŏ p'yŏnch'anwiwŏnhoe 2008: 20–21).[15] Government leaders shared the idea that the sentiment of weak-power realism could no longer provide a philosophical basis for the ROK's foreign policy, given the ROK's rising national capabilities. The concept of middle power which the Roh Moo-hyun government proposed was an antithesis of the concept of weak power.

Thirdly, the ROK has set up its foreign policy goals through the lens of the middle power concept. As well as describing the country's international status, as mentioned above, the notion of middle power has begun to shape the aims and agendas of the ROK's foreign policy. This third context is based on the belief that as the country has developed to a higher level, that of a middle power, it is required to play roles corresponding to its status. In other words, ROK governments have suggested middle power as a symbolic term representing the country's will to seek new foreign policy aims and subsequent strategies that correspond to its change of status. For example, Kim Yong-jik insists that the Roh Tae-woo government's *Nordpolitik*[16] was a policy of medium power reflecting both the progress of international dynamics such as the dissolution of cold war structures and the ROK's attempts to extend the scope of its foreign policy based on its rising

---

[15] The Roh Moo-hyun government perceived the term 'weak state realism' as indicating that as the ROK was a peripheral country in the hierarchy of international politics, it had to align itself with strong countries.

[16] The Roh Tae-woo government developed the diplomatic policy of *Nordpolitik* in the 1990s as a means of establishing diplomatic relations with the Soviet Union, China and other communist countries and of improving relations with North Korea (see Kim 2001: 262).

status as a leading democratic country amongst newly industrialised countries (Kim 2001).

More recently, the Roh Moo-hyun government, in seeking to strengthen its political autonomy in relation to the great powers, in particular the US (Moon 2011: 263; Lee Soo-hyung 2009), took the view that the ROK as a middle power was both entitled and able to transform itself from a passive object into an active subject of international politics. The Lee Myung-bak government also uses the notion of middle power in this context. Shin Kak-soo, pointing to the volume of the ROK's economy as evidence that the ROK is such a power (Shin 2010), argues that it is time for the ROK to pursue a new diplomatic paradigm of multilateral diplomacy beyond its long-held focus on North Korea and issues of the Korean peninsula. It is a view supported by Chun Young-woo, national security advisor to the Blue House, who sees multilateral dialogues as providing important opportunities for middle power countries to enhance their influence on international society (Chun 2010).

Such co-opting of the term 'middle power' by ROK governments has its limitations. It is difficult to say that these governments have invoked the term on the basis of a conceptual understanding of it. The notion has conveyed varied meanings and has been suggested in varied contexts, sometimes to denote economic success, at other times to represent the ROK's role in the political order of Northeast Asia. This inconsistency is attributable to the fact that ROK governments, in using the term have been driven by political purposes or policy objectives.

The problem, in the author's eyes, is that in recent years, the notion that the ROK has become a middle power goes beyond the country's mere self-perception of its status in the international order. The concept plays heavier roles, such as formulating the ROK's foreign and security policy agenda, with the corresponding possibility that an inappropriate application of the concept might cause policy mistakes by the ROK government and subsequently a bigger political problem beyond the Korean peninsula in light of the ROK's rising political weight in Northeast Asia and the degrees of intervention of neighbouring countries in Korean issues.

4 THE ROK'S FOREIGN AND SECURITY AFFAIRS IN CONTEXT

4.1 *Vital issues in the ROK's international relations*

It can be argued that there are several vital aspects to the ROK's foreign relations. First among them is the continuing subject of war. The armistice agreement that ended the Korean War in 1953 has served as a backbone to the political structure of the Korean peninsula, and even after nearly sixty years, issues indirectly and directly related to the state of armistice have constituted a large part of the ROK's foreign and security policy agenda.[17] The issue of war continues to work as an important or at least inescapable factor in the ROK's foreign affairs. Furthermore, China, and the US signing for the United Nations Command were signatories of the armistice agreement and have been indispensable actors in dealing with issues touching on the security of the Korean Peninsula and beyond. In recent times, the two countries have been intervening more actively in Northeast Asia including the Korean peninsula. The US, faced with China's rise, particularly its military build-up, has sought under the Obama administration to extend US influence and presence in East Asia (see Bader 2012). As one measure, the Obama government has improved relations with its key partners including the ROK and Japan, both concerned over China's new assertiveness.

At the interstate level, the two Koreas have maintained close security relationships with these two big powers, the ROK with the US through the ROK–US Mutual Defense Agreement of 1953 and the DPRK with China through the Sino–North Korean Treaty of Friendship, Cooperation and Mutual Assistance of 1961. In addition, since 1992, when the ROK established diplomatic relations with China, Sino–ROK interaction has also progressed rapidly.

At the state level, the gap in overall national capability between the two Koreas has been widening. The DPRK, now in a phase of leadership transition after the death of Kim Jong Il, has continued to develop its nuclear capability in spite of continuing economic difficulties. Within the ROK, contingency scenarios for a sudden change in North

---

[17] Major foreign policy agendas of the ROK governments since the Kim Dae-jung administration may be cited as examples: Kim Dae-jung's engagement policy; the Roh Moo-hyun government's Policy for Peace and Prosperity and its Northeast Asian Cooperation Initiative; and the Lee Myung-bak administration's Vision 3000: Denuclearisation and Openness (aimed at North Korea).

Korea such as a collapse of the regime continue to be discussed in a cautious manner. Neither South nor North will officially give up their determination to lead Korean reunification, although, in this situation, their discourses on the subject can be considered as mere political propaganda. The important point is that reunification would mean a revision of the status quo in the Korean peninsula and Northeast Asia and subsequently would have a substantial impact on the political interests of neighbouring countries.

Within this framework, the following two points may be made with respect to the main features of South Korean foreign affairs. Firstly, security matters still occupy a critical place in the country's foreign policy agenda. For example, the government's review of major foreign policy issues from the Kim Dae-jung administration to the Lee Myung-bak government, presented in diplomatic white papers covering the years 1998 to 2011, gave first place to the following: South Korea's engagement policy with North Korea, and the first summit between the two Koreas (Kim Dae-jung government); the Six Party Talks for dealing with the North Korean nuclear problem, the issue of establishing a peace regime on the Korean peninsula, and the rearrangement and development of the US–ROK alliance (Roh Moo-hyun government); and the *Cheonan* (*Ch'ŏnan*) and Yeonpyeong (Yŏnp'yŏng) incidents along with the unresolved North Korean nuclear stand-off (Lee Myung-bak government) (Ministry of Foreign Affairs and Trade of the ROK 1998–2011). These were all security matters. The North Korean nuclear problem is not only a regional security concern, but also a wider global issue from the viewpoint of proliferation. The engagement policy and the issue of establishing a peace regime are linked to the security matters of the Korean peninsula and Northeast Asia because they are attempts to find a new political structure to replace the current state of armistice. The *Cheonan* and Yeonpyeong incidents were warlike provocations against the South Korean navy and territory, resulting in the death of South Korean citizens and soldiers.[18]

The second feature is that the ROK has necessarily interacted with its large neighbours in dealing with the above issues. With regard to the North Korean nuclear issue, North Korea has sought normalisation

---

[18] Although the international civil-military joint investigation team (JIG) composed of the ROK, US, Sweden, Australia and the UK concluded that the ROK corvette *Cheonan* was sunk by a North Korean torpedo attack, North Korea has denied its intervention. China and Russia have not yet confirmed who sunk the ship.

of the relationship with the US and the conclusion of a peace treaty in return for abandoning its nuclear programme. Considering the substantial parties to the current armistice pact and the ROK–US and the Sino–North Korean alliances, the process for solving the nuclear stand-off is an issue with which at least the two Koreas, the US and China are concerned. Accordingly, the main diplomatic framework for dealing with the North Korean nuclear problem and discussing the Korean peninsula peace regime has been the Six Party Talks, along with the trilateral or quadripartite contacts among the above players. The *Cheonan* and Yeonpyeong incidents have also not remained at an inter-Korean level. According to Glaser, China gives precedence to maintaining stability and the status quo on the Korean peninsula (Glaser et al. 2010: 2–4). However, the warlike nature of the *Cheonan* incident and the growing rigidity in the Sino–DPRK relationship brought about by North Korea's deepening isolation drove China directly and indirectly to intervene in the incident and as a result, the handling of the *Cheonan* incident rapidly took on a wider aspect.[19]

4.2 Existing research on the ROK from the middle power perspective

As seen above (section 3.1), discussion on the concept of middle power has grown within the ROK's foreign policy circles. However, research on the concept among IR academics working on South Korea would not appear to reflect this mounting discussion. The volume of middle power-related studies is not large and most of them have been conducted over the last decade. The author's contention with this research is that it explains the ROK case on the basis of existing middle power perspectives without first reviewing the ROK's political context and features. Several of these studies are introduced here, in chronological order.

Robertson, writing on the Kim Dae-jung government, applies the behavioural perspective to an analysis of the features of the 'Sunshine policy' and argues that it could be considered as an exemplary middle

---

[19] Some observers point out that the core of the handling of the *Cheonan* and Yeonpyeong incidents was the Sino–ROK relationship. According to Victor Cha, in the aftermath of the *Cheonan* incident, members of the ROK national security team claimed that 'China had now shown its true face', and a senior officer of the ROK government stated that the ROK's strategic calculations over China had changed in dealing with the *Cheonan* incident (Cha 2011: 41–42).

power policy (Robertson 2007). According to him, the Sunshine policy displayed typical middle power tendencies such as preferring compromise in international disputes, having a vested interest in the maintenance of the status quo and encouraging third-country engagement. However, the essence of the Sunshine policy was not whether it had typical middle power tendencies or not, but that the Kim Dae-jung government had the political motivation to take the initiative in inter-Korean affairs through exercising a relatively self-reliant North Korean policy.[20] In this respect, Robertson's analysis, from the perspective of middle power, does not look into the critical aspect of the Sunshine policy.

The focus of Shin Soon-ok's research is the Roh Moo-hyun government (Shin 2009). She suggests the 'MP identity' as a crucial variable for studying the features of middle power.[21] In this respect, Shin argues that the Roh Moo-hyun government had a strong middle power identity and that this was well demonstrated by its 'balancer initiative', which proclaimed a balancing role for the ROK in the power structure of Northeast Asia.[22] Shin's research is meaningful because it attempts to reconstruct a notion of middle power with a review of both the theory of IR and the ROK case. However, it is questionable whether the ROK's identity as a middle power can be decided solely by its state-level attributes. Considering the essence of IR and the ROK's political context, a relationship with the great powers is a factor that cannot be overlooked in discussing the ROK's international politics.

During the Lee Myung-bak government, discussion on the concept of middle power flourished with the holding of the G20 Seoul summit.

---

[20] Im Dong-won, former unification minister and a key architect of the Sunshine policy during the Kim Dae-jung government, has said that the policy created a new trend in inter-Korean relations. It was the first time that the ROK led the inter-Korean relationship and North Korea followed the ROK's initiative. According to him, the Sunshine policy confirmed that the main actors in the Korean peninsula were Koreans and accordingly other countries could not formulate and implement North Korean policy without the ROK's consent (Sindonga 2000).

[21] According to her explanation, a country internalises a middle power identity through a sequence of self-conceptualisation, that is, the aspiration to promote itself as a certain type of power in order to establish who it is and what its values and interests are, and self-identification, that is, recognition of the self as a distinctive entity through engaging with a normative framework in the international system (Shin 2009: 8–10).

[22] Although there has been debate on what the 'balancer' meant, former US secretary of state Rice understood it as the ROK's argument for playing the role of balancer between the US and China (Rice 2011: 528).

For instance, Balbina Hwang and Jo Youngji argue that the summit provided the ROK with an opportunity to seize the mantle of global leadership and capitalise on its unique development experience as a middle power (Hwang and Jo 2011: 53). In a similar context, Kalinowski and Cho discuss the emergence of the ROK as a middle power with regard to its positioning in global affairs (Kalinowski and Cho 2012). They review the ROK's role in international institutions, its evolving economic globalisation strategy and official development policies. Their review is significant in that they explain the ROK's various roles in various international fields. However, given that security affairs take up a large part of the ROK's foreign affairs, these middle power discourses could be said to have the same problem as the existing middle power perspectives: they talk about the ROK's international status without exploring the essence of the country's international politics.

In this respect, Chun Chae-sung and Kim Sang-bae approach the main issue of this paper, the ROK as a middle power, from different viewpoints. While discussing the concept of middle power in Korean contexts, Chun Chae-sung focuses on the political situation in Northeast Asia. In a situation where competition between the US and China has been increasing in that region, he reviews the ROK's necessary positioning and strategy as a middle power in relation to the US and China in order to secure its national interests (Chun 2012). Analysing the middle power features of the ROK, Kim Sang-bae in a series of studies examines the notion of power in IR theories and elaborates on the concept of 'network power' as a new source of power (Kim 2008; 2009; 2011).[23] Kim argues that through developing network power, a middle power such as the ROK can exert an influence beyond its national capabilities (in his wording, the 'node-based' capabilities), formed by military and economic resources along with ideal, non-

---

[23] According to Kim, a network is a collection of nodes connected to each other by links. Kim views current IR work as a network. Nodes are diverse levels of units with states and sub-states as actors, and links are diverse relationships formed by the units. Kim argues that the political phenomena of current world politics tend to happen beyond the unit-level boundary such as national sovereignty. Accordingly, power is exerted not only by unit-level variables such as one country's national capabilities, but also by multiple levels of relations constituted by different levels of units. Kim categorises sources of network power into: power of the network (collective power), power on the network (positional power), and power from the network (structural power) (Kim 2008: 46–49).

tangible factors such as its ideology, knowledge and cultural impact.[24] As an example, he posits that the ROK's successful positioning as a critical hub within East Asian politics will allow it to possess influence at the regional level.

5 Conclusion

The established middle power perspectives have contributed to filling the gap between theories and realities in IR. In the explanations offered by IR, the concept of middle power focuses on the role of 'agents', which the mainstream structure-level of theories have overlooked (Cooper et al. 1993: 13). Research into the concept and roles of middle power provides a tool to analyse those states which are considered as neither great powers nor weak states. In this respect, middle power perspectives are meaningful for studying the ROK's foreign affairs in terms of theory and practice. If structural factors such as the polarity posited in IR and the relationship among great powers decide everything, as mainstream IR theories assume, the ROK will be considered only as an object in the power politics between the US and China and subsequently there will be no room for discussing the ROK's attempts to achieve an autonomous foreign policy, reflected in the efforts in recent years by ROK governments to take initiatives in dealing with the regional or global affairs related to it. In this situation, the notion of middle power is in the position of offering a perspective enabling researchers and foreign policy practitioners alike to examine the ROK's foreign affairs in a much more thorough manner.

However, as this paper has argued, existing middle power discussions in both policy and academic circles have limitations when they come to be used as a framework for analysing the middle power features of the ROK and surveying its foreign and security policy. The concept of middle power is used inconsistently in the ROK policy field, since it has been deployed mostly for internal political purposes. As a result, a gap has emerged between the meaning of middle power as ROK governments have used it and its meaning as IR academics

---

[24] In recent years, the concept of network power has begun to be discussed as a new foreign policy strategy within the ROK government. For example, in 2010 the ministry of foreign affairs and trade held a series of conferences reviewing the concept in terms of theory as well as its application. Online: http://www.youtube.com/watch?v=ZlBMxl5R5bI.

have developed it. In the author's view, existing middle power perspectives in the IR academic field display weaknesses in terms of theory, a tendency towards liberalist criteria, and a state-centred point of view. He argues that they fail to reach countries which have security matters and conflict rather than co-operation with other countries at the front of their foreign policy. In this respect, he maintains, these perspectives are less suited to an analysis of the middle power features of the ROK.

This paper proposes, therefore, that the concept of middle power should be revised in such a way as to consider the realist factors of IR, such as power relationships with other countries, even including great powers, that embrace 'hard politics' issues, as main determinants in identifying middle power countries. In this respect, judging whether the ROK has become a middle power or not solely by its successful holding of big international conferences such as the G20 meeting might lead to illusions on the part of ROK governments about the country's capability and roles in Northeast Asia as well as in the current world order. The author suggests Chun's approach mentioned above (section 4.2) as an example for such a revision. Analysing and comparing a series of cases which convey the ROK's attempts to influence big neighbours such as the US or China over security matters might also be considered as a way to investigate the middle power features of the ROK.[25] Finally, the author offers the following working definition of middle power:

> A middle power is a state actor that has restricted influence on deciding the distribution of power in a given regional system, but is capable of deploying a variety of sources of power to change the position of great powers and to defend its own position on matters related to the security affairs of the region to which it belongs.

Such a revision might offer an opportunity for the concept of middle power to expand its theoretical boundaries to include countries which have similar political contexts to the ROK that current MP perspectives accordingly do not well explain. Furthermore, this revision might provide academic grounds for discussing the capability, roles and autonomy of middle power within the realist trends of IR, which have mostly considered great powers as sole meaningful actors.

---

[25] The author offers the ROK–US differences over North Korea and the US–ROK alliance during the Kim Dae-jung and Roh Moo-hyun governments and the different views of the ROK and China on North Korea in dealing with the *Cheonan* and Yeonpyeong incidents as research cases.

References

Bader, Jeffrey A. (2012), *Obama and China's Rise: An Insider's Account of America's Asia Strategy*, Washington DC: Brookings Institution Press

Cha, Victor (2011), 'Fundamental Realism: Korean Assessments of U.S. Power', in: Craig S. Cohen and John J. Hamre (eds), *Capacity and Resolve: Foreign Assessments of U.S. Power*, Washington DC: Center for Strategic and International Studies, pp. 30–43

Ch'amyŏchŏngbu kukchŏngunyŏng paeksŏ p'yŏnch'anwiwŏnhoe [Committee for publication of white papers of the Roh Moo-hyun government] (2008), *Ch'amyŏchŏngbu kukchŏngunyŏng paeksŏ 5* [White paper of the Roh Moo-hyun government 5], Seoul: Kukchŏng Hongboch'ŏ

Chapnick, Adam (1999), 'The Middle Power', in: *Canadian Foreign Policy*, 7 (2), pp. 73–82

Chun, Chae-sung (2012), 'Mijungkyŏngjaengsidae, kallimkire sŏn han'guk oegyo' [Era of Sino–US competition: the ROK's diplomacy at a crossroads], lecture to *Chisik Maru Talk: SNS Saengbangsong* [Knowledge-sharing talk: SNS live broadcast], 28 February 2012, in: *East Asia Institute*. Online: http://www.eai.or.kr/type_k/panelView.asp?bytag=p&code=kor_multimedia&idx=10890&page=3 (accessed 26 March 2012)

Chun, Young-woo (2010), 'Haegŭi yangmyŏnsŏnggwa haek anbo chŏngsang hoeŭi' [The significance of hosting the second Nuclear Security Summit], in: *Joongang Ilbo*, 17 April 2010. Online: http://article.joinsmsn.com/news/article/article.asp?Total_ID=4115097 (accessed 8 November 2011)

Cooper, Andrew F., Richard A. Higgott and Kim Richard Nossal (1993), *Relocating Middle Powers: Australia and Canada in a Changing World Order*, Vancouver, British Columbia: UBC Press

Economist (2011), 'What Do You Do When You Reach the Top?', 12 November 2011. Online: http://www.economist.com/node/21538104 (accessed 20 December 2011)

Foreign Affairs and International Trade Canada (2011), 'Canada and the World: A History, 1939–1945: The World at War', in: *The Department in History*. Online: http://www.international.gc.ca/history-histoire/index.aspx?menu_id=8&view=d (accessed 15 February 2012)

Fox, Annette Baker (1959), *The Power of Small States: Diplomacy in World War II*, Chicago IL: University of Chicago Press

Glaser, Bonnie, Scott Snyder, See-won Byun and David J. Szerlip (2010), *Responding to Change on the Korean Peninsula: Impediments to U.S.–South Korea–China Coordination*, Washington DC: Center for Strategic and International Studies

Higgott, Richard A. and Andrew F. Cooper (1990), 'Middle Power Leadership and Coalition Building: Australia, the Cairns Group, and the Uruguay Round of Trade Negotiations', in: *International Organization*, 44 (4), pp. 589–632

Hill, John R. (1986), *Maritime Strategy for Medium Powers*, London: Routledge

Holbraad, Carsten (1984), *Middle Powers in International Politics*, London: Macmillan

Hurst, Lynda (2007), 'On World Stage, a Best Supporting Actor', in: *The Star*, 29 September 2007. Online: http://www.thestar.com/columinsts/article/261324 (accessed 20 October 2011)

Hwang, Balbina and Youngji Jo (2011), 'Bridging the Global Gap: Korea's Leadership Agenda for the G-20', in: *Joint U.S.–Korea Academic Studies*, 21, pp. 53–72

IISS (International Institute for Strategic Studies) (2010), *The Military Balance 2010*, London: Routledge
Kalinowski, Thomas and Hyekyung Cho (2012), 'Korea's Search for a Global Role between Hard Economic Interests and Soft Power', in: *European Journal of Development Research*, 24 (2), pp. 242–60
Kang, Man-gil (1973), 'Yu Kil-chunŭi nonmun chungnimnon' [Yu Kil-chun's article: strategy for neutrality], in: *Ch'angjakkwa pip'yŏng [Quarterly Changbi]*, 30 (4), pp. 1129–41
Kim, Chi-wook (2009), 'Kukchechŏngch'i punsŏk tanwirosŏ chunggyŏn'gukka' [Middle power as a unit of analysis of international relations: its conceptualisation and implications], in: *Kukchechŏngch'i nonch'ong [Korean Journal of International Studies]*, 49 (1), pp. 7–36
Kim, Sang-bae (2008), 'Network kwŏllyŏgŭi segye chŏngch'i: chŏnt'ongjŏkin kwŏllyŏk ironŭl nŏmŏsŏ' [Questing for the network theory of world politics: beyond three assumptions in the realist theory of international politics], in: *Kukchechŏngch'i nonch'ong [Korean Journal of International Studies]*, 48 (4), pp. 35–61
Kim, Sang-bae (2009), 'Smart powerŭi kaenyŏmjŏk ihaewa pip'anjŏk kŏmt'o: chunggyŏn'guk network kwŏllyŏkronŭi sigak' [Critical understanding of the concept of smart power: a perspective on middle power's network power], in: *Kukchechŏngch'i nonch'ong [Korean Journal of International Studies]*, 49 (4), pp. 7–33
Kim, Sang-bac (2011), 'Networkro ponŭn chunggyŏn'guk oegyochŏllyak: kujojŏk kongpaekkwa wich'ikwŏllyŏk ironŭi wŏnyong' [Middle power's diplomatic strategies in the perspective of networks: applying theories of structural holes and positional power], in: *Kukchechŏngch'i nonch'ong [Korean Journal of International Studies]*, 51 (3), pp. 51–77
Kim, Yong-jick (2001), 'The Nordpolitik as President Rho Tae Woo's New Foreign Policy, 1988–1992', in: *Segye chiyŏk yŏn'gunonch'ong [Journal of World Area Studies]*, 23 (1), pp. 261–77
Lee, Myung-bak (2010), *The 34th Presidential Radio Address*, 8 February 2010. Online: http://www.president.go.kr/kr/community/radio/radio_list.php (accessed 20 October 2011)
Lee, Soo-hyung (2009), 'Chunggyŏnkukkawa han'gugŭi oegyoanbochŏngch'aek' [Middle power theory and security and foreign policy of the Roh Moo-Hyun government], in: *Kukpang yŏn'gu [Journal of National Defence Studies]*, 52 (1), pp. 3–27
Ministry of Foreign Affairs and Trade of the Republic of Korea (1998–2011), Diplomatic White Papers, Seoul: Ministry of Foreign Affairs and Trade [for the years 1998–2011]
Ministry of Foreign Affairs and Trade of the Republic of Korea (2011), Second Complex Diplomacy Conference, 19 April 2011. Online: http://www.youtube.com/watch?v=ZlBMxl5R5bI (accessed 10 April 2012)
Moon, Jae-in (2011), *Moon Jae-inŭi unmyŏng* [Moon Jae-in's destiny], Seoul: Kagyo
Moravcsik, Andrew (1992), 'Liberalism and International Relations Theory' in: Center for International Affairs Working Paper Series, 92 (6). Online: http://www.princeton.edu/~amoravcs/library/liberalism_working.pdf (accessed 15 March 2012)
Morgenthau, Hans J., Kenneth Thompson and David Clinton (2005), *Politics Among Nations: The Struggle for Power and Peace*, 7th ed., New York: McGraw-Hill Higher Education

Neack, Laura, Jeanne A. K. Hey and Patrick J. Haney (1995), *Foreign Policy Analysis: Continuity and Change in its Second Generation*, New York: Prentice Hall

Neufeld, Mark (1995), 'Hegemony and Foreign Policy Analysis: The Case of Canada as a Middle Power', in: *Studies in Political Economy*, 48 (3), pp 7–29

Nye, Joseph S. (2009), 'South Korea's Growing Soft Power', in: Project-Syndicate.org, 11 November 2009. Online: www.project-syndicate.org/commentary/nye76/English (accessed 1 October 2011)

Ping, Jonathan H. (2005), *Middle Power Statecraft: Indonesia, Malaysia, and the Asia Pacific*, Aldershot, UK: Ashgate Publishing Ltd.

Rice, Condoleezza (2011), *No Higher Honor: A Memoir of My Years in Washington*, New York: Crown Publishers

Robertson, Jeffrey (2007), 'South Korea as a Middle Power: Capacity, Behaviour, and Now Opportunity', in: *International Journal of Korean Unification Studies*, 16 (1), pp. 151–74

Roh, Moo-hyun (2005), Address by President Roh Moo-hyun at the High-level Plenary Meeting of the 60th Session of the United Nations General Assembly, 14 September 2005. Online: http://www.un.org/webcast/summit2005/statements/rok050914eng.pdf (accessed 20 October 2011)

Roh, Tae-woo (1991), Address at Hoover Institute, Stanford CA, US, 29 September 1991. Online: http://www.pa.go.kr/online_contents/speech/speech02/1307684_4248.html (accessed 20 October 2011)

Shin, Kak-soo (2010), 'Kagyooegyo kusang: han'guktajaoegyo ŭi saeroun paradingmŭl ch'ajasŏ' [Bridging diplomacy: in search of a new paradigm for Korea's multilateral diplomacy], in: *Kukchegwan'gye yŏn'gu* [*Journal of International Politics*], 15 (1), pp. 293–324

Shin, Kak-soo (2011), 'Kukkyŏge kŏlmannŭn sŏnjinoegyo p'yŏnda' [South Korea's diplomacy initiative: Global Korea], in: *Financial News*, 9 January 2011. Online: http://www.fnnews.com/view?ra=Sent1801m_View&corp=fnnews&arcid=110109183413&cDateYear=2011&cDateMonth=01&cDateDay=09 (accessed 8 November 2011)

Shin, Soon-ok (2009), 'A Failed "Regional Balancer": South Korea's Self-Promoted Middle Power Identity', paper presented at the International Studies Association Convention, New York, February 2009

Sindonga (2000), 'DJ T'ongil Dramaŭi yŏnch'ulga Im Tong-wŏn Kukchŏngwŏnjang' [The main architect of the DJ's unification policy, Im Dong-won], in *Sindonga*, 1 August 2000. Online: http://shindonga.donga.com/docs/ magazine/shin/2006/09/13/200609130500025/200609130500025_4.html (accessed 10 March 2012)

SIPRI (Stockholm International Peace Research Institute) (2011), *The SIPRI Military Expenditure Database*. Online: http://milexdata.sipri.org (accessed 3 January 2012)

Ungerer, Carl (2007), 'The "Middle Power" Concept in Australian Foreign Policy', in: *Australian Journal of Politics and History*, 53 (4), pp. 538–51

Ungerer, Carl and Simon Smith (2010), 'Australia and South Korea: Middle Power Cooperation and Asian Security', *Strategic Insights*, 50, Barton: Australian Strategic Policy Institute

Waltz, Kenneth N. (1979), *Theory of International Politics*, New York: Random House

NORTHERNERS ON SOUTHERN SCREENS: FROM *SHIRI* (1999) TO *THE YELLOW SEA* (2010)

Mark Morris

Abstract

This paper presents a broad survey of a range of films that have appeared in South Korea during the past few years, some dealing with North Korea and North Korean characters, some with the *chosŏnjok* from China's Jilin province. A small number of other films have looked at South Korean society from the point of view of North Korean refugees. Two significant films from 1999 and 2000 which indicated a kind of cultural Sunshine policy towards North Korean characters are examined first, then a selection of films from the Sunshine years between 2000 and 2008, together with some of the general themes that evolved during the decade. A final section presents more recent cinematic visions of the North. The aim is to provide pointers to some interesting films and to suggest some interpretive co-ordinates for people interested in the intersection of history, politics and culture in the contemporary ROK.

Key words: North Korea on film, *chosŏnjok*, Korean War films, *t'albukja*/defectors

Prologue

Any attempt to assess representations of North Korea or of North Korean characters on South Korean screens has to be accompanied by a keen sense of humility. For no matter what the impact may have been of images moving across screens in multiplex theatres, computers, net-pads or smart phones, those images were probably not as powerful nor as ubiquitous as the DPRK's own self-dramatising televisual imagery of late 2011. The announcement of the death of Kim Jong Il on 19 December, then the funeral cortège telecast on the 28th combined to leave scenes of grieving crowds bundled up against the Pyongyang cold and of a chubby young man with a retro haircut as indelible images which many of us around the world have carried into the new year of 2012.

1 INTRODUCTION

During the past few years over a dozen films have appeared in South Korea which deal with North Korea and North Korean characters. Some of them may seem reliant on a simplistic condemnation of the Democratic People's Republic of Korea (DPRK), stuck in an anti-communist—or at least anti-DPRK—time-warp, while others give a more humane, even humorous or sentimental representation of Northerners, albeit often with a strong dose of condescension. One new focus of attention has been the northerners north of the North: the *chosŏnjok*, ethnic Koreans from the Yanbian (Korean: Yŏnbyŏn) Autonomous Region of Jilin province of China, many of whom have come looking for work all the way to South Korea, some legally and some clandestinely.

Perhaps even more interesting are a small number of films that have looked at the society of South Korea through Northern eyes, adopting the point of view of North Korean refugees—people generally referred to by the ideologically loaded term *t'albukja*, literally 'escapees from the North' and usually translated as 'defectors'—or of impoverished *chosŏnjok* migrant workers. Such films present a vision of South Korea far removed from its positive self-image. The South is a cold, grasping place, harsh enough to make Northerners dream of becoming *t'alnamja* and 'escaping from the South' back to a poorer but more humane home in the North.

Before analysing some of these recent films, however, it is worth going back to the early years of the take-off in South Korea's film industry; because either side of the momentous opening to the DPRK made by President Kim Dae-jung of the Republic of Korea (ROK) in his visit to Pyongyang in June 2000, two significant films were released, both of which indicated a kind of cultural Sunshine policy vis-à-vis the way North Korean characters might be represented in mainstream cinema, a cultural opening that proved successful at the box office. A following section will look at a selection of films which appeared during the Sunshine years between 2000 and 2008 and will consider some of the general themes that evolved during the decade, before a final section considers more recent cinematic visions of the North released in 2010 and 2011.

2 BACK STORY CIRCA 2000

Many elements converged by the late 1990s to boost the South Korean film industry from something of a business and cultural backwater into the highly successful New Korean Cinema. The International Monetary Fund crisis of 1997 brought a redeployment of human and investment capital into large entertainment conglomerates with modern business nous and plans for integrating production, distribution and exhibition; government regulations were eased, permitting the emergence of independent film producers; theatres were renovated or replaced by multiplexes; conglomerates and talent agencies attracted a new generation of actors; the film schools began consistently turning out graduates with acting, technical, scriptwriting or directing skills; and most importantly, a young generation of South Koreans with disposable income and a new-found pride in going to see films produced by their own national cinema, often by film-makers close to their generation, made film-going a major part of their netizen cultural lives. A screen quota system, requiring exhibitors to show a certain percentage of South Korean films, played its part, but it had often been circumvented and was less significant as attendance figures for local films began to exceed those for imports. Still, the quota system proved a rallying point from the late 1990s for some dramatic demonstrations in defence of the film industry against the Hollywood juggernaut (Paquet 2009: 68–70).

South Korea's new cinema was also helped by the removal of the censorship in place during the years of the Park Chung-hee and Chun Doo-hwan administrations. Kim Suk-Young has reminded us how difficult the National Security Law made it to portray North Koreans outside of the official Cold War propaganda and how little room it left 'for humanistic portrayal of North Koreans' (Kim 2007: 221). Gradual reforms, eventually leading to a less political ratings system, made films like those discussed here possible to produce and exhibit.

2.1 *Shiri* and *Joint Security Area*

Into this conjuncture arrived two films which, it is generally agreed, marked a take-off for a New Korean Cinema: Kang Je-gyu's *Shiri* in 1999, and Park Chan-wook (Pak Ch'an-uk)'s *Joint Security Area: JSA* in 2000. *Shiri* ran for four months, sold well over six million tickets, and turned an investment of US$2.3 million into takings of US$27.6 million (Paquet 2009: 71). It told the story of a band of renegade North Korean special-force agents on a suicidal mission to steal a South Korean secret weapon and to explode it at a friendly football match between the DPRK and ROK. The match would be attended by leaders of both nations, intent on moving towards reunification on terms which these terrorists could not accept. Here was a Korean-made film which could compete with Hollywood on its own terms: in Darcy Paquet's words, '*Shiri* featured shootouts on urban streets, exploding buildings, car chases, ticking bombs and other narrative/visual clichés of big-budget action films from Hollywood and Hong Kong' (Paquet 2009: 71). The critics had their doubts, but audiences showed up in record numbers. A bit of a cinematic *hallyu*—'the Korean wave'—was begun when the film was sold to Japan for US$1.3 million (Paquet 2009: 71). *Shiri* set the pattern for the emergence of the South Korean blockbuster, firstly by obviously setting the story in Korea and among Korean characters; secondly, as J.Y. Lee and Julian Stringer observed, by 'tackling national or political subject matter'; and thirdly by 'appealing to universal values, such as family, friendship, love and humanity, as well as generic cinematic pleasures' (Lee and Stringer 2010: 62).

The film wove a love story in and around the main action. A key South Korean intelligence agent is engaged to an attractive young woman who, it turns out, is herself an undercover North Korean agent. We finally realise that she is the same woman we met in the violent opening scenes acting as a ruthless assassin. This may sound rather far-fetched, but Korean cinema had been there before. The first post-Korean War film about espionage was Han Hyŏng-mo's *The Hand of Fate* (1954). There, an undercover North Korean agent works as a bar hostess; she saves a young man from a beating and the two fall in love. Only belatedly does she discover he is in military counter-intelligence, and he that she is a spy. At the film's climax, she forces him to finish her off. And, in Kang Je-gyu's *Shiri*, that is pretty much the way things conclude. The female agent, surrounded by a circle of hyper-equipped SWAT team shooters, contrives to be gunned down by her lover.

The romantic angle no doubt adds a kind of human dimension to this North Korean female assassin-spy; the beauty of the actress playing her, Kim Yun-jin, goes a long way to melt Cold War prejudice. Yet it is another Northern character who gets the best lines. Choi Min-shik plays the scruffy, fanatical leader of the rogue special forces. In his own final showdown with the opposition right before the death of his key female agent, he growls out this message:

> People in the North are falling dead beside the roads from hunger and disease. Have you ever seen a mother and father eating the flesh of their own child dead from starvation?! How on earth could bastards raised on lousy cheese and cola and hamburgers understand the likes of that! (Seo 2008: 57–58).

However briefly, these words spat out by a man in his last extremity demand recognition of the fundamental humanity of people in the North, here couched in terms of the devastating famines of the mid-1990s, which people in the South were well aware of. It also holds up a mirror to democratising, consumer-capitalist South Korea and asks that most awkward of questions when it comes to North–South debates: who are, where are, the real Koreans?

Joint Security Area: JSA was released in September 2000, only three months after Kim Dae-jung's trip to Pyongyang for the summit with Kim Jong Il. The film was able to take advantage of the mood of optimism, temporary though it turned out to be, towards a possible shared future. As Kim Suk-Young summed it up, the historic meeting was followed by 'an explosive amount of publications about North Korea, high interest in North Korean culture, and numerous occasions for cultural exchange'. In 2000 alone, exchanges exceeded those of any previous year (Kim 2007: 224).

Park Chan-wook's *JSA* took a different cinematic route. Kang Je-gyu is a master of the linear, loud and colourful narrative drive, as suits the blockbuster. Park is generally considered to have more in common with directors such as Bong Joon-ho (Bong Jun-ho) or Kim Ji-woon (Kim Ji-un), standard-bearers of the new cinema who can match genre expectations with the sort of complex narratives and artistic cinematography once most associated with European art-house film-making.

A more complex film than *Shiri*, *JSA* is not easy to sum up. Five soldiers, two from South Korea and three from the North, have been involved in an incident at the Joint Security Area (JSA) on the Demilitarised Zone (DMZ) that has claimed the lives of two from the North and left one ROK soldier wounded physically and mentally. Through a series of flashbacks which follow a UN Swiss-Korean investigator's efforts to undercover the truth, the audience learns how two men from each side had gradually become friendly, fraternising on a regular basis at an isolated border outpost on the Northern side; the ill-timed appearance of a North Korean officer led to the shooting. Seeing men in their different uniforms sitting together, chatting, drinking, swapping snacks and cigarettes and communicating easily in the same if differently accented language was a cinematic first for viewers. The timing of the film's release, in the wake of the Pyongyang summit, was effective. *JSA* did not break *Shiri's* box office record but it did sell almost six million tickets and went on to considerable success internationally.[1]

Here, too, casting was important. Lee Byung-hun (Yi Byŏng-hŏn), as the wounded South Korean soldier, and Lee Young-ae (Yi Yŏng-ae), as the UN investigator, were already bankable stars. It was Song Kang-ho, however, playing a North Korean sergeant, who made the strongest impression. Song has an extraordinary range, shifting from hulking menace to bumbling shyness to slapstick mugging almost without effort. It was a very clever piece of Sunshine casting to make the main North Korean soldier funny and, in the end, the wisest survivor. Not everyone was ready for the kind of cultural and political détente that *JSA* seemed to represent. Not long after the film's release, a group of ROK Army veterans stormed the offices of the company which produced the film, demanding an apology and the addition of notices at the beginning and end of the film asserting the purely fictional nature of its narrative (Paquet 2000).

That the film sold some 5.8 million tickets in its first four-month run was, however, a sign that old hardline attitudes were changing. During these months, in October and November 2000, a social scientist, Shin Gi-Wook, happened to conduct an in-depth survey of South Korean attitudes towards the North and the abiding question of reunification. The findings did more than give statistical backing to com-

---

[1] Information on box office figures and annual film ranking has been gleaned from Darcy Paquet's still valuable if hibernating website Koreanfilm.org.

monsense notions of a shared ethno-nationalism that might provide a basis for eventual reunification. Shin found that many respondents not only recognised significant and valid differences between the two societies, but almost one-third were willing to support a unified Korea 'based on elements equally from North and South, suggesting a willingness to accommodate' (Shin 2006: 200; see also 185–203).

3 THE SUNSHINE YEARS: ROM-COM NORTHERN SPIES, *T'ALBUKJA*, WAR COMEDIES

Rather than attempt a comprehensive catalogue of all South Korean films focused on North Korea or North Koreans produced in the years following *Shiri* and *JSA*, I will suggest a few general trends in the way the North came to be portrayed and indicate a few absences as well.

To begin with a telling absence. After his success with *Shiri*, Kang Je-gyu got to work on his next blockbuster, the first war epic of the new cinema industry, *T'aegŭkgi hwinallimyŏ* ('Our flag is flying')— usually known by the shorter title *T'aegŭkgi* or the English-international label *Brotherhood*. Jinhee Choi has noted the curious lacunae scattered through this big-budget tale of two brothers set amidst the Korean War:

> Kang prioritizes the evolving conflict of the two brothers over the depiction of the war. The film provides the viewer with minimum information regarding the war's progression ... [and] viewers, as well as the characters themselves, are kept in the dark with regard to the specific development of the war or the significance of each battle (Choi 2010: 45).

None of the Inmingun—the DPRK People's Army—soldiers are given any real personality. *T'aegŭkgi* was planned as a Korean response to *Saving Private Ryan* (1998). This entailed all the wizardry of the latter's battlefield hyper-realism, followed by extensive post-production treatment. The skills developed by the high-tech and other South Korean professionals involved have been appreciated in the local industry and successfully marketed in China since. Yet not only is the actuality of the war largely absent from the film, the enemy often seems reduced to a chaos of anonymous young men in Northern uniforms hurling themselves about anonymous hillsides in a rage. There are no North Koreans in this film.

3.1 *Rom-com Northern spies*

In an concise examination of representations of North Korea, Stephen Epstein has raised an important question about popular cultural post-Sunshine policy, pointing out that in the last decade, productions from South Korea 'have often treated the North in modes that draw on comedy, irony or farce in preference to more straightforward, solemn readings', and hypothesing that

> [t]he ironic mode has also become a strategy for dealing with a growing sense of heterogeneity on the Korean peninsula. If North Korea is no longer viewed as an evil portion of the South Korean Self, but rather as another country and one with a special relationship to South Korea, the South Korean imaginary becomes freer to treat these differences as humorous rather than threatening (Epstein 2009).

A first effort towards an ironic treatment of espionage was Jang Jin's *The Spy*, released the same year, 1999, as *Shiri* with its deadly serious terrorists. The film took the risk of extracting humour from the plight of a hapless North Korean agent landed on the east coast with the mission of stealing DNA samples of a new breed of super-pig; the far from ironic fact of the 1990s Northern famines and the DPRK government's need to increase food production at all costs sits uneasily with a number of humorous and romantic subplots. (For a detailed interpretation, see Kim Suk-Young 2007: 226–31.)

More directly aimed at the youth market was a group of comic stories about clumsy spies and North-South romantic entanglements, which followed Jang Jin's pioneering attempt. The silliest may be *The Whistling Princess* (2002). The daughter of the North Korean leader goes walkabout while performing with a dance troupe visiting the South. She meets up with a local rock musician, while the CIA joins in the hunt: a quasi-political rock rom-com non-thriller. The following year this short-lived subgenre sprouted *Love Impossible* [a.k.a. *Love of North and South*] and *North Korean Guys*. The former brings together a Southern college student, a lazy womanising slacker but also son of the head of ROK intelligence, with a North Korean archaeology student whose father is a top general: the plot contrives to have two teams of students from each country co-operating on a dig for Koguryŏ tombs in Yanbian, whence the romance can lurch into life. The latter film is the slapstick tale of two Northern sailors who very much by accident find themselves washed up at a Southern beach resort. On the coat tails of these two came *Spy Girl* (2003). A Northern female agent is on the tracks of a spy who embezzled crucial funds. She joins a long-established cover-family and, in order to keep an eye on an intersection where the rogue spy might be likely to be spotted, takes the perfect undercover job, working behind the counter at the local Burger King. She, of course, becomes the 'angel' drooled over by all the guys. The Northern spy juxtaposed to Big Whoppers certainly suggests heterogeneity but is a long way from the admittedly genre-bound seriousness of *Shiri*.

3.2 *T'albukja: the coming of the defectors/refugees/migrants*

In a more thoughtful, though often romantic and/or sentimental, vein were feature films which focused on the fate of Northern refugees. The terminology applied to people who had left North Korea and eventually arrived in South Korea is complicated and politically loaded. The word *t'albukja*, 'defector from the North', implies a kind of conscious political rejection of the DPRK and a concomitant control over the direction of one's fate that seem a bit grandiose for the majority of those who have felt pushed by hunger, lack of basic medicines and other problems, or by fear of arrest and incarceration to take the hazardous roads which may only eventually lead south. The term 'refugee' is unacceptable to the Chinese government, which refuses to grant such status and supply the kind of treatment and facilities international agreements would require of a nation which found itself host to political refugees. The newer South Korean term *saet'ŏmin*, 'new settler', seems at once overly optimistic and too emptied of any acknowledgement of hardship endured or current marginality (see Schwekendiek 2010: 250–51).

The famines of the 1990s drove thousands of North Koreans to leave the country either temporarily in search for food or medicine over the border into China, or into a fugitive residence in China and other Asian countries, from where, after several years, many began to enter South Korea in significant numbers (Tanaka 2008; Schwekendiek 2010: 247–70). Before this wave of forced migration, there had always been a slow leak of better-off defectors. One such family is at the centre of An Pan-seok's *South of the Border* (2006). Gangling, shy Sŏn-ho is the son of a privileged family, in love with Yŏnghwa, a young woman who is happy working as a museum guide. When Sŏn-ho's father makes contact with the family's grandfather, supposedly an honoured martyr of the Korean War, but actually alive in Seoul, plans are made to defect. Sŏn-ho, who had pledged to bring his fiancée out as soon as possible, wanders aimlessly in Southern society until taken up by an older woman. He fails to find a reliable broker to help Yŏng-hwa escape, only to learn that she has married someone else up North; resigned, he decides to settle down with his new partner and help run their restaurant.

Then one day, six years after Sŏn-ho had left North Korea, Yŏng-hwa shows up in Seoul. Rumours of her marriage were false, she remained true to Sŏn-ho during the ordeal of the years in between and her less privileged road to South Korea. He squirms with shame through several encounters with her, before the truth of his new life comes out. The film has some moving scenes, especially involving the two female leads, the veteran Shim Hye-jin as the older wife, and Cho Yi-jin as Yŏng-hwa: both do their best to make up for the hulking 'star' Cha Seung-won (Ch'a Sŭng-wŏn). Details of the life of North Koreans from even a well-off background reduced to scraping a living down South are fleshed out with care. But this is melodrama, not docu-fiction. We are led to suffer with the impossible situation of Sŏn-ho, and are all but undone by the tearful, beauty of Yŏng-hwa.

This may be the first film to recreate life at a Hanawŏn resettlement centre. All North Koreans who make it to South Korea are processed through intensive interviews. Then they usually undergo a period in one of the centres where newcomers can be taught about 'South Korean culture, history, computer literacy, and cooking, among other things ... and are introduced to religious congregations' (Tanaka 2008: 7; see also Gluck 2002). How to manage a bank account and find a job are presented as well. Some data on Hanawŏn were made available by the Ministry of Unification in 2012: the facility includes a main centre and one branch facility that 'together can accommodate 400 people simultaneously and 2,400 in one year'. Since operations began in July 1999, a total of 10,333 North Korean defectors had passed through Hanawŏn programmes up to the end of December 2007 (Ministry of Unification 2012). More recently the project has itself needed to be augmented: in March 2009, 'additional community centres for the 15,000 "new settlers" were opened in Seoul, Pujŏn and Taegu', aimed at supporting North Korean defectors after they had completed the three-month resettlement programme (Burghart and Hoare 2010: 63). The picture presented in *South of the Border* of life in Hanawŏn, like the whole reception and resettlement process, is very positive. The more recent film *Dance Town* (2011), discussed below, gives a far less rosy portrayal.

Crossing (2008) was a much more ambitious treatment of Northern refugees, made under strong Christian influence. Actor Ch'a In-p'yo plays a poor Northern working-class father with one son and a pregnant wife suffering from tuberculosis. Desperate to find money to buy medicine nowhere available in his mining region, the man crosses into Yanbian hoping to earn enough to buy the medicine and return to save his wife. Everything goes horribly wrong. He has to flee from Chinese police swoops on illegal workers, eventually joining up with a group of other refugees who take the desperate step of forcing their way into the local German consulate. This action eventually earns him passage to South Korea and help from Christian organisations. In Seoul he learns that the medicine he has risked his life for is available free of charge for the initial treatment. Back in the North, his wife and unborn child have died. The famine has worsened and his son is caught trying to flee the country in his turn. He is thrown into a hell-hole of a children's prison staffed by sadistic guards. The father learns of his family's tragedy and pays a broker to get his son out. The boy ends up with a group attempting to flee through northeast China into Mongolia; when a Chinese border patrol cuts them off from the Mongolian border, the boy escapes and wanders over the border into the Gobi desert where he dies alone during a freezing cold night.

The grimness of the story no doubt reflects the experiences of the defectors whom the director, Kim Tae-gyun, says he met and talked with in preparation of the film. Much of the film is visually impressive, making good use of locations in China and Mongolia. But the actual presentation often tips over into the bathetic; the barely two-dimensional adults and the melodramatic build-up to the boy's demise can leave a viewer feeling more manipulated than educated about a critical situation. Before release, the film found itself caught up in a bitter battle over plagiarism (HanCinema, 14 July 2008), and Kim Tae-gyun's knowledge of a scenario being developed for another director based on one particular defector's experiences rather undercut claims about his independent research. Yet the film had enough industry and political support to be nominated as South Korea's entry for the foreign language film category of the Oscars in 2009 (Han 2008). Ch'a In-p'yo has taken his role as Northern defector very much to heart. He has recently been in the news for his active participation in protests against China's policy of returning defectors to the DPRK (HanCinema, 24 February 2012).

Crossing was far from a hit, but its 900,000 box office tickets look good compared to the modest returns of around 250,000 of *South of the Border*. One other film worth noting in the context of defectors and refugees is *Silk Shoes* (2005). A gangster wants to honour the last wishes of his grandfather; the confused old man wants to go back North to his home in Hamgyŏng province to die. A hapless film director, in debt to the gangster, is called in to stage a fake return, complete with a clutch of hammy actors in Northern drag. Critics pointed out that this story sounds much like the plot of the successful 2003 German film *Good Bye, Lenin!* Others have insisted that the film arose independently, growing out of the geo-political parallels of the two divided nations (Hartzell 2006). This slight film does insist on one important lesson in the way it builds humour from the worst-kept secret in South Korea. When elderly neighbours of the grandfather hear about plans for his return, they show up with armloads of letters and presents for their own people back home: half the pensioners in the area seem to have come from Hamgyŏng. South Korea, in recent years trying to find a place for thousands of North Korean defectors/refugees/migrants, is already a very Northern country. Waves of migration from the North, from the colonial era through the dislocations of the post-liberation era and the Korean War, form a deeply sedimented portion of the ROK.

3.3 War comedies

One other general theme which emerged during the first decade of the new century was that of war as comedy. Two films that appeared in 2005 explored war comedy through distinctly off-beat narratives. *Heaven's Soldiers* mixed politics, science-fiction time-travel, broad humour and a strong dose of patriotism. Two trios of soldiers, one each from North and South, are transported by the appearance of a mysterious comet back to the year 1572. Along with them go a nuclear device and a wise-cracking female physicist. The small band is just in time to help fend off an attack by bloodthirsty Manchu bandits and to rescue from his own weaknesses a small-time ginseng smuggler fated—we and soldiers soon realise—to become the great general and heroic defeater of Hideyoshi's hordes, Yi Sun-shin.

The first sequences are among the most interesting. We see two American-looking fellows monitoring news footage of the Pyongyang summit of 2000. They seem perturbed by the scene of Kim Dae-jung and Kim Jong Il shaking hands and toasting one another. 'Shit!' exclaims the younger one, tossing his earphones onto the table. Then we fast-forward a number of years to an underground bunker near the border where a team of DPRK and ROK officers and advisors discuss the fate of the nuclear warhead the two Koreas have jointly produced. The Americans want it handed over to them, and China and Japan agree. Later in the cafeteria our physicist muses aloud: given that the ICBM which the two Koreas have also developed is undetectable by American radar, gosh, 'we would be the only country who could launch a pre-emptive strike against the US'.

This black humour of war, and jibes directed against the US, are taken further in the surprise hit of 2005, *Welcome to Dongmakgol*. Two small bands of soldiers from South and North have become lost somewhere in the hills of Kangwŏn province during the Korean War. They encounter one another in the small, Shangri-La village of Dongmakgol. Their mutual hostility and suspicion take a while to convert into co-operation, but the good-hearted villagers gradually win them over. The scenario is based on a successful play by Jang Jin, a playwright, stage-director and director, among other films, of *The Spy*, discussed above. Jang Jin's script supplies some trenchant black humour. In an early confrontation the opposing soldiers argue about who started the war. When the youngest Northern soldier vehemently rejects an ROK squaddie's claim that the North did, his officer coolly cuts him short: No, we invaded alright, thus reducing the most controversial issue in modern Korean history to a well-timed joke: set-up, then punch line.

A more elaborate kind of grim comedy is saved for the film's finale. The now reconciled soldiers learn that the US Air Force is about to mount a massive raid on the village, which Allied 'intelligence' suggests might be a communist stronghold. The group tries to save Dongmakgol by staging a diversion nearby in order to attract the bombers their way, lighting fires, grabbing every weapon they can find, and even being helped by a wounded American airman hiding out in the village. The computer-generated fleet of bombers and dive-bombers headed for them seems to have been designed to look especially unrealistic, more Marvel Comics than Spielbergerian hyper-realism. The American planes do their over-kill best to obliterate our fictionally reunified Korean heroes.

I doubt that there is anything very subversive in the jokey criticism levelled at the US in both *Heaven's Warriors* and *Welcome to Dongmakgol*. There is a sense of Koreans putting on screen what they say to each other all the time, and putting it in humorous terms to blunt both the underlying bitterness about current geopolitical realities and the weakness of both Koreas in the face of the hand history has dealt them: humour as the other side of the coin of *han*. It may, however, be one of the ironic achievements of the arrogance and aggression underwriting the foreign policy of Bush-era America—much of which, but particularly that vis-à-vis North Korea, rubbed against the sentiments of many South Koreans—that Southern film-goers ended up buying more than eight million tickets for a modest production like *Welcome to Dongmakgol*.

Kim Kyung Hyun has recently argued that the films coming out of the Sunshine Policy era ultimately 'helped create one-dimensional stereotypes about North Koreans in the South that rarely moved beyond the creation of a pathetic Other' (Kim 2011: 109). Much more sceptical than Stephen Epstein, Kim argues that the new portraiture of Northerners was part of an ideological manoeuvre, a 'liberal form of otherization' aiming 'to transform North Korea (in due time, and at least in the popular imagination) into a subject willing to embrace reforms that remain in the best interests of ... South Korea' (ibid.: 108).

4 CONTEMPORARY VISIONS, 2010-2011: WAR, LIFE AND DEATH UP NORTH, REFUGEES, *CHOSŎNJOK*

The openness towards the North followed by both Kim Dae-jung and his successor Roh Moo-hyun allowed, at a time when the entertainment industry had become less burdened by censorship and was focusing on a youthful and optimistic audience, for a similar openness towards North Koreans and their country on Southern screens. The success of *Shiri* and *JSA* suggested the wisdom of such an approach. The decade of the 2000s gave Northern themes a comic twist, while treating the fate of refugees generally in the mode of sentimentality and melodrama. The past few years have seen a proliferation of films which share in this decade-long experiment in translating Korean history and geopolitics into cinematic form, yet which suggest, on the one hand, a few regressions and, on the other, a new critical focus on the society of South Korea. Four central concerns emerge: war, life and death in North Korea, refugees, and the *chosŏnjok* Chinese-Koreans.

4.1 *War*

The 60th anniversary in 2010 of the outbreak of the Korean War did not pass unnoticed by TV producers or film-makers. Close to 25 June, the date of the North Korean invasion, both the Korean Broadcasting System and Munhwa Broadcasting Corporation launched big 20-part dramas.

Yi Jae-han (a.k.a. John H. Lee)'s film production *71: Into the Fire* was released in mid-June. In some ways it is a straightforward, guts-and-glory combat film. Yet it has higher aspirations of telling the story of 71 student volunteers who in the summer of 1950 found themselves thrown into the fighting near Pohang on the Pusan perimeter. The film seems to have much in common with *T'aegŭkgi*, discussed above, and like the 2004 blockbuster, it seems to owe a lot to *Saving Private Ryan*. It shares the American film's mission of offering an action-filled, special-effects spectacle, while claiming to serve as a sober memorial to the heroic dead. There is certainly plenty of frantic battle action, particularly in the opening scenes, as ROK forces fall back before the onslaught of the Inmingun. Full use is made of computer-generated imagery (CGI) and big orange explosion (BOE) pyrotechnics, of steady-cam and very unsteady cam, and of all the wizardry of digital editing; add to these stunt work and a lot of blood, and the spectacle of war is delivered with a visceral impact.

That *71:Into the Fire* intended to commemorate the sacrifices made by real student soldiers is made clear by the explanatory text at the beginning of the film and through old photos of the real boy soldiers, which appear as the final credits roll past. *T'aegŭkgi* similarly framed its narrative with a literal exhumation of the remains of fallen soldiers. However, this kind of commemorative moment, like any thoughtful examination of the contexts of the war itself, has to work hard for attention amid the spectacle of such big-budget war films.

The battle between North and South is embodied in the two main protagonists: the effective leader of the band of students and delinquents, played by Choe Sŭng-hyŏn (K-pop star T.O.P.), and the commander of the Northern soldiers, a part taken by deep-voiced Ch'a Sŭng-wŏn (mentioned above in the film *South of the Border*). Ch'a's character is a cardboard cut-out villain of a storm trooper; the other Northern soldiers are cyphers, dressed in standard uniforms. The attack on the boys seems driven by macho frustration, not tactics. Angered that mere lads should have beaten his men in an initial skirmish, the commander decides to destroy them, even though bypassing them would be quite easy. The finale is a rooftop showdown between the two leads. Yi Chae-han's *71: Into the Fire* seems stuck in Cold War anti-communist clichés about Northern soldiers as a 'demon army'; the use of the survivors' tale and of their photos to validate the production cannot help but seem cynically contrived.

The 2011 war film *The Front Line* is a very different kind of offering. It is the third film from the young director Jang Hun, a former assistant to Kim Ki-duk (Kim Ki-dŏk). Its Korean title *Kojijŏn* means 'battle for the heights'. The Korean War genre, not surprisingly, contains a number of films focused on desperate struggles to take or hold high ground. In Jang Hun's film the action is set after the main waves of fighting up and down the peninsula have resulted in a bloody stalemate. Insubordination, fraternising with the enemy, drugs, the apparent murder of an officer, a hidden massacre of soldier comrades, alongside gritty humour—*The Front Line* includes a corrosive package of subplots alongside spectacular, almost vertical action sequences. The fraternising takes place indirectly. On one occasion, when the Southern soldiers retake the hilltop at the centre of the story, they find an empty ammunition box buried in the floor of the hilltop bunker. They open it and find a grotesque version of a booby-trap: before retreating, their opponents had shat in it. The ROK lose the hill, take it back again, and when they once again dare to open the box, this time it contains a bottle of strong Northern *soju*. This begins a series of exchanges: tins of food and beer, letters from the Northern soldiers to families in the South, photos, and so on.

Scenes cut back and forth between the two sides, even though most of the story follows the ROK Army characters. There is only one scene in which a junior officer stirs the men back into action one last time with a patriotic speech oddly dissonant with the rest of the film. In a futile battle for the hill in the hours before the 1953 armistice takes effect, US fighter-bombers rain down ordinance indiscriminately, leaving the hill strewn with corpses. One dying DPRK officer sits in the bunker with a ROK Army officer after the air raid; they can only laugh when the radio announces the final cease-fire. The man dies, and the Southern soldier staggers back down the hill though the carnage.

The film perhaps tries to do too much: the high-tech excitement of the battle scenes is mixed with sentimentality about buddies killed, a bit of old-fashioned patriotism, all threaded along an anti-war theme. Certainly no humour is involved in the depiction of the US as a dangerously reckless ally. The ROK Army maintains a kind of battered nobility even while finding the fighting for a useless hilltop senseless. The Inmingun characters—battle-scarred commander, gawky young commissar, cute but deadly female sniper—are a scruffy lot with unclear motivation, but they fight and die as fellow Koreans, not monsters.

Two other films that appeared in 2011 are worth mentioning. *Dreams Come True* is not, strictly speaking, a war film, but a film about the contemporary stand-off between the two Koreas that is always a kind of war in the waiting. It is set at the time of the 2002 World Cup and follows football-mad Northern soldiers on the DMZ trying to find out how the matches are progressing, with eventual help from soldiers on the other side of the line. The group of DPRK troops are generally affable if naive. The trouble comes, as it did in *JSA*, from martinet-like officers. *In Love and War*, set in the early months of the Korean War, is an uneasy blend of the humour of *Welcome to Dongmakgol* with one standard anti-communist plot, the Inmingun occupation of a rural Southern village. Here again, despite the humanity of many of the thinly-sketched Northern characters, the officers are deadly. The villagers have been ordered to dig a massive pit as an 'air-raid shelter', but the Northern high command intends that the pit should become their grave. There is a final showdown between the more humane soldiers and the hard-liners, at which point the US Army arrives guns blazing, blasting both soldiers and peasants. What seemed a witty if bitter joke about the US military in *Heaven's Soldiers* and certainly in *Dongmakgol* already seems a cinematic cliché. The division of Northern soldiers into more-or-less good ones versus true villains may be a simple reflection of how production companies try to appeal to mainstream opinion. As Shin Gi-Wook had found from his survey in 2000, since the majority of South Korean people conceive of national identity through a common sense of ethnic nationalism, those who believe in a shared bloodline between Koreans are more likely to blame Kim Il Sung for national division. To the contrary, as members of the same Korean ethnic nation, the people of North Korea are portrayed as innocent victims of the North Korean regime (Shin 2006: 201).

4.2 Life and death up North

Given the large number of North Koreans entering South Korea and the difficulties many face integrating into ordinary occupations, it is not surprising that some have chosen the entertainment industry as a place where Northern origins may be an advantage. Kim Hye-yŏng has become a well-known singer and actor since coming over the border in 1998. Her training at Pyongyang Theatre and Film University no doubt made the transition easier (HanCinema, 19 August 2008). There was even a Northern girl band, Tallae Ŭmaktan, which made a brief splash in 2006 (Epstein 2009: 3–6).

Of more interest are two film directors from the North. Kim Gyu-min's *Winter Butterfly* (2011) is set in North Hwanghae province at the time of the famines of the 1990s. The story is as stripped down as the lives of the people: a young mother and her young son struggle to survive the effects of hunger and the brutal treatment of local police and military. The trailer runs the following Korean phrases, written in white on a black background, in between scenes of the worsening situation of the two focal characters: 'This film treats actual events which took place in North Korea./ The brutal conditions of North Korea conveyed by a defector director./ Their life without dreams or hopes. What has made them like this?/ A story of people who merely exist, living to eat and eating to live' (see YouTube *Winter Butterfly* trailer). This is a very difficult film to watch; the ending is especially shocking. Director Kim left the North in 2001, making his way through China and into Mongolia. In South Korea, he studied drama and cinema at Hanyang University before working his way into the film business. This included stints on some of the films mentioned above, such as *Crossing* and *South of the Border*. During their shooting, he often served as a speech coach, helping the exclusively Southern actors to come up with passable Northern accents (Lee 2011).

Another defector turned director is Jeong Seong-san (Chŏng Sŏng-san). He is a more controversial figure, mainly through a project that preceded his recent film *Ryang-gang-do: Merry Christmas, North!* That project was a full-tilt Lloyd-Weberian musical, *Yodŏk Story* (see YouTube *Yodŏk Story* trailer). The BBC reported on its opening in 2006, calling it 'probably the least cheerful musical since Les Miserables—a three-hour extravaganza set in one of North Korea's notorious labour camps' (Scanlon 2006). Another defector helped with choreography. Perhaps in reaction to the criticisms directed at the grotesque contrasts of singing and dancing, plus a love story, with the setting of a prison camp, Jeong's film project took a different tack. *Ryang-kang-do* focuses on the world of children. At Christmas time a group of happy South Korean kids puts presents for children in the North in pouches attached to big helium balloons, the kind used to send propaganda leaflets over the North. While some of the balloons are shot down over the DMZ, one makes it way to a poor village. The presents include a Santa Claus suit and a posh hand-console-operated robot. The effects on the Northern kids of this sudden bounty are electric—though one of the problems proves to be just that when the robot's batteries run out. The sentimentality creeps in though a subplot about a seriously ill younger brother. The local kids try to scam enough petrol for the ambulance ride to Pyongyang but to no avail. In the spirit of *Silk Shoes* and *Good Bye, Lenin!* they stage an elaborate fake snowy Christmas for the dying boy.

Jeong's own story is perhaps more interesting than either his play or his film. He came from a well-off family, his father being one of the people who import the stylish cars favoured by the DPRK elite. He studied at Pyongyang Theatre and Film University, had started his military service but ended up in a prison camp when caught listening to broadcasts from South Korea. His journey to the South was by way of China and Vietnam. Once there by 1995, Jeong picked up his studies of drama and film again, focused on scriptwriting and found work as accent coach for both *Shiri* and *JSA* (HanCinema, 4 February 2012). When in *Shiri* Choi Min-shik makes his chilling statement about people starving in the North, it is made to sound all the more convincing in a voice shaped by Jeong Seong-san.

4.3 *Refugees*

Recent films about the experiences of refugees within South Korea have shifted emphasis from the awfulness of the conditions that sent them South to the hardships of life in their new home. Kim Kyŏngmuk's *Stateless Things* was screened at the 2011 London Film Festival and at other festivals that year. It splices together the tales of two young men, one an illegal immigrant from the North. He scrapes along in menial work under abusive treatment, until ending up as a male prostitute. In this underworld he encounters a young man who is the kept toy boy of a married businessman. Both are stranded in a kind of stateless limbo amid the shiny wealth of the contemporary South.

The Journals of Musan (2010) is another downbeat independent film, one which has had even greater exposure through the international film festival circuit, often the only route for controversial, low-budget films in an age of growing monopolisation by conglomerates headed by the massive CJ Entertainment. It tells the story of refugee Jeong Seung-cheol (Chŏng Sŭng-ch'ŏl), a bumbling, mop-haired man adrift in Southern society. No one seems to want to offer him a real job; a friendly detective tries to help him adapt, but to little avail. Through the church he attempts to befriend a woman in the choir by basically stalking her. She turns out to have another life, working evenings at a *norae-bang* (karaoke bar). His stint as a waiter there is disastrous. South Korea seems a place full of people with no time for outsiders and with too much money to care. No one would doubt the sincerity of the film or film-maker. Bak Jeong-beom (Pak Chŏngbŏm) scraped to make the film, becoming producer, scriptwriter, director and lead role. He has explained in interviews how he intended the work as a tribute to his best friend, Jeong Seung-cheol, a Northern refugee and fellow cinephile, who died from cancer six years into a new life in the South.

> I was already resigned to the fact that the film would naturally be labelled a 'defector film' [*t'albukja yŏnghwa*]. It would, I thought, seem to have been made to exploit the subject matter. And so I set myself the goal of making a film which Seung-cheol would not have been ashamed of (Go 2011).

Perhaps the finest film treating similar themes and characters is Chŏn Kyu-hwan's *Dance Town* (2011). The film begins in North Korea, with a very ordinary couple in early middle age. The husband's position takes him occasionally to China; he brings back simple consumer goods, including hand cream for wife Chŏng-nim and the odd erotic video for both to watch. We learn through brief flashbacks about the wife's earlier marriage to a cheating husband, and understand that her present life with her staid-looking husband is a haven to her. All this falls apart when the husband is reported for dealing in contraband; in desperation he arranges for a *chosŏnjok* acquaintance to help smuggle her out. He is arrested and eventually shot, as we find out much later.

Her arrival in the South is followed by brutal questioning; the interrogator growls at her, 'Tell the truth, or we'll kill you.' She seems utterly lost while at a Hanawŏn centre, yet is soon released under the watchful eyes of a resettlement security agent. The female agent assigned her case sits in a car outside Chŏng-nim's apartment building and monitors her new charge through CCTV cameras following the unsuspecting woman around her flat. This hard-edged portrayal of what it is like for a North Korean even to make the first steps of integrating into the South contrasts starkly with the soft-focus account presented in a film such as *South of the Border*. The director gives his narrative greater complexity and critical force by weaving the stories of two other women into that of Chŏng-nim. One concerns her security case-worker, an unmarried woman in her thirties, whose stylish clothing and soignée appearance seems a thin carapace between herself and the world. At home her mother saddles her with caring for an aunt lost in dementia. The other parallel life is that of a middle-school student who gets pregnant; her poor mother, for a time a co-worker of Chŏng-nim at a dry-cleaning shop, has to borrow money from all around to pay for the girl's abortion. The film ends with Chŏng-nim in hospital after an attempted suicide, the social worker sitting mute by the bedside of her aunt, and the school girl sniffing glue and passing out. It may be the quality of the acting and the subtle, unobtrusive settings and camera-work which keep the film from sliding into bathos (as does *The Journals of Musan*) or self-defeating bleakness. A reviewer in *Cine21* noted that

> seeing the web of hell-like relationships enfolding *Dance Town* ... you may wonder whether there really are people like that around us, but director Jeon Gyu-hwan's staging is all too realistic and never for a moment unconvincing (*Ssine21*, 31 August 2011).

The most unusual variation on the theme of a refugee narrative is provided by the action film *Poongsan* (2011). Its director, Jun Jae-hong, was an assistant to Kim Ki-duk; Kim wrote, produced, and generally managed to have his hyperbolic style all over this production. A mute loner takes goods and people back and forth right through the

DMZ. He can fetch an important defector's young lover over in three hours flat, round trip, is the claim. With the aid of a handy telescoping vaulting-pole to clear fences, well-practised skills in swimming the river, and a great deal of suspension of disbelief on the part of the audience, he manages the task, but falls fatally in love with the woman he has rescued. Here, North Korea and a very porous DMZ are little more than props to add a bit of geopolitical spice to a tale of doomed lovers.

4.4 *Chosŏnjok*

Until quite recently, few films made in South Korea dealt explicitly with the Korean-Chinese *chosŏnjok* community. One melodrama from the late 1990s and a documentary or two were about all that was produced until the last decade. A few years ago, *Innocent Steps* (2005) reworked rom-com spy film terrain in the form of a dance film. A young Korean-Chinese woman joins up with a jaded dance professional to help revive his career. The film was more a vehicle for its female star Mun Gŭn-yŏng—'Korea's Kid Sister'—to show off her steps and her *chosŏnjok* accent than to present any real knowledge about the region her character had come from. (For a very intricate reading, see Kim Kyung Hyun 2011: 115–19.)

Since the release of his first film in 2003, Jang Ryul (Chinese, Zhang Lu) has emerged as the premier Korean-Chinese film director. He came to prominence with his second film *Grain in Ear* (2005), an award-winner at the 2005 Pusan International Film Festival. Jang's reputation has attracted funding from the Korean Film Council and the French Centre National de la Cinématographie, and he himself has worked to produce other film-makers from his region. His fifth feature, *Dooman River* (2010), is probably the best film yet about *chosŏnjok* people. The Dooman (more often romanised as Tuman) river runs between North Hamgyŏng province and Jilin province of China, before flowing past the border with Russia into the East Sea. The crucial area for movement between North Korea and the Yanbian region is the shallow portion upstream where, in winter, the river freezes over. Jang Ryul's film tells a quietly devastating tale of life on the border during one winter in a rural commune. People cross over from the Korean side simply to look for food, others as the start of the hazardous refugee trail further into China, and some have come smuggled over by a local van driver. The people on the Chinese side try to help, poor as they are. As hunger drives more people over and they begin stealing food and animals, local people start to turn against them. Most of the action and film's point of view is centred on the children on the Chinese side of the border. Out of a combination of communal ill-will and personal grudges, some local boys start to use violence against the even poorer boys coming over the frozen river. The film has a tragic ending that may seem a bit artificial, but the strength of the story and the beauty of the winter landscapes make it an artistic achievement that matches anything produced in South Korea in recent years.

Jang Ryul includes in his film mundane details of daily life north of the North, in what might seem the furthest outpost of Koreanness, that may surprise non-Korean audiences. The most striking may be the interconnected nature of a Chinese country township with the economy of South Korea. The phone rings in one small house; the voice on the other end is that of the family's mother ringing from down South. She is working to earn as much as possible before heading home. One young girl is living with her uncle and family because, we learn from stray comments, her parents died in a factory fire in a small South Korean city. An old man and his grandson go to the post office to send herbal medicine to the boy's mother in Seoul; the woman behind the counter agrees that this sort of thing costs a fortune down South, she had struggled working there before giving up and coming home. Since the normalisation of relations between China and the ROK in 1992, a good proportion of working-age Korean-Chinese people have made their way to the South, for a short or longer sojourn, by one means or another. They make up the majority of Chinese immigrants in the country. Where once before, and during the colonial era, Koreans might emigrate to the Chinese northeast to find land or work and send remittances home to Korea, now Korean-Chinese head South and send crucial financial assistance back to China.

Na Hong-jin's action thriller *The Yellow Sea* (2010) depicts a far different kind of Korean-Chinese society. The opening section is set in Yanji, the main city of Yanbian. Cab driver Ku-nam has two serious problems. His wife has left to work in the South and he needs to pay off money owed the people who arranged her visa; he also has a gambling habit that has saddled him with a dangerous amount of additional debt. The local gang boss makes him an offer: get into South Korea and fulfil a contract to kill a man, and I'll forget about the debts. The second section takes him on the illegal migrant trail, by train, by bus, in the hold of a small cargo ship, and eventually onto an inflatable boat which lands him and other surviving migrants on the South Korean coast. Ku-nam heads for Seoul, and goes looking for his wife in Karibong-dong, a Korean-Chinese neighbourhood. After his plans for the hit unravel, and he gradually discovers the truth about his wife's murder, the film descends into long, bloody action sequences down in Pusan, involving local gangsters, the head of the Yanji mob and his crew, and the much battered Ku-nam.

Yanji is depicted mainly through its underworld. Ku-nam spends his free time in noisy mahjong dens. The main outside location scene takes place at the dog market, where the grizzled gang boss rules over a primitive bazaar of barking dogs in steel cages and men dressed in leather and furs. The scene suggests that the *chosŏnjok* are not simply a different group of ordinary, modern Koreans, but an ur-race, akin to the primitive Koreans of the pre-Koguryŏ dynasties who people the bit parts in television dramas like *Chumong*. Much later, the Yanji gangsters hide out in Pusan. Battered and bloodied, they are having a meal, chatting and munching on great hunks of dog meat, as a television relays the KBS late-night farewell behind them, the South Korean national anthem playing as the national flag waves in the breeze. It is an unusually sharp-edged sort of black humour for a ponderous action film. Yet less humorous is the fact that in *The Yellow Sea* the image of the *chosŏnjok* as impoverished, possibly illegal and maybe criminal elements within South Korea is not balanced by much of the ordinary humanity ever-present in Jang Ryul's *Dooman River*.

5 Conclusion

It is not difficult to connect the openness of South Korea towards North Korea during the presidencies of Kim Dae-jung and Roh Moo-hyun with the openings provided by a democratising society for a renascent film industry to incorporate new types of stories and new kinds of characters drawn from new conceptions of the North. Yet cinema always has two pressures other than the political shaping its narratives: the financial realities of a competitive market and the globalised imaginary of film genre. Most of the films discussed above were commercial products. Many were made to sell tickets, not to change minds. Often their stories were acceptable to investors and producers, eventually to audiences, and sometimes successful because whatever risks they might take stepping into a new, non-confrontational way of looking North, they conformed to genres known from long acquaintance with both Hollywood and earlier Korean film genres, and often were chiefly following the lead of a recent or rival production.

It is hard to judge how much a different kind of politics has affected films about North Korea made since the Lee Myung-bak regime took power in 2008; but the hard-line stance, the reverse course as regards the DPRK, the almost predictable increase in tension generally and dangerous incidents sporadically (Burghart 2011), have not really reversed cinema's course of relative, if only liberal and qualified, openness towards the North.

Filmography

71: Into the Fire/Pohwasogŭro, dir. John H. Lee (Yi Che-han) (2010)
Brotherhood/T'aegŭkgi [hwinallimyŏ], dir. Kang Je-gyu (Kang Che-gyu) (2004)
Crossing/K'ŭroshing, dir. Kim T'ae-gyun (2008)
Dance Town/Taensŭ taun, dir. Jeon Kyu-hwan (Chŏn Kyu-hwan) (2011)
Dooman River/Tumangang, dir. Jang Ryul (Chang Ryul) (2010)
Dreams Come True/Kkumŭn irujinda, dir. Kyu Yun-shik (2011)
The Front Line/Kojijŏn, dir. Jang Hun (Chang Hun) (2011)
Grain in Ear/Manjong, dir. Jang Ryul (2005)
The Hand of Fate/Unmyŏngŭi son, dir. Han Hyŏng-mo (1954)
Heaven's Soldiers/Ch'ŏn'gun, dir. Min Chun-ki (2005)
In Love and War/Chokgwaŭi tongch'im, dir Pak Kŏn-yong (2011)
Innocent Steps/Taensŭŭi sunjŏng, dir. Pak Yong-hun (2005)
Joint Security Area: JSA/Kongdong gyŏngbi guyŏk, dir. Park Chan-wook (Pak Ch'an-uk) (2000)
The Journals of Musan/Musan ilgi, dir. Park Jeong-beom (Pak Chŏng-bŏm) (2010)
Love Impossible/Namnam bungnyŏ, dir. Chŏng Ch'o-shin (2003)
North Korean Guys/Tonghaemulgwa Paektusani, dir. An Chin-u (2003)
Poongsan/P'ungsangae, dir. Juhn Jaihong (Chun Chae-hong) (2011)
Ryang-gang-do: Merry Christmas, North!/Ryanggangdo aidŭl, dirs. Kim Sŏng-hun and Chŏng Sŏng-san (2011)
Shiri/Swiri, dir. Kang Je-gyu (Kang Che-gyu) (1999)
Silk Shoes/Pidan kudu, dir. Yŏ Kyun-dong (2005)
South of the Border/Kukkyŏngŭi namjŏk, dir. An P'an-sŏk (2006)
The Spy/Kanch'ŏp Ri Ch'ŏl-chin, dir. Jang Jin (Chang Chin) (1999)
Spy Girl/Kŭnyŏrŭl morŭmyŏn kanch'ŏp, dir. Pak Han-chun (2003)
Stateless Things/Chult'ak tongsi, dir. Kim Kyŏng-muk (2011)
Welcome to Dongmakgol/Welk'ŏm t'u Tongmakgol, dir. Pak Kwang-hyŏn (2005)
The Whistling Princess/Hwip'aram kongju, dir. Yi Jŏng-hwa (2002)
Winter Butterfly/Kyŏul nabi, dir. Kim Kyu-min (2011)
The Yellow Sea/Hwanghae, dir. Na Hong-jin (Na Hong-chin) (2010)

References

Burghart, Sabine (2011), 'Relations between the Two Koreas in 2010', in: Rüdiger Frank, James E. Hoare, Patrick Köllner and Susan Pares (eds), *Korea 2011: Politics, Economy and Society*, Leiden and Boston: Brill, pp. 59–70

Burghart, Sabine and James E. Hoare (2010), 'Relations between the Two Koreas in 2009', in: Rüdiger Frank, James E. Hoare, Patrick Köllner and Susan Pares (eds), *Korea 2010: Politics, Economy and Society*, Leiden and Boston: Brill, pp. 55–65

Choi, Jinhee (2010), *The South Korean Film Renaissance: Local Hitmakers, Global Provocateurs*, Middletown CT: Wesleyan Press

Epstein, Stephen (2009), 'The Axis of Vaudeville: Images of North Korea in South Korean Pop Culture'. Online: http://www.japanfocus.org/-Stephen-Epstein/3081

Gluck, Caroline (2002), 'Korean Defectors Learn Basics', *BBC News*, 27 May. Online: http://news.bbc.co.uk/1/hi/world/asia-pacific/2006411.stm

Ko, Kyŏng-sŏk (2011), 'Pak Jŏng-bŏm kamdok: "'Musan ilgi' kwabunhanp'yŏngga padatta"' (int'ŏbyu) [Director Park Jeong-beom: '*The Journals of Musan* has been overly praised' (interview)]. Online: http://movie.daum.net/movieinfo/news/movieinfoArticleRead.do?articleId=1556048

Han Sunhee (2008), 'S. Korea picks "Crossing" for Oscars', *Variety*, 7 August. Online: http://www.variety.com/article/VR1117990204/

HanCinema (14 July 2008), 'Film "Crossing" May Be Banned From Theaters'. Online: http://www.hancinema.net/film-crossing-may-be-banned-from-theaters-14638.html

HanCinema (19 August 2008), 'Actress Defector to Marry S. Korean Actor'. Online: http://www.hancinema.net/actress-defector-kim-hye-young-to-marry-s-korean-actor-20559.html

HanCinema (4 February 2012), 'Jeong Seong-san's Long Struggle to Make Film About N. Korea'. Online: http://www.hancinema.net/jeong-seong-san-s-long-struggle-to-make-film-about-n-korea-38349.html

HanCinema (24 February 2012), 'Actor Cha In-pyo Campaigns for N. Korean Defectors'. Online: http://www.hancinema.net/actor-cha-in-pyo-campaigns-for-n-korean-defectors-39160.html

Hartzell, Adam (2006), *Silk Shoes*, review. Online: http://koreanfilm.org/kfilm06.html#silkshoes

Kim, Kyung Hyun (2011), *Virtual Hallyu: Korean Cinema of the Global Era*, Durham NC and London: Duke University Press

Kim, Suk-Young (2007), 'Crossing the Border to the Other Side', in: Frances Gateward (ed.), *Seoul Searching: Culture and Identity in Contemporary Korean Cinema*, Albany NY: State University of New York Press, pp. 219–42

Lee, Claire (2011), '"Winter Butterfly" tells poignant tale of suffering in N.K.'. *Korea Herald* (1 June 2011). Online: http://www.koreaherald.com/entertainment/Detail.jsp?newsMLId=20110601000601

Lee, J.Y. and Julian Stringer (2010), 'Korean Blockbusters: Yesterday, Today and Tomorrow', in: Daniel Martin and Mark Morris (eds), *Discovering Korean Cinema*, London: Korean Cultural Centre UK, pp. 57–69

Ministry of Unification (2012), 'Settlement Support for Dislocated North Koreans'. Online: http://eng.unikorea.go.kr/CmsWeb/viewPage.req?idx=PG0000000536

Paquet, Darcy (2000), *Joint Security Area*, review. Online: http://koreanfilm.org/kfilm00.html

Paquet, Darcy (2009), *New Korean Cinema: Breaking the Waves*, London and New York: Wallflower Press

Scanlon, Charles (2006), 'Musical Brings Korean Horrors Home', *BBC News*, 4 March 2006. Online: http://news.bbc.co.uk/1/hi/world/asia-pacific/4841876.stm

Schwekendiek, Daniel (2010), 'A Meta-analysis of North Koreans Migrating to China and South Korea', in: Rüdiger Frank, James E. Hoare, Patrick Köllner and Susan Pares (eds), *Korea 2010: Politics, Economy and Society*, Leiden and Boston: Brill, pp. 247–70

Seo, Seung (ed.) (2008), *Che Min-shiku: Kōdō suru yakusha* [Choi Min-shik: an actor in action], Kyoto: Ritsimeikan Daigaku Koria Kenkyū Senta

Shin, Gi-Wook (2006), *Ethnic Nationalism in Korea: Genealogy, Politics, and Legacy*, Stanford CA: Stanford University Press

Ssine21 (31 August 2011), 'Talbuk yŏsŏngŭi kot'ongsŭrŏun Seoul chŏkŭnggi "Taensŭ t'aun"' [*Dance Town*: painful record of a female defector's experience of Seoul], review. Online: http://www.cine21.com/do/movie/detail/review?movie_id=29704

Tanaka, Hiroyuki (2008), 'North Korea: Understanding Migration to and from a Closed Country'. Online: http://www.migrationinformation.org/Profiles/display.cfm?ID=668

YouTube, *Winter Butterfly*, trailer. Online: http://www.youtube.com/watch?v=0t3NTRpXxZ4

YouTube, *Yoduk Story*, trailer. Online: http://www.youtube.com/watch?v=uuYtSIovxuc

All online sources were consulted during February 2012.

A NEW DEAL: GRAPHIC NOVEL REPRESENTATIONS OF FOOD ISSUES IN POST-FAMINE NORTH KOREA

Martin Petersen[1]

ABSTRACT

On the basis of a close reading with especial focus on the particular scope of the graphic novel as a multi-modal medium, this paper suggests that the North Korean graphic novel *A Strange Letter* from 2001 may be viewed as the regime striking a new deal with its citizens. More than a model of, and prescription as to how young citizens ideally should behave and orient themselves, the novel presents a variety of explanations as to what went wrong in the late 1990s, why it went wrong, and what must be done to protect and strengthen the nation in the post-'Arduous March' period. *A Strange Letter* illustrates what the regime expects of its citizens. Interestingly, it also seems to imply what citizens can now expect of the regime. This claim is based mainly on the interaction between the police officers depicted in the novel as reflective of critical introspection on the part of the regime.

Key words: North Korea, graphic novels, famine, food, cultural representation

1 INTRODUCTION

With the disintegration of the communist bloc and economic policies under pressure, increasingly hostile foreign relations forming around the nuclear issue, the unforeseen demise of the national leader and natural calamities partly caused by short-term agricultural policies, the early to mid-1990s were a troubled phase in the history of the Democratic People's Republic of Korea (DPRK). In the mid- to late 1990s,

---

[1] The author gratefully acknowledges the assistance of Mrs Choi Hyun Joo in the preparation of the translations from the Korean in this article. He has also reproduced six illustrations by Kim Ryung in support of his analysis of narrative techniques. Unfortunately, he has not been able to secure the artist's permission for reproduction of these images.

North Korea went through a famine with devastating social consequences, and immense loss of human life. Studies of the famine estimate that between 220,000 and 3.5 million people lost their lives in the period (Haggard and Noland 2007; Lee Suk 2005; Smith 2009). With the state unable to play its traditional role as provider of food through the public distribution system, a main pillar in the social contract between the regime and its citizens broke down. Households had to rely on their own efforts to secure food through farming, trade and barter. Small-scale units in all sectors initiated entrepreneurial coping behaviour, and the regime to a large extent had to tolerate this expanding sphere of market activity. Already by late 1998, however, the North Korean regime began to signal that the worst crisis was over, and within the national master- narrative the preceding period was separated off as the 'Arduous March' (konanŭi haenggun) in allusion to Kim Il Sung's anti-colonial guerrilla movement of the late 1930s.[2] The immediate post-famine period (1999–2002) has been characterised as a period of cautious economic reform and opening in which the regime eventually launched the July 2002 economic management reform measures in a defensive move to reassert control.[3]

An ensuing trend in the literary and arts production of the early 2000s was an engagement with social themes connected to the Arduous March. This relatively speaking more critical literature also included an engagement with food issues. The 98-page graphic novel *A Strange Letter* (*Isanghan p'yŏnji*) written by Kim Yŏng-sam and Chŏn Yŏng-il, illustrated by Kim Ryong and published in April 2001, is one such narrative. It depicts the unravelling of a foreign attempt at poisoning North Korean military food reserves in the post-Arduous March period, but notably, it also indicates that there are some internal reasons why the poisoning scheme almost succeeded.

On the basis of a close reading that focuses on the particular characteristics of the graphic novel as a multi-modal medium (characteristics that include braiding (Groensteen 2007), metalepsis (Kukkonen 2011), panel transition (McCloud 1994) and focalisation (Horskotte and Pedri 2011)), this paper argues that *A Strange Letter* must be understood in the context of the North Korean regime's attempt to strike

---

[2] Gabroussenko (2008) notes that by 1997 the regime was already beginning to announce the termination of the 'march of hardship' (as she translates the term). She adds, however, that in the following period there were continuous references to the concept.
[3] For a short overview of approaches to recent DPRK reforms, see Park (2009).

a new deal with its citizens. More than merely a model of how citizens ideally should behave in times of crisis and post-crisis, *A Strange Letter* can be seen to present a variety of explanations as to what went wrong in the mid- to late 1990s and what the regime expects of its citizens to better those circumstances in the early 2000s. More interestingly, perhaps, the novel also seems to imply what its citizens can now expect of the regime. This claim is mainly based on the interaction between the police officers depicted in this graphic novel, which can be seen as reflecting a measure of critical introspection within the regime. The impression is conveyed of a more dialogic aspect to North Korean literature and arts than is often acknowledged.

2 NORTH KOREAN CULTURAL PRODUCTION IN THE 2000S

From a contemporary and historical perspective, North Korean cultural production must be understood in the context of state engagement and control. Literature and arts were swiftly placed under the aegis of party and state in the post-liberation days of 1945 and have remained so. As a nationally adopted 'socialist realism in our style' (*urisik sahoejuŭijŏk sasilchuŭi*) is the approved vehicle of literary and artistic policy in North Korea, writers and artists are required to depict 'socialist society' without hostile classes, oppression or exploitation. David-West (2007) describes the situation as '[t]otal subordination of literature to the party, political suppression of ideas, and valorization of populism and anti-foreignism—this is the essence of North Korean *socialist realism*' (106).

Graphic novels (*kŭrimch'aek*) and comics (*manhwa*), too, have the explicitly stated function of instilling regime values in their readership. The encyclopedia *Chosŏn T'aebaekkwa Sajŏn* (p. 392) stipulates the accessible character of the medium, its persuasive power, but also broad reader base and didactic function (the education of workers, youth and children). Considering the heated debates about the social harm that comics may cause adolescent readers (Beaty 2005), it is interesting to note that at least from the perspective of encyclopedic authority, the graphic novel in the DPRK is regarded as a 'safe', controlled zone for regime communication.[4]

Several studies have examined how contemporary literary fiction (Epstein 2002; Ryang 2002, 2009; Myers 2010; Gabroussenko 2008, 2009, 2011; David-West 2007, 2009; Cho 2007; Lim 2007), film (Lee Hyangjin 2000), the arts (Frank (ed.) 2011), opera (David-West 2006), performance art (Kim Suk-Young 2010), children's illustrated books (Zur 2010) and schoolbook narratives (Hart 1999) have been utilised as instruments for ideological education in North Korea.

The anthropologist Sonia Ryang (2002) shows how novels from the 1980s are intended to be appropriated by readers as vehicles for the reflection, management and perfection of the self. In other words, novels are integral to the way the state puts forward model types so that North Korean individuals may strive to become model citizens. The crises of the 1990s did not change regime appropriation of cultural production, but inevitably had an impact on how these models were put forward. Gabroussenko (2011), while rejecting the notion of a literary thaw, has noted a recent tendency in rural fiction of the 2000s towards depictions of the countryside that carry more focus on dynamics and conflict and on the representation of South Korea. Cho (2007) provides various examples of how after the famine of the mid-1990s novels became more candid in their depiction of economic difficulties. In particular, *Yŏlmang* (*Aspiration*) by Kim Mun-ch'ang from 1999 and Ri Sin-hyŏn's *Kanggye chongsin* (*Kanggye Spirit*) from 2002 depict food shortages, starvation and death. While literary works from the period highlight factors external to the food situation such as imperialists' sanctions and their attempts at isolation, the irresponsible attitude is also treated, as is the defeatism of 'executive members' and 'chronic maladies such as bureaucracy and routine which are far removed from true revolutionary attitudes' (Cho 2007: 10). Importantly, these themes are never broached in isolation, but serve in the narrative economy to underline the outburst of revolutionary optimism which the crisis calls forth. In her study of fiction dealing with the arduous march, Gabroussenko (2008) states that '[w]hile documentary writings of North Korean refugees invariably refer to this period as an apocalypse, which brought unimaginable horrors to Korean soil (sometimes to the extreme of cannibalism of family mem-

---

[4] For a short introduction to North Korean graphic novels, see Petersen (forthcoming).

bers), ... the North Korean literary discourse divests the "march of hardships" from its unpalatable core' (40).

3   THE REPRESENTATION OF FOOD IN NORTH KOREAN GRAPHIC NOVELS

Food, and issues related with the production and consumption of food, is also a theme that occurs frequently in North Korean graphic novels. The 1990 comic collection by Kim Sang-bok, *A Sick and Rotten World* (*Ssŏkko pyŏngdŭn sesang*), employs documentary-style graphic narratives of the consumption of food in the depiction of a degenerate capitalist world. Here are both the story of an American food competition in which some competitors literally eat themselves to death and the story of a group of wealthy South Korean housewives drinking snake blood. Not surprisingly, this 'sick and rotten' world of culinary excess finds its positive opposite in images of purity in the consumption of food in the distributed ritual essence of Kim Il Sung. Thus, in *Operation Special* (*Tŭksu chakchŏn*) by Choe Hyok, published in 2001, a DPRK patriot about to be sent on a mission in the Korean War beyond the 38th parallel is offered natural water from the wells of Mangyŏngdae in farewell. He timidly consumes this sacrosanct water from Kim Il Sung's birth place with his face turned reverently away from his senior, who has distributed this essence of the regime.[5] In Chin Yong-hun's *Guard the Cradle* (*Yoramŭl chik'yŏ*) from 2009, another patriot about to be sent off into South Korea during the Korean War is offered a noodle dish as part of his spiritual and material preparation. The undercover agent is then embraced by his senior party official in farewell. Both sequences underpin the nation-as-family theme which also includes images of food and commensality—another central theme in contemporary graphic novel production.

The proliferation of graphic motifs of food consumption forms a constitutive part of the nation-as-family master-narrative. In parallel, the protagonists in some the seemingly few graphic novels dealing with current North Korean society are depicted as also being keenly

---

[5] Later in the story, a female patriot about to be abused as a comfort woman during the Pacific War by Japanese troops avoids personal and national catastrophe by harming herself with hydrochloric acid, in this manner keeping her patriotic body pure.

aware of these motifs.⁶ In Kim Yong-hyon's *The True Identity of Pear Blossom* (*Paekot'ŭi chŏngch'e*) (2004), a mother—she is in fact not the biological mother, but a landlord's daughter working undercover as a spy for the American CIA—skilfully employs the social codes of her maternal care for her 'son', who is working on the completion of a project of importance for the national economy and defence, to spy on his plans. Armed with chicken broth, she forces her way into the restricted zone in which he is working.

The graphic novel *Whistle in the Misty Mountains* (*Angaeryŏngŭi kijŏksori*, hereafter *Whistle*) by Kim Sang-bok, published in 2003 in the collection Pangt'anbyŏk (Bulletproof), in its turn deals with a North Korean family of national and class traitors, a father and two sons, who attempt to sabotage a train in the Arduous March period. In the introductory caption, the narrator authenticates the story as follows: 'This story is based on actual events that took place in the severe days when our nation was on the Arduous March' (137). These three internal enemies are actively trying to prepare the crisis-ridden North Korean society of the 1990s for violent overthrow. They want to destroy socialist society in order to regain days of splendour and full stomachs, we learn through the father's lecture to his sons: 'The socialist order as it goes through ordeals must be torn down so that we can regain our world with full bellies and grand lives' (144). This group of dispossessed men is shown to respond almost instinctively to systemic crises and food deficiencies. Aside from railroad sabotage, one son has also tried to put fire to a threshing floor (*t'algokchang*)—a part of the local food production and distribution infrastructure. Giving credibility to the existence, if not prevalence, of such narratives in contemporary North Korean society, whereby internal enemies are blamed at least in part for the destruction of food distribution facilities, the South Korean *Chosun Ilbo* (online edition, 2 November 2011) cited Radio Free Korea for a news story apparently based on North Korean institutional sources, which claimed that recent fires had been

---

⁶ A substantial part of the recent North Korean graphic novel output is preoccupied with the fight against imperialist Japan and the American aggressor in the 'Fatherland Liberation War' (1950–53), often depicted through narratives of North Korean undercover agents deeply embedded in enemy territory on patriotic missions.

instigated by internal 'impure elements' and enemies sponsored by South Korea.⁷

In *Whistle*, the regime arguably employs the particular scope of the graphic novel to link by association the crisis of the mid-1990s with images of internal traitors of reactionary class background and foreign imperialist sympathies. While one favourite theme in foreign media dealing with North Korea is internal dissent, or, as is more often the case, explanations for its absence, *Whistle* is an example of how such dissent is depicted in popular media in the DPRK. The resolution of the crisis unfolded in the last pages of the novel is exemplary Military First-era revolutionary realism. A young female soldier on patrol in the misty mountains recognises one of the brothers from a 'wanted' poster. She immediately intercepts the sabotage attempt and single-handedly defeats the family, before bringing the train to halt moments before certain doom. In a key scene, the train personnel and passengers witness the heroine, who insists on remaining anonymous, as she denounces the class enemies: 'See this, all of you! The class enemies are making frantic efforts up to their dying moment' (157). After this communal ritual they all assist in reassembling the railroad.⁸

This finale fully resonates with mobilisation campaigns calling for united, selfless efforts and self-sacrifice for the common good of the nation embodied in literature of the late 1990s and 2000s (Gabroussenko 2008). Although the resolution of the crisis is overly simplistic, *Whistle* arguably deals with current issues with some degree of directness in comparison with literary works and films from the period.⁹ As a first point to make, current North Korean society, otherwise mostly described in North Korean socialist realism as 'conflictless', is here shown to be threatened by internal enemies, who even formulate an ideological agenda. They are not the usual North Korean citizens, who merely fail to live up to regime expectations of the good citizen, as is often the case in literary fiction. Studies of North Korean cultural output infer that truly negative characters in this output as it deals with current society are mostly external enemies. Brian Myers (2010) thus

---

⁷ Chosun.com, 'Pukhan, t'algokchang kongjang sisŏl itan hwajae ... "Namhan sohaeng" sŏnjŏn', 2 November 2011. Online: http://news.chosun.com/site/data/html_dir/2011/11/02/2011110201802.html (accessed 3 April 2012).

⁸ Train scenes also occur in key moments in other graphic novels such as *Guard the Cradle* (2008–09) and *The True Identity of Pear Blossom*.

⁹ For an overview of negative characters in North Korean film production, see Sŏ Chŏng-nam (2002: 88–97).

claims that '[m]id-level bureaucrats are sometimes criticized as a social class, but individual North Koreans are never singled out as true villains' (90). A second point to make, albeit with some caution, is that the attack on the communal threshing floor and the villainous family's dream of long gone days of luxury may be seen as a way for the regime, through the vehicle of popular culture, to address children's and young readers' experience of the failure of many communal food production and distribution facilities and infrastructure by giving graphic form to internal dissent.

4 A STRANGE LETTER

Where unpleasant images of food as a theme of conflict are at the periphery of *Whistle in the Misty Mountains*, *A Strange Letter* actively engages with the food issue (Figure 1). In this graphic novel of 2001, Ch'a Sŏn-il travels abroad to take care of a matter related to the imports of premium wheat flour destined for Changsang Provisions Factory (*Changsang Singnyo Kongjang*). He frequently travels abroad on such import business. After completing the deal, a man asks him to bring back home a letter to a man named Hong Myŏng-dŏk working in the factory. We later learn that on earlier occasions this same man, whose nationality is not quite clear, has given Sŏn-il presents and money. On their first encounter, three years earlier, he put money into Sŏn-il's pocket with the words: 'You are really doing a good job with the "Arduous March". It's not much, but please use it' (64). Sŏn-il reluctantly brings the letter back to Changsang along with expensive clothes for his daughter and wife. He senses that something is wrong and is puzzled at the enigmatic contents, and so instead of delivering the letter himself he asks a random schoolgirl in the street to deliver it for him. The schoolgirl, Ch'oe Ok-kyŏng, coincidentally happens to be the new friend of Sŏn-il's daughter, Hŭi-suk. (At this point, though, no one is aware of this connection.) Ok-kyŏng immediately gets suspicious and contacts the police (or, as we are told, the relevant authorities, the *haedang kigwan*). Sŏn-il feels guilty and makes an anonymous phone call to the police to inform them of the strange letter. A team of police officers, a section chief (*kwajang*) and two young staff members (*puwŏn*), investigates the case and soon finds out that there is something fishy about the new storage chief (*ch'anggojang*) of the Changsang factory, Rim Pyŏng-sŏp, and the janitor (*kyŏngbiwŏn*), Om

Pong-tal. Pyŏng-sŏp, who picked up the letter inside the food factory, has replaced Hong Myŏng-dŏk as chief as a consequence of a fire in the storage facility, a fire that he blamed on Myŏng-dŏk, who was then transferred to menial labour.

Figure 1 Character gallery of *A Strange Letter*

With the assistance of the informing schoolgirl, the police find out that Sŏn-il was the courier who brought the letter into the factory and that he is also identical with the anonymous phone caller. Chin-ho, the male police staff member, suggests summoning him right away, but the section chief decides to wait patiently for Sŏn-il himself to report the matter to them. In the meanwhile Ok-kyŏng has paid a birthday visit to Hŭi-suk's new residence in an apartment building, and on this occasion realised that the strange man with the letter was none other than her friend's father. After consulting the police officers, she hints to Hŭi-suk that her father's travels abroad may have brought trouble. Hŭi-suk returns home, confronts Sŏn-il and rejects his gifts from abroad. Infuriated at this juvenile insubordination, he slaps her, but then, on second thoughts and at long last, hastens to reports the matter to the section chief.

Now the police can solve the matter. With clever schemes they send the female staff member, Ye-suk, into the factory to reveal, arrest and interrogate Pyŏng-sŏp and Pong-tal. The son and nephew of a landlord from North Hwanghae province, both turn out to be US spies. The letter from abroad instructed them to arrange together with a third man the poisoning of the premium-quality wheat flour imported by Sŏn-il in a 'star star snow snow'-labelled bag, which was specially reserved for the North Korean military. The scheme was first plotted when, according to the narrator, 'the nation was undergoing temporary ordeals'—another reference to the famine years of the mid- to late 1990s. Test results indicated that the polluted flour made the victims languid and caused death within a year. On the final page, Ok-kyŏng, the schoolgirl who swiftly informed on the basis of her suspicion, is rewarded in front of her school, Sŏn-il, his daughter and Hong Myŏng-dŏk, the now rehabilitated former storage chief.

4.1 *Meta-authorial reading*

Over the following pages I will employ three readings of this graphic novel: a meta-authorial, an ironic, and a reader-recognisant meta-authorial reading. Following David-West (2009) (who notably warns against the pitfalls of the meta-authorial reading), we may loosely define such reading as being primarily based on the premise that the regime with its profession of monolithic solidarity defines how the North Korean writer must write and the North Korean reader must read. North Korean literature is 'intended as a mirror of the official nationalist-Stalinist "monolithic" ideology' (David-West 2009: 23), thus making of it a political subject, which accordingly 'requires a critical approach that can competently interpret its inherently partisan modes of meaning' (ibid.).

In many aspects, *A Strange Letter* fits into a reading for the meta-author; a reading, in other words, which approaches this cultural text as an expression of regime intentionality with inherently partisan modes of meaning. This in itself is hardly surprising, considering the state-controlled character of North Korean cultural production. While it does not deal with the Arduous March as its main theme, *A Strange Letter* serves as a narrative frame, as one model of how young North Korean readers should remember and put behind them this period, comprehend the present day (the early 2000s) and employ this comprehension for the reflection, management and perfection of self (Ryang 2002). The point here is not that the graphic novel presents a model for how to remember the Arduous March. The case seems rather to be that improved conditions have made North Korea an increased target for hostile aggression. *A Strange Letter* graphically renders the danger of a 'return' to the crisis of the Arduous March period if members of society do not all stay on alert.

A Strange Letter was published in 2001, the year in which the largest food aid deliveries to North Korea, amounting to one million tonnes of food worth some US$240 million, were made through the UN World Food Programme (Smith 2009). Surely the story does not deal with food aid but suggests a more equal relationship between the DPRK and the outside world in the form of trade and food imports. Moreover, no foreigners are depicted inside North Korea in the narrative. Judging from the images of the foreign cityscape, the locals, and Sŏn-il's return by train, the implied trading partner is likely to be the Russian Far East, which was not a major trade partner at that period (Haggard and Noland 2007). The Rajin–Sŏnbong (Rasŏn) foreign economic trade zone created in the early 1990s, with a rail link to the Russian city of Khasan, has been slow to develop as planned (see Hassig and Oh 2009: 82–83). Around 2001, food aid and food imports came mainly from Japan, China, the United States, South Korea and the European Union. The novel in any case gives only visual hints as to a location possibly in the far eastern corner of the former communist bloc, in this way leaving room for general inferences of interaction with an unspecified foreign trading partner. There was a marked rise in the imports (including aid) of cereals around 2000–2001, suggesting why imports—and the poisoning—of high-quality wheat flour were selected as a topic and also making it likely that readers would have encountered foreign foodstuffs and/or bags with foreign labels in their everyday life. It should be noted, however, that refugee surveys in the mid-2000s indicated that 40 percent of respondents were unaware of food aid and only 3.4 percent of respondents acknowledged having received any such aid (Haggard and Noland 2011).

In *A Strange Letter*, the import and consumption of foreign foodstuffs comes under danger from the United States. The actual threat is caused by the mysterious man of unknown nationality, who bribes Sŏn-il, the North Korean import representative, and who later incites his accomplices inside the Changsang Provisions Factory to poison the wheat flour in bags labelled with snow and stars. The plot is thus informed by a rather universal insecurity concerning foodstuffs produced abroad. Further examples of North Korean graphic novels depict foreign imperialists scheming to inflict damage on North Korean society through harming bodies. They achieve this concretely, as in Pak Hong-ju's *Misty Island* (*Angaetŏp'in sŏm*) (2002), which deals with wartime bacteriological experiments; and subtly, as in Chin Yong-hun's *Guard the Cradle* (2008–2009), in which a Japanese spy undergoes facial surgery so as to impose as a North Korean patriot.

This hypersensitivity to the foreign underpinning *A Strange Letter* also extends to North Koreans who interact with foreigners. The foreign spy working for the imperialist US gradually draws Sŏn-il into his net though interpersonal charity: money and generous gifts. These sequences covering Sŏn-il's foreign sojourn show how North Koreans travelling abroad or, by extension, merely interacting with foreigners are targeted for suspicion, confirming one of the widespread Western beliefs that the regime does not tolerate interpersonal interaction.[10]

Sŏn-il's character embodies the ambiguous feature of opportunity and exposedness in North Koreans' dealings with foreigners. He may be seen as representing a class of merchants and officials who during the famine of the 1990s were able to an unprecedented degree to make careers through economic transactions beyond the control of state and party. The flash-back sequence that focalises Sŏn-il's visits abroad shows a feeble and reluctant Sŏn-il gradually giving in to the material temptations offered by the 'capitalist demon'.[11] Smith (2009), who has examined the North Korean famine as a causative agent of economic transition, argues that proximity to foreigners and foreign capital was one important survival strategy during the famine period and beyond. In dealing with Sŏn-il, the novel under discussion signals that state and party are back in control and that proximity to foreigners is a risky business. Graphically, the patiently waiting section chief in his office is repeatedly depicted in front of a world map. It is he, not Sŏn-il (and the real-life mercantile prototypes whom it is reasonable to expect have inspired the character), who knows how to, and is authorised to, navigate the world. The widely disseminated image of Kim Jong Il

---

[10] For an analysis of racialised segregation between North Koreans and foreigners in DRPK cultural production, see Brian Myers (2010: 131).

[11] For Horstkotte and Pedri (2011), the focalisation-marking resources of graphic novels 'serve to cue readers to imaginatively transfer to the storyworld by constructing what Alan Palmer would call an "embedded narrative," that is, the way in which the story is experienced by one particular character and thus under that character's aspectuality' (351).

standing before a globe with a resolute gesture and pointer in hand attended by regime elites and his highly satisfied father is the master-narrative of which the world map image is a small-scale resonance.[12]

Figure 2   Sŏn-il watched by the section chief
(*A Strange Letter*, page 74)

At long last, standing before the section chief, below his world map, Sŏn-il bows his head, unburdens his heart and then, the narrator informs us in a caption, 'Cha Sŏn-il, as if a heavy burden had been lifted from his shoulders, walked with a happy mind as that of a child, and light as if flying' (*A Strange Letter*: 74) (Figure 2). He has been, not degraded, but re-inscribed into a position as child within the nation-as-family—or the General's household (*Changgunnimuŭi siksol*, as the slogan in a scroll hanging in the school office states.[13] Kim Suk-Young (2010) has noted the 'simulation of eternal childhood' within

---

[12] See Fauna (19 December 2011), 'Photo of an oil painting featuring Kim Il-sung and Kim Jong Il', in: *North Korea Leader Kim Jong-il Dies, His Life in 59 Photos*. Online: http://www.chinasmack.com/2011/pictures/north-korea-leader-kim-jong-il-dies-his-life-in-59-photos.html (accessed 3 April 2012).

[13] Such hanging scrolls are also seen as decorative-functional elements in other graphic novels.

the imagined family of the nation-state (144), and how in North Korean cultural production traditional patriarchs are often marginalised in the family unit by the state patriarch, and projected as 'emasculated characters who do not function as traditional providers for the family' (ibid.: 146). Brian Myers discerns this feature of idealising citizens as innocent, spontaneous, gullible children, who leave initiatives to the party and state, as the idealisation of *sobakham*, emotional spontaneity. David-West (2007) de-emphasises this aspect, pointing out that *sobakham*, '[a]ffecting the ability to function optimally for the sake of the "fatherland" ... assumes the undesirable form of personal weakness' (111). In *A Strange Letter* this *sobakham* is not idealised as a permanent state of mind, but is a key element in the self-reforming process of the wayward father. His state of mind is a gateway back into sanctioned social life. Sŏn-il has become unburdened of his bad conscience, but also divested of authority to interpret and navigate the world. This 'fixing' of the father's social role is simultaneously a re-negotiation of the preceding flash-back sequence focalised in Sŏn-il's narration to the section chief. The flash-back sequence rendered him, if not in directly hostile, then in 'messy' foreign settings in street vistas with coarsely built and sloppily dressed Caucasians, among whom the foreign spy preys on Sŏn-il.

Sŏn-il is temporarily led astray, and mildly castigated (and castrated) for this, but he is reformable. In comparison, the true internal enemies are beyond the reach of the national family and its emasculated salvation. They are doubly inscribed with externality. Firstly, these spies carrying names such as 'black snake' and 'racoon' are working for the US—a common type of antagonist in DPRK graphic novels—and they have a family background as landlord—another archetypical enemy category (Hart 1999): a background, we are told, they have eliminated from their identity papers.[14] While officially North Korea is a classless society with various social strata, refugee- and defector-based research has extensively pointed to the prevalence of a *sŏngbun* stratification system in which status as a 'hostile stratum' is related to a 'reactionary' family past in the colonial and post-liberation periods, with significant influence on life prospects.[15] *A Strange Letter*, as is also the case with *Whistle* and *Pear Blossom*, un-

---

[14] For the falsification of identity papers, see Lee Keum-Soon et al. (2009: 184) and Kim Yong's testimony (2009).

[15] See Lee Keum-Soon et al. (2009). Some interviewees indicate reduced or even no discriminatory practices with regard to family and class background.

derpins this stigmatisation of a landlord's descendants in its villain typology.

A Strange Letter lucidly presents one narrative model of how to bring collective closure to the traumatic years of the mid- to late1990s and sketches the opaque imperialist forces and internal class enemies waiting to overthrow North Korea in the vulnerable post-famine period. In this narrative, the nation is regaining strength, but class enemies and foreign imperialists are constantly scheming. In a sense, the process of bringing collective closure is ongoing, never ending. In this context, the use of the food poisoning attempt against the People's Army as a plot subtly engages popular understanding of how even within the privileged military, symptoms of constipation, disease and death occurred, and may still occur. Although the military was highly prioritised during the crisis of the mid- to late 1990s, being enlisted in the military was not in itself a guarantee of food supplies, even if, at the least, it enabled opportunities for diversion and coercion (Haggard and Noland 2007: 108–25), an issue that is not dealt with in the novel.

Concurrently, the novel presents its young readership with a model of behaviour. This model is primarily embodied in Ok-kyŏng, the schoolgirl, who relayed her suspicions to the police and urged her friend Hŭi-suk to confront her father. Hŭi-suk is a secondary role model. She transgresses (what we may broadly term) Confucian family norms by defiantly opposing her father, and thereby steers the whole family towards the imagined community. The regime's message is discernible here: young people may contribute to maintaining the Fatherland as a safe haven by being alert to irregularities in society, by not hesitating to inform the police and, importantly, by confronting friends and family members temporarily led astray. These youth values are also disseminated in the public space of Pyongyang with road posters urging members of society to be alert towards spies. The novel does in fact show Ok-kyŏng's doubts. Her realisation that the strange man with the letter is the father of her friend Hŭi-suk gives substance to her doubts as to whether she did right in informing the police. Notably, however, these doubts are presented neither as personal introspection in thought bubbles nor in dialogue with her family (who is absent from the story). They are addressed to the younger police officer, who swiftly reassures her that she is doing the right thing. In a short flash of comic relief, the narrative has Hŭi-suk think to herself that Ok-kyŏng is like a question mark, who even makes her school teachers sweat through her constant questions. This is one instance in which the novel is focalised so as to make the reader see the story-world from the perspective of the less-than-perfect figure. Epstein (2002) describes the narrative effect of this feature in turn of the millennium North Korean fiction as follows: 'The protagonists engage the reader's empathy but fall short of others so that events can bring about a subjective realization in which the reader may participate' (45).

The narrative abundantly rewards 'Question Mark' for being too much so. The final image has the community celebrating 'Question Mark'. This scene is focalised in such a manner that the celebrating community seems in fact to be celebrating the reader. The young reader is thereby provided with an opportunity to ponder what it must feel like to be in Ok-kyŏng's shoes. The manner in which the community gazes may be said to address readers 'by breaking the fourth wall of the window pane' (Kukkonen 2011: 224), a narrative device which is described as ascending, rhetorical metalepsis (ibid.). Metalepsis is a term from narrative theory that marks the transgression of boundaries of the fictional world. Ascending, rhetorical metalepsis also occurs in the final frame of a few other recent DPRK graphic novels and serves to transcend the epistemological gap between the social realist characters of the story-world and the young North Korean readers. This feature resonates with Kim Suk-Young's notion of 'the reversal of mimesis', 'when producers of theater and film regard everyday reality as inferior to represented reality, and invent utopia versions of reality and present them for audiences to emulate'; 'theatricality becomes the key notion, the staged version of reality when the representation of everyday life exceeds everyday life itself' (Kim 2010: 14).

4.2 Ironic reading

One problem with a blanket subscription to this understanding of North Korea as 'a theatrical state par excellence' (Kim 2010: 14) and with the meta-authorial reading is that while both approaches address the need to understand that the regime's intentions are undoubtedly at play in cultural texts, such a reading does not enable us to question the intricate relationship between regime and author, reader and text. At worst, it reduces a cultural text to an automaton of the regime, and reduces regime, writers and readers to monolithic sameness.

Using the term 'ironic reading', Lee Hyangjin (2000) concerns herself with the 'uncontrolled' response of cultural consumers (spectators and readers) to cultural productions in the socialist realist tradition, which insist on a social reality that conflicts with their lived experience as active interpreters of the social world in which they exist (253). In a similar vein, Epstein (2002) shows how 'the texts rely on the reader's "willing acquiescence in belief" and eagerness to suppress cognitive dissonance in favor of the interpretation the texts themselves wish to dictate. The reader's role in the implicit contract established with the state and author, then, is to allow his or her faith in the system to be reaffirmed' (48). The moment willing acquiescence does not occur, an ironic reading may take place. Whether the 'ironic reading' as it is virtually forced upon readers through the sheer contrast between regime 'reality' and their personal experience of everyday life, is permeated with disillusion, cynicism, amusement or merely an absence of interest is an altogether different question, which is at least to some extent closely related with the reader's or spectator's social status, living standards, educational background and access to information.

A number of cognitively dissonant or ironic readings in *A Strange Letter* are possible points where the reader's willing acquiescence in belief is particularly challenged. Related to the question of food security, the fact that the two villainous cousins working in the factory as storage chief and janitor have been able to live with falsified papers and hide their true class background (and evil intent) contradicts the image of the all-knowing surveillance apparatus graphically rendered in the world map and in the image of the section chief standing in the open window in front of fluttering curtains, smilingly observing Sŏn-il run off as a child.

The North Korean reader who does not suppress cognitive dissonance may likewise ponder what the police and political and administrative authorities connected with the provisions factory were doing when Rim Pyŏng-sop schemed to oust the upright storage chief, Hong Myŏng-dŏk. Were they merely sitting in an office nicely decorated with world maps waiting for people (not) to come to them when a group of misled foodstuff factory personnel passed judgment on the wrong person? And where were the local party officials? According to Haggard and Noland (2007), 'county-level warehouses are controlled by the county-level People's Committees, which are made up of Party functionaries and senior administrative cadre' (53). From 1996 onwards, so-called corn guards were employed to guard granaries in response to instances of pre-harvesting and diversion. This solution to the problem of monitoring was challenged by the fact that these corn guards were soon entangled in local coping strategies (ibid.: 111). Corn guards are not part of the narrative, but the spontaneous mass denouncement of Myŏng-dŏk presents the Changsang factory as a troubled locale, a place temporally deserted by the 'All-seeing Eye'. *A Strange Letter* does not give the impression of the factory as a place where the party is firmly handling matters of employment and management. It depicts a more communal, almost autonomous process in the flash-back scene of the storage fire, which is focalised in Myŏng-dŏk's explanation to the section chief. Here we find Myŏng-dŏk surrounded by co-workers. Pyŏng-sŏp takes the lead in blaming Myŏng-dŏk for reckless handling of cigarettes and inflammable liquids inside the granary. He ends the accusation with a pointing finger and the words: 'All people here stand witness!' (35) (Figure 3). This is the counter-image, the nightmarish vision of the communal gathering depicted in *Whistle*, where the female solider in a similar circle points towards the dying father lying on the ground and passes her judgment (see below) (Figure 4).

Figure 3 Myŏng-dŏk under accusation
(*A Strange Letter*, page 35)

In stylistic terms, the uncanny resemblance between the righteous communal group passing judgment on a class traitor and the misled masses witnessing the judgment of a righteous man is not coincidental. Both graphic novels were, as already related, illustrated by Kim Ryong. There is one important difference in these two scenes which guides reader encodings, namely the focalisation of the 'accused'. Where we find the villainous father in *Whistle* lying on the ground, face pressed downwards, bemoaning his fate, Myŏng-dŏk is also physically present in his scene of conviction, but depicted from a perspective which makes him appear larger than both the accuser and the human circle. Most importantly, Myŏng-dŏk does not respond to the accusation in self-pitying words, or with a defeatist body language (which would effectively have disqualified him as a hero, and model of emulation), but stares towards the reader situated beyond the fourth wall of the window pane, again if not in a radical breach of the story, then still in a mild degree of ascending, rhetorical metalepsis that strengthens reader identification with the good person.

Figure 4   The soldier gives her judgment
(*Whistle in the Misty Mountains*, page 157)

A reading against the grain illuminates the dilemma of the food poisoning story, which celebrates all the good and reformable citizens, but as a 'by-product' exposes how one of the cornerstones in the North Korean social contract—the infrastructure of food distribution—is not fully under the regime's control. Narrative dynamics have caught up the meta-author in contradictions.

A counter-argument to this ironic reading is that this particular graphic novel intentionally enables and stimulates such cognitively dissonant readings. As already mentioned, it is not unusual to find critical portraits of DPRK officials in North Korean cultural products (Cho 2007; Myers 2010). We should thus be careful not to conflate the police officers (and the non-present party officials) in *A Strange Letter* with the regime per se; that is, to view them as cultural representations. Cultural works may produce critical representations of government officials without for that reason being critical towards the regime as such. Yet *A Strange Letter* in no way intends an understanding of the police officers as faulted. We therefore need to supplement the meta-author and his ironic reader approach to better understand regime intentions and the implied reader in *A Strange Letter*.

4.3 *Reader-recognisant meta-authorial reading*

Before considering this third reading, let us briefly recall the political context. *A Strange Letter* appeared in April 2001 in what is commonly described as a period of cautious economic reform and opening (1999–2002). Less than a year after the summit between Kim Daejung and Kim Jong Il, about half a year after Secretary of State Madeleine Albright's visit to Pyongyang in October 2000, and a few months after Kim Jong Il's major state visit to China in January 2001, the novel was published in a period in which the relatively reform-oriented cabinet had the institutional lead over the ideologically conservative party and pragmatically conservative military on issues such as the economy and South Korean matters (McEachern 2010). In this context, *A Strange Letter* may be seen to propose a 'New Deal', a return to better days, where everyone (except for a few villains and scapegoats) will have a positive communal role.

Graphically, this new deal is rendered on the very last page. As already related, the first panel shows a humble Ok-kyŏng receiving an appreciation from the section chief, while the head master (*kyojang*) and a teacher applaud her. The second and final panel in a simple aspect-to-aspect transition depicts a group of people applauding her as she receives the appreciation.[16] In the background are seen numerous

---

[16] For a discussion of intra-panel relations, see Scott McCloud (1994). With aspect-to-aspect transition, 'rather than acting as a bridge between separate moments,

schoolchildren, mainly girls. In the foreground stand father, Ok-kyŏng and Hong Myŏng-dŏk. They are focalised in such a manner that the celebrating masses appear to be looking outwards, celebrating us the readers. I have already discussed how this renders in graphic fashion the award that will be bestowed upon children who, after reading the novel, emulate the behaviour and embody the values of 'Question Mark'. This group image is an instance of 'braiding', a term coined by the comics scholar Thierry Groensteen to comprehend the rhyme effect across the network constituted by a graphic novel as a totality, 'the remarkable resurgence of an iconic motif (or of a plastic quality) ... concerned primarily with situations, with strong dramatic potential, of *appearance* and of *disappearance*' (2007: 151–52). This scene is the re-negotiated, rectified and conflictless image of group behaviour, which rhymes with, and thoroughly replaces, Myŏng-dŏk's nightmarish vision of misled group behaviour in the storage fire scene.

In this new deal, the honest, hardworking officials, who have been marginalised with the breakdown of the socialist public distribution system, will be reinstated. Those forced into entrepreneurial coping behaviour in order to secure food for their households with the virtual demise of food distribution or who have taken the opportunity to live luxuriously will be welcomed back into the social contract and (re)gain their status as children to the party, nation and leader; that is, if they comply with party rules, accept the nation-as-family contract and render themselves merrily as children passing under the omnipresent eye of the party, the state and its patriarchs. This 'mild' deviance is epitomised in the image of daughter and wife trying on the fancy foreign dresses brought home from abroad by the father, who pleasurably watches their 'fashion show' (Figure 5). In this context, the sequence where Ok-kyŏng pays a birthday visit to Hŭi-suk's new home is also of interest. We learn that Sŏn-il's family has recently moved into an apartment from a one-storey building—the intense childhood dream of the protagonist in the film *The Schoolgirl's Diary* (2006).[17] The novel does not contemplate whether the family's newfound success will be affected by their 'return' to the nation-as-family.

---

the reader here must assemble a single moment using scattered fragments' (McCloud 1994: 79).

[17] *The Schoolgirl's Diary* (*Han Nyŏhaksaengŭi ilgi*), directed by Jang In-hak, relates a North Korean schoolgirl's struggle to understand that her father to all appear-

Figure 5 A fashion show
(*A Strange Letter*, page 57)

Most critical, however, to the understanding of this new deal is the representation of the police. They will reinvigorate their power and reinstate a just order, wholesome social values and safe access to healthy foodstuffs. Most notably, this will be done not in the impatient and somewhat legalistic manner of the young male police officer, Chin-ho, but in the humanistic, patient manner of his senior, Sŏk-ch'ŏl.

Conversation between these two male policemen is a recurrent theme throughout *A Strange Letter*. Their conversations, rendered in sequences of varying length, occur seven times (at pages 18, 23–24, 29–30, 44–45, 75–76, 79, 88–89) and culminate in their joint interrogation of the two criminals (90–92). In the first two sequences, the two merely exchange opinions. This exchange, however, is both verbally and visually hierarchised. The two men address each other employing different speech levels, indicating the seniority of the section chief. In addition, Chin-ho gazes attentively at his senior, whose manner of listening is more a matter of gauging Chin-ho's comprehension of the case than a way of obtaining fresh perspectives.

In the third conversation sequence, the section chief for the first time challenges the junior's opinion, when the latter suggests that Myŏng-dŏk is an accomplice in the scheme. In yet another instance of

---

ances has left his family in difficult circumstances so that he can contribute to the success of the nation.

'discrete' ascending, rhetorical metalepsis, the questioning, testing, consensus-oriented attitude of the senior is replaced by a lecturing of the junior. This lecturing is graphically rendered by an image of the senior's face in shadow on a dark background, sternly looking through the fourth wall of the window pane towards the virtual position of the reader: 'I always emphasise this, but as much as our work is directly linked to the fate of all kinds of people, make sure to always contemplate deeply and sufficiently when you make your judgment' (*A Strange Letter*: 30).

In their fourth conversation, immediately after Ok-kyŏng has identified Sŏn-il as the anonymous man with the letter, the junior asks whether they should summon him. The senior with only a slight variation repeats his lecture: 'Of course, our work would be easy if we summoned him for questioning, but wouldn't that leave a stain in his life? Right now, he is agonising' (44). This second lecturing of the younger official in emphatic police conduct is graphically rendered in a reversal of the previous sequence. This time, the senior is standing with his back to the junior (and the readers), looking out of his office window. In the following panel, in what appears to be a scene-to-scene transition (McCloud 1994: 60–93), both junior and senior look out of the window. The junior points at Sŏn-il passing by in the street below, exclaiming: 'Wait. That's him.' The senior responds: 'Hmmm. He doesn't seem to be a stranger after all!' (44–45).

Like the group motif, the police officials surveying people from an elevated point is also a graphic rhyme. It is a motif braided across the graphic network of *A Strange Letter* with the effect of manifesting regime omnipresence. In another 'version' of this motif, we find the senior official leaving the Changsang People's School after having inquired about Myŏng-dŏk's past and looking back over his shoulder at the school buildings in deep contemplation. Not only through the conversation scenes, then, but also through the braiding of the elevated surveillance motif, the novel endorses the emphatic attitude of the section chief, whose patience bears fruit when Sŏn-il comes running to his office to report on the matter, and he exclaims with outstretched arms: 'I am glad to see you. I knew you would come. Matter of fact, I was waiting for you to come' (62). Moments after, the rhyming of the elevated surveillance motif culminates when Sŏn-il hurries off happily below the police office window.

In the three subsequent scenes of dialogue between senior and junior on the appropriate timing and manner of arresting the two criminals in the Changsang Provisions Factory, the same pattern of patience/impatience is fleshed out in the two male police characters, but the duality of empathy/legalism is replaced by a search for the most effective way to expose the criminals. Here, another side to the section chief is conveyed in a close-up of his claw-like, clenched right hand as he exclaims: 'Like catching mudfish, you have to bury the palm of your hand in the sand to seize its last breath' (79) (Figure 6).

Figure 6 How to catch mudfish
(*A Strange Letter*, page 79)

In dealing with these two criminals, a female junior is involved. The role of this third police official is mainly played out in Chapter 3, 'It was a trap'. The female police assistant is not involved in the male dichotomies of patience/impatience, empathy/legalism, but is employed as a bait so as to trick the criminals into action. The sequence in which Ye-suk performs the 'catch mudfish' game with the janitor and storage chief is the closest this novel gets to slapstick. We find the two villains engaging in playful dialogue with her and posing in what for the lack of better description may best be described as 'uncle-flirtatious' poses. While this sequence mainly seems to provide brief comic relief in a narrative which otherwise emphasises model behaviour and engages readers with a predominantly didactic message, this gendered 'digression' falls squarely within the repertoire of female representations in North Korean cultural production. As pinpointed by

Kim Suk-Young (2010): 'Sexuality can be used as the means, so long as the ends signify the patriotic cause. While the only positive placement of women outside the traditional family is related to the process of social awakening, the only allowed type of female sexuality is the one instrumentalized to expunge enemies from the fatherland'(215).

Key to this third reading of a regime offering a new deal through the emphatic senior is thus, firstly and basically, that we accept the premise that the novel is about regime communication, and, secondly and specifically, that the interaction between the police authorities—the hero and his two side-kicks—and their justly suspended action weaves the theme of regime reflexivity and of 'self-criticism' across the network of this graphic novel.[18] It is, in other words, a concession to North Korean cultural consumers, whose suspension of disbelief has been stretched too far.

If this third reading of 'soft power' regime communication is viable, what we see is definitely not a literary thaw as emphatically noted by Gabroussenko (2009). On the contrary, it is a graphic novel with quite escapist models of crisis solution and authoritarian nation-as-family values. Nevertheless, *A Strange Letter*, through the patient and just senior officer, who holds back his impatient junior from dealing swiftly with not only the unjustly victimised citizen but also the basically good citizen temporarily led astray, only to unleash his other junior at the true criminals like the palm of a hand buried in sand to catch mudfish, facilitates a controlled and restricted dialogue with its implied readers.

Whether, and to what extent actual readers of this graphic novel have positively engaged in this dialogue is an altogether different matter. The modestly reformist tenor of the early 2000s was short lived. Renewed confrontations over nuclear issues and George W. Bush's post-9/11 axis of evil speech were just around the corner, tipping the balance between party, military and cabinet. Most importantly, the food situation—for the vast majority—got only slightly better than it had been during the Arduous March of the mid- to late 1990s, '[t]he state never regained economic capacity sufficient to re-establish state control of the production, supply and distribution of goods including food' (Smith 2009: 245), and real-life Sŏn-ils were still engaging in

---

[18] For a discussion of the theme of self-criticism in DPRK fiction, see Sonia Ryang (2009).

coping strategies in a 'system of marketisation without liberalisation' (ibid.).

5 CONCLUSION

As already suggested, *A Strange Letter* illustrates what the regime expects of its citizens, but interestingly also what its citizens can expect of the regime, at least in terms of regime officials as represented by the police officers the novel depicts.

This is noteworthy for two reasons. Firstly, it conveys the impression of a dialogic aspect to the ideological function of North Korean graphic novels. While not dismissing the meta-authorial perspective (arguably employed by Gabroussenko, Myers and in part by Ryang and Kim Suk-Young), but also not quite following the counter-intuitive and ironic readings (as developed by David-West, Epstein and Lee Hyangjin), this paper suggests that the regime does control the graphic narrative and does not leave much room for creative agency, but that the 'openings' and 'cracks' in *A Strange Letter* are not uniformly unintended ironic paradoxes, but show the regime reaching out to its citizens in the early 2000s so as to draw back lost power. It is a question open for interpretation whether we should ultimately understand this 'New Deal' as a palm buried in the sand patiently waiting to catch mudfish.

As we well know, the promulgation of turning points is more the rule than the exception in DPRK regime rhetoric. Yet, and this is the second noteworthy aspect of the novel, it pinpoints what was seen as a turning point in recent North Korean history at the time of its production; namely, the moment when the DPRK declared it had left the Arduous March behind and was striving for a new and better era.

REFERENCES

Beaty, Bart (2005), *Fredric Wertham and the Critique of Mass Culture*, Jackson MS: University Press of Mississippi
Cho, Jeong-Ah (2007), *The Changes of Everyday Life in the Aftermath of their Economic Difficulties,* Seoul: Korea Institute for National Unification
Choe, Hyok (2001), *Tŭksu chakchŏn* [Operation special], Pyongyang: Chosŏn Ch'ulpanmul Kyoryu Hyŏphoe
Chin, Yong-hun (2008), *Yoramŭl chik'yŏ,* che 1 bu [Guard the cradle, vol. 1], Pyongyang: Kŭmsŏng ch'ŏngnyŏn ch'ulpansa
Chin, Yong-hun (2009), *Yoramŭl chik'yŏ,* che 2 bu [Guard the cradle, vol. 2], Pyongyang: Kŭmsŏng ch'ŏngnyŏn ch'ulpansa
David-West, Alzo (2006), 'Nationalist Allegory in North Korea: The Revolutionary Opera *Sea of Blood*', in: *North Korean Review,* 2 (2), pp. 75–87
David-West, Alzo (2007), 'The North Korean Positive Hero in *The People of the Fighting Village*', in: *North Korean Review,* 3 (2), pp. 101–118
David-West, Alzo (2009), 'The Literary Ideas of Kim Il Sung and Kim Jong Il: An Introduction to North Korean Meta-Authorial Perspectives', in: *Cultural Logic,* pp. 1–31. Online: http://clogic.eserver.org/2009/David-west.pdf (accessed 2 March 2012)
Epstein, Stephen (2002), 'On Reading North Korean Short Stories on the Cusp of the New Millennium', in: *Acta Koreana,* 5 (1), pp. 33–50
Frank, Rüdiger (ed.) (2011), *Exploring North Korean Arts*, Nuremberg: Verlag für moderne Kunst
Gabroussenko, Tatiana (2008), 'Calls for Self-Sacrifice in North Korean Creative Writing in the Late 1900s to 2000s', in: *Journal of Korean Studies,* 13 (1), pp. 29–56
Gabroussenko, Tatiana (2009), 'North Korean "Rural Fiction" from the Late 1990s to the Mid-2000s: Permanence and Change', in: *Korean Studies,* 33, pp. 69–100
Gabroussenko, Tatiana (2011), 'From Developmentalist to Conservationist Criticism: The New Narrative of South Korea in North Korean Propaganda', in: *Journal of Korean Studies,* 16 (1), pp. 27–62
Groensteen, Thierry, trans. Bart Beaty and Nick Nguyen (2007), *The System of Comics*, Jackson MS: University Press of Mississippi
Haggard, Stephen and Marcus Noland (2007), *Famine in North Korea: Markets, Aid, and Reform,* New York: Columbia University Press
Haggard, Stephen and Marcus Noland (2011), *Witness to Transformation: Refugee Insights into North Korea*, Washington DC: Peterson Institute for International Economics
Hart, Dennis (1999), 'Creating the National Other: Opposing Images of Nationalism in South and North Korean Education', *Korean Studies,* 23, pp. 68–93
Hassig, Ralph and Oh Kongdan (2009), *The Hidden People of North Korea: Everyday Life in the Hermit Kingdom,* Lanham MD: Rowman and Littlefield
Horstkotte, Silke and Nancy Pedri (2011), 'Focalization in Graphic Narrative', in: *Narrative,* 19 (3), pp. 330–57
Kim, Mun-ch'ang (1999), *Yŏlmang* [Aspiration], Pyongyang: Munhak Yesul Chonghap Ch'ulpansa
Kim, Sang-bok (1990), *Ssŏkko pyŏngdŭn sesang* [A sick and rotten world], Pyongyang: Kŭmsŏng Ch'ŏngnyŏn Ch'ulpansa

Kim, Sang-bok (2003) *Angaeryŏngŭi kijŏksori* [Whistle in the Misty Mountains], in: *Pangt'anpyŏk* [Bulletproof] Pyongyang: Kŭmsŏng Ch'ŏngnyon Ch'ulpansa, pp. 137–60
Kim, Suk-Young (2010), Illusive Utopia: Theater, Film, and Everyday Performance in North Korea, Ann Arbor MI: University of Michigan Press
Kim, Yong, with Kim Suk-Young (2009), *Long Road Home: Testimony of a North Korean Camp Survivor*, New York: Columbia University Press
Kim, Yong-hyon (2004), *Paekot' ŭi chŏngch'e* [The true identity of Pear Blossom], Pyongyang: Kumsŏng Ch'ŏngnyŏn Ch'ulpansa
Kim, Yŏng-sam and Chŏn Yŏng-il (2001), 'Isanghan p'yŏnji' [A strange letter], in: *Kŭdŭrŭn torawatta* [They came back], Pyongyang: Kŭmsŏng Ch'ŏngnyŏn Ch'ulpansa
Kukkonen, Karin (2011), 'Metalepsis in Comics and Graphic Novels', in: Karin Kukkonen, Sonja Klimek (eds), *Metalepsis in Popular Culture*. Berlin: Walter De Gruyter, pp. 213–31
Lee, Hyangjin (2000), 'Conflicting Working-Class Identities in North Korean Cinema', in: *Korea Journal*, 40 (3), pp. 237–54
Lee, Keum-Soon, Soo-Young Choi, Soo-Am Kim, Kyu-Chang Lee and Soon-Hee Lim (2009), *White Paper on Human Rights in North Korea: 2009*, Seoul: Korea Institute for National Unification
Lee, Suk (2005), *The DPRK Famine of 1994-2000: Existence and Impact*, Seoul: Korea Institute for National Unification
Lim, Soon-hee (2007), *Value Changes of the North Korean New Generation and Prospects*, Seoul: Korea Institute for National Unification
McCloud, Scott (1994), *Understanding Comics: The Invisible Art*, New York: Harper Perennial
McEachern, Patrick (2010), *Inside the Red Box: North Korea's Post-totalitarian Politics*, New York: Columbia University Press.
Myers, Brian (2010), *The Cleanest Race: How North Koreans See Themselves—And Why It Matters*, Brooklyn NY: Melville House
Pak, Hong-ju (2002), *Angaetŏp'in sŏm* [Misty island], Pyongyang: Kŭmsŏng Ch'ŏngnyŏn Ch'ulpansa
Park, Phillip H. (2009), 'Introduction: Economic Reform and Institutional Change in the DPRK', in: Phillip H. Park (ed.), *The Dynamics of Change in North Korea: An Institutionalist Perspective*, Seoul: IFES, Kyungnam University, pp. 3–41
Petersen, Martin (forthcoming), 'The Downfall of a Model Citizen? Family Background in North Korean Graphic Novels', in: *Korean Studies*, 35
Ri Sin-hyŏn (2002), *Kanggye chŏngsin* [Kanggye spirit], Pyongyang: Munhak Yesul Ch'ulpansa
Ryang, Sonia (2002), 'Technologies of the Self: Reading from North Korean Novels in the 1980s', in: *Acta Koreana*, 5 (1), pp. 21–32
Ryang, Sonia (2009), 'Biopolitics or the Logic of Sovereign Love—Love's Whereabouts in North Korea', in: *North Korea: Towards a Better Understanding*, Sonia Ryang (ed.), Lanham MD: Lexington Books
Smith, Hazel (2009), 'North Korea: Market Opportunity, Poverty and the Provinces', in: *New Political Economy*, 14 (2), pp. 23–56
Sŏ, Chŏng-nam (2002), *Sŏ, Chŏng-nam ŭi Pukhan Yŏnghwa T'amsa* [Sŏ Chŏng-nam exploring North Korean film], Seoul: Saenggakŭi Namu
Zur, Dafna (2010), 'Textual and Visual Representations of the Korean War in North and South Korean Children's Literature', in: Rüdiger Frank, James E. Hoare, Patrick Köllner and Susan Pares (eds), *Korea 2010: Politics, Economy and Society* Leiden: Brill, pp. 271–303

SPECIAL ECONOMIC ZONES, TRADE AND ECONOMIC REFORM: THE CASE OF RASON SPECIAL CITY

Bernhard J. Seliger[1]

ABSTRACT

The recent rebound of Rason (Rasŏn) after two decades of an uncertain existence has been largely unobserved. This is astonishing, since of the North Korean special economic zones, Gaeseong (Kaesŏng) Industrial Complex, Hwanggumphyong (Hwanggŭmp'yŏng) Whihwa, the defunct Geumgangsan (Kŭmgangsan) Tourism Zone, and Rason, the latter is the only one driven by economic forces, not political ones. This makes Rason an interesting object of study for the question of whether the SEZ policy has a greater meaning for North Korea's overall economic reform. This article looks at this issue by tracing back the origins of Rason, its economic meaning, in particular for China, and the 'trickle down' effect of investments. While Rason is far from being comparable to the market economy experiments China undertook in the early 1980s with an SEZ like Shenzhen, nevertheless the economic forces driving the development of Rason as well as its geographic position will make it more viable and less inherently unstable than the other North Korean SEZ and thereby might allow a longer-term experiment with new, institutionalised and state-sanctioned forms of market development.

Key words: Rason Special City, North Korea, foreign investment, Special Economic Zones, China, Greater Tumen Initiative

1 INTRODUCTION

The special economic zones (SEZ) of North Korea have been keenly observed in the past decades. The opening of Gaeseong Industrial Complex (GIC), the most successful and today the only surviving project among the many economic co-operation projects from the Sun-

---

[1] The author has been leading a co-operation project with the Rason Economic Administration since 2009 and has visited the area numerous times. The views are strictly those of the author, not of the Hanns-Seidel-Foundation.

shine policy era, has been heralded as a potential first step to a market economy. The development of Geumgangsan Tourism Zone and the aborted attempt at a special zone in Sinuiju were equally seen as steps towards the market (see Seliger 2003, 2006). However, the two inter-Korean projects in particular were essentially political in nature. Investment was only possible through a mixture of large-scale state investment in infrastructure and state guarantees against debts of private firms by the government of South Korea. And political trouble brought both projects to the brink of closure, and one, Geumgangsan, beyond. This does not mean that the zones have had no economic effect. The impact of the GIC on the North Korean economy is tremendous, and on the South Korean economy is at least sizable. Moreover, the fact that around 50,000 North Korean workers now work according to the rules of the market, in modern factories enjoying a more or less stable supply of raw materials, energy and other utilities, is of the utmost importance. It might be true that North Korea's ever-increasing dependence on earnings from the zone explains why this zone has been exempted from the general decline in inter-Korean relations since 2008. But equally, it might well be true that North Korea cannot afford to let 50,000 of its workers go idle, return to their hometowns (since by now, many of the workers no longer come from Gaeseong itself) and report on the labour conditions in the complex as being incomparably better than in most North Korean factories.

Rason, which acquired the status of a special city in January 2010, lying at the border of North Korea, China and Russia, at the delta of the Tumen river, an area euphemistically called a 'golden triangle', has received much less attention in scholarly circles and among policy-makers alike. This can be traced back to two views on Rason, which are not per se wrong, but which need an urgent updating. The first, that of Rason as a policy failure, dates back to its early existence up to the mid-2000s. Indeed, the original vision of Kim Il Sung to make Rajin-Sonbong (Sŏnbong) the 'Singapore of the East' seemed doomed from the outset, and Rason was not able to attract any significant amount of investment. It was good only for occasional exotic or bizarre notes, as when the casino run by a Hong Kong tycoon and immodestly called the 'Emperor hotel' (see Figure 1) opened and, later, had to close again due to Chinese pressure, after several Chinese officials gambled away money which did not belong to them in this casino. The second idea about Rason often encountered is that since

Figure 1   Emperor hotel

The hotel and casino is one of the Rason landmarks. Chinese pressure forced the notorious casino in the left annex to close, but a more discreet and smaller casino still operates on the upper floor.

its development is mainly driven by Chinese interests, it is an interesting annex (and, as some politicians in Korea secretly fear, a potential goal for annexation) to Chinese development plans for the northern Chinese provinces of Heilongjiang, Jilin and Liaoning, but because of its remote geographical position has only a negligible impact on the rest of North Korea.[2] While it is true that Rason's economic development is dependent on Chinese initiatives, this does not mean that its impact on North Korea should be underestimated. Indeed, when Chinese planning, which began at least ten years ago, led to practical steps, such as the restoration of the bridge over the Tumen river in 2010, this was accompanied by renewed North Korean interest in the zone. The visit by Kim Jong Il in December 2009 and the installation

---

[2] In its most extreme form, this argument is restated as a claim that North Korea has 'sold' Rason or that there are indeed in total 'four northeastern provinces of China', which, in respect of North Korea, include Rason. This view can be also found among North Koreans, though they are not candid enough to talk about it in such blunt terms.

of a former trade minister as head of the Rason economic administration were the turning points when North Korea began again to take Rason's economic potential seriously. At the same time, Chinese involvement and seeming dominance should not lead to the belief that Rason is merely a convenient port for China—the last years have seen many quarrels between China and North Korea regarding Rason, at central as well as local level, including the Chinese attempt to establish a foothold in Chongjin (Ch'ŏngjin) as an alternative to Rason.

There is thus a serious interest in Rason, and the remainder of this paper will focus on its importance for North Korea's economy and its potential to become more than a mere transport corridor, namely a veritable experimental zone for a market economy. The second section looks back to the rationale to introduce special economic zones and the first, dismal one-and-a-half decades of Rason's existence. Section 3 discusses Rason as a transport corridor for northeast China. Recent developments showing that Rason's special role and status also has a wider impact on its economy are discussed in section 4, followed by a conclusion that looks at the difference between Rason and the Chinese SEZ and draws some consequences for policies to improve Rason's status.

2 PROMISES, UNFULFILLED DREAMS AND FAILURE

2.1 *SEZ: concept and practice*

The introduction of SEZ in North Korea was not a policy innovation, but followed a pattern established long ago in other countries. Trade liberalisation from the late second half of the 20th century in many countries was the result of a change of trade policy from import substitution to export orientation. To establish a superior export base, foreign direct investment rather than protection was seen as critical. It provided both the capital and the technology and know-how necessary for export industries. To attract foreign capital, many countries designed specific regions as locations for export industries and offered advantages, especially regarding taxes and customs, for investors. None of these experiments has received so much attention as the introduction of SEZ in China from 1979. High growth rates in exports and Gross Domestic Product in China have been to a large extent the result of the performance of the SEZ. This contrasts with the economic difficulties that the countries of Central and Eastern Europe and the former Soviet Union experienced in economic transition. It explains why China became a role model for transition countries in East Asia.

However, China was by no means the first state experimenting with export zones. The first Export Processing Zone (EPZ) was established in Shannon in Ireland as early as 1958, followed by EPZ in Puerto Rico in 1962, in Mexico in 1964, and in Canada in 1965. From there the movement spread to Asia, with EPZ in Taiwan in 1966, in South Korea in 1971 and in the Philippines and Malaysia in 1972. The more countries abandoned protectionist trade policies, the greater the number of EPZ became. Today, there are more than 850 EPZ or Special Economic Zones worldwide. While in most East Asian states EPZ were successful, in other regions the results were mixed. This is especially true fort the EPZ in Latin America and in South Asia, e.g. in India. In both cases their attractiveness for foreign investors was relatively low. Industries that were mainly labour intensive settled in the EPZ, and transfer of technology and of management knowledge was rare. The principal reasons for failure were wrong economic policy decisions, for example high bureaucratic hurdles in the case of Indian EPZ by the provincial governments, which were sceptical about the concept of the EPZ. Other reasons included the establishment of EPZ, often motivated by regional development goals, in regions where the infrastructure for a successful EPZ was lacking; see the comparative studies by Ryan (1985), Shoesmith (1986), and Kundra (2000).

The concept of Special Economic Zones, sometimes used interchangeably with that of Export Processing Zones, is more comprehensive. It means especially a more comprehensive approach to economic reform, including reforms aiming to introduce the market mechanism in the domestic market, e.g. in housing, and the creation of preconditions for growth, such as a sufficiently modern infrastructure for foreign investors. The Chinese case of SEZ was widely recognised and Shenzhen near Hong Kong in particular became a symbol of successful transition.[3] Among the many remarkable features of the development of the Chinese SEZ is that they indeed achieved the transformation from places for the production of low-technology, labour-

---

[3] It should be noted that the role of SEZ is slowly changing in China, due to a proliferation of SEZ as well as to the economic transition in the rest of the country. For the development of Shenzhen see Seliger (2009).

intensive products to high-technology, human-capital intensive products. This transformation, which requires technology transfer, was among the goals of EPZ and SEZ originally aimed for but rarely achieved elsewhere in the world. But SEZ are confined not only to transition countries and emerging markets. OECD countries too have used the combination of regionally confined tax incentives and special regimes.

SEZ theory has accordingly focused on a number of institutional arrangements tailored to very different economic situations. A number of studies have examined SEZ in developing countries and as a policy instrument of such countries (Schweinberger 2003a, 2003b). They include many country studies, especially on China (Litwack and Qian 1998; Jones, Li and Owen 2003). Generally, the question of how SEZ can overcome the structural problems of peripheral regions is addressed, for example, in the framework of new economic geography (Weisman 1998). In OECD countries, SEZ were mostly seen as an opportunity for such peripheral regions, for example, in the discussion about an SEZ to alleviate the high unemployment in Eastern Germany after unification (see Ragnitz 2002). However, another strand of literature analysed the possibility of beggar-thy-neighbour policies and regional protectionism through SEZ (see Sonin 2003) and the consequences on federal systems, as in the United States (Mossberger 2000). The microeconomic consequences of locational policies have also been debated and models of optimal incentive structures have been developed (see Mauer and Ott 1999).

These studies have so far not been conclusive, major reasons for which have been the proliferation of SEZ and the diversity of their institutional design as well as the institutional embeddedness of SEZ in the economic policy of a region or country. While models of optimal incentives work only under the radically simplified conditions of neo-classical theory, the interaction of institutions in the real world makes ex ante judgements on SEZ extremely difficult. In North Korea, the lack of transparency in the national economy as well as in the direction of economic policy is an additional problem to be considered. In this respect, the development plan unveiled at the 1st Rason Trade Fair (see below), unrealistic as it is, is a first step in the right direction, namely the definition of policy goals. Transparency regarding economic data in North Korea is still missing, as much a consequence of secrecy as of the inability to assemble accurate figures.

2.2 Rason: early operations, early failures

Rajin and Sonbong are two small counties, with a total population of around 170,000 inhabitants (as of 2010), at the border of North Korea, China and Russia. In 1991, they were together declared the 'Rajin–Sonbong Free Trade Area', and on 31 January 1993, the Standing Committee of the Supreme People's Assembly adopted the Law of the Democratic People's Republic of Korea on the Rason Economic and Trade Zone.[4] It has since been revised several times, most recently on 3 December 2011.[5] The administrative centre of the zone is Rajin, which also has the largest port in the zone. During Soviet times, trade between the Soviet Union and North Korea via the area was important. In particular, there was a large-scale, now defunct petrochemical factory and, in Sonbong, a port through which lumber from the Russian Far East was imported (now also defunct). For oil imports, the port of Sonbong, which is somewhat small, was linked by a pipeline to the open sea, where larger oil tankers could unload their freight. The development of Rajin–Sonbong was also embedded in the larger context of hopes to develop the so-called Greater Tumen area, a project in which the UNDP co-operated with the Chinese and Russian governments as well as with North Korea (Peverelli 2007).

From the North Korean point of view, three reasons were named why Rason, as the merged city was renamed in 2001, became a free trade zone.[6] First, the port was ideally located for transit trade. Two islands in front of the harbour protect the area from typhoons, and in the winter the port remains largely ice free, a fact that makes it attractive also for Russia, whose ports on the Far Eastern coast freeze over. A road links the zone to Wonjeong (Wŏnjŏng) at the border with China, and the port was used in its heyday for transportation to Russia, Japan (until the first nuclear test in October 2006), and, during the Sunshine policy era, to Seokcho (Sŏkch'o) and Busan in South Korea as well. Second, Rason, with its beautiful and unspoiled beaches, was ideally located to attract tourists from China and Russia. Indeed, sev-

---

[4] The text of this law is available at the North Korean Economy Watch website. Online: http://www.nkeconwatch.com/nk-uploads/Law-on-Rason.pdf.
[5] The text of this revision may be downloaded from the North Korean Economy Watch website. Online: http://www.nkeconwatch.com/2012/03/19/kcna-publishes-dprk-sez-laws/.
[6] Conversation with director Kim Hwang Rim, Rason Economic Administration Investment Department, December 2009.

eral thousand Chinese tourists and a considerably smaller number of Russian tourists (mostly confined to one resort) visit the area every year for holidays, though this is far from the expected potential.[7] Lastly, liberal legislation (by North Korean standards) was designed to attract foreign investment. This, however, was largely unsuccessful, for reasons discussed below. The Rason experiment was closely watched by the outside world, and experts saw a successful opening of Rason as a way to overcome the immense economic difficulties of North Korea in the 1990s (Cotton 1996).

North Korea admits that the first phase of Rason, after some initial success, was characterised by stagnation. It attributes this stagnation firstly to a relatively inexperienced administration that had little knowledge about investment promotion and carried out barely any form of marketing.[8] The main contact point for foreign investors was and still is the representative office of Rason in Yanji, capital of the Yanbian Korean Autonomous prefecture of Jilin province of China. This is of importance, not only because Yanbian is directly adjacent to Rason, but also because many of the medium- and small-scale investors and traders with Rason come from the ethnic Korean minority in Yanbian. The second reason for Rason's misfortunes in its first decade of existence was the lack of reliable transportation (more on that in the next section) with regard to utilities like electricity and clean water. Foreign companies had to work with their own electricity generators, Korean firms mostly without. While there has been some domestic investment in hydropower (in Hi-chon, outside Rason, but with the intention of generating electricity for the zone), and some foreign investment in a wind power station (a small-scale American initiative) and an oil power station (by a Taiwanese firm), all of this was not enough to guarantee reliable electricity. Third, co-operation between North Korea, China and Russia in the 'golden triangle' lacked depth.

While these reasons are important, problems within the Korean government over the concept of a free trade zone should also be mentioned. Originally, North Korea may indeed have seemed to envisage

---

[7] Among the current projects of the Greater Tumen Inititative (GTI, the reborn former UNDP-led Tumen River Area Development Project) is one on multi-country tourism in the Tumen river area. Although North Korea left the GTI, it has recently begun to co-operate again informally with the organisation and might profit from these projects.

[8] There has been, however, certain support by UNIDO and the UNDP, among them an investor brochure published in 1998; UNIDO (1998).

something similar to China with its SEZ, but later the licence was revoked. The head of the zone was demoted for corruption, and the zone again came under the control of North Hamgyeong (Hamgyŏng) province. Probably more importantly, the lack of adequate transportation on the land side to China was a sign of a general unpreparedness on China's part to start co-operation in earnest. While today the difference between the modern and developed Chinese side of the border in Hunchun and the North Korean side at Wonjeong is obvious (or rather, was obvious, until China began to invest massively in infrastructure in Rason), until 2007 the road to the extremity of the 'golden triangle' on the Chinese side was equally a dirt road, as in North Korea, and the villages along the border were not developed at all and used the same non-mechanised methods of agricultural production as those in North Korea.

2.3 *Rason's economic activities*

Designation of the Rajin and Sonbong Economic and Trade Zone was not, however, completely unsuccessful, and after the first decade, a curious mix of companies could be found in the zone, originating, according to North Korean sources, from ten countries, though 90 percent of the investment came from China. One of the most important foreign firms was a Thai firm providing important telecommunication services. Communications are in general one of the weak points of the North Korean special zones. The Thai firm Loxley (recently reportedly crowded out or bought out by the new national provider of hand phone services, Orascom) offered telecommunication and hand phone services in the zone. The harbour was used by some Chinese firms and even by a Swiss company dealing in magnesite for its exports.

However, most important for the zone were the Korean state factories and the Chinese-invested factories in the area of fish and marine products. For example, Rajin Fish Exporting Company, founded in the early 1980s, is a main producer of squid, sea cucumbers, sea urchins, shellfish, and other marine products.[9] More than 400 workers are employed either in fishing or in processing. A small company-owned boat delivers the produce to Russia and, before the South Korean government's measures of 24 May 2010 banning trade with North Korea,

---

[9] Conversation with director Dong Gi-Myong, December 2009.

delivered also to South Korea. Every year, 80 tons of sea urchin eggs, 5,000 tons of squid and 10,000 tons of shellfish were processed, partly from its own fishing fleet, partly from other companies, since the company has relatively modern facilities, including a super-freezer. Among the export goals were China and South Korea (until May 2010), but even Australia and Europe, via processing factories in China.

Another company working in the field is the Rason Daehung Trading Company, which in December 2009 was visited by Kim Jong Il. This company was founded only in 1996, but with 500 workers is the largest Korean company in the region. It deals in octopus, squid, crabs and shells and each year produces 5,000 tons of crabs and 1,000 to 1,500 tons of squid, mostly for export to Japan (until 2006), China and Australia. A side business is a strong liquor based on the local pine mushroom, which is exported to Southeast Asia, as well as medicine, vinegar and soy sauce in a distillery employing 40 workers. .

All in all, 20 companies are active in the field of marine products, according to the Rason Economic Administration 14 of which work only for the local market, and five for international markets, with a higher degree of professionalism. The biggest problem is that these companies, including the larger ones producing for foreign markets, lack either the equipment for storing and, in particular, freezing, and/or the electricity to keep this equipment in constant use. From the beginning Chinese traders and investors were interested in North Korean maritime products, which have a good reputation on the market (including the South Korean and Japanese markets). Initially, they started to invest in some of the companies in Rason, but soon found that reliable production in the zone was not possible due to the lack of equipment and electricity. While it was possible to solve the first problem through investment, the second could only be solved through the difficult process of making companies self-sufficient in energy through generators. Therefore, traders soon began merely to export Korean products in large transporters. The value-added processing, which is considerable for marine products, thus occurred in China and no longer in Rason. This is a source of constant complaint by the Rason Economic Administration. Trade relations and investment therefore in this field, which is currently one of the main businesses between both countries, remain small.

Another group of companies are represented by the small-scale activities of American, often Korean-American, missionaries. These missionaries work on farms and a fruit farm, but also produce other items like glasses or sanitary towels.[10] These 'investments' are in reality mostly not for profit. One company works, for example, by paying the workers not in cash, but in 600 g of rice (the official daily ration under the Public Distribution System, which, however, is nowhere achieved in reality). Profits are reinvested or spent on social projects. The Rason authorities know that these activities are motivated by religious zeal; indeed, missionaries are allowed to bring in their own private bibles, but any form of proselytising is strictly forbidden. Among these activities the Rason International Catholic hospital should be mentioned (see Figure 2).

Figure 2   Rason Catholic hospital

The hospital was erected with aid from the Catholic church, in particular the Benedictine order, and is one of the largest aid projects in Rason. Outside, the English, but not the Korean title points to the origins of the hospital, but inside, it contains the usual pictures and slogans of the leadership cult of North Korea.

---

[10] A very important social product in Rason, where women are usually confined to the use of dry grass. This practice often leads to painful infections and other diseases.

It was erected with money collected principally by the Benedictine order, again, mainly by German and South Korean Benedictines. Before the division of Korea, the order had a monastery in Wonsan (today Wonsan Agricultural College), and was interested in undertaking humanitarian relief work in North Korea. Currently, the hospital is a major source of medical treatment for the population of Rason, and a new outpatient clinic is being built.[11] Korean officials term this hospital an investment, though it is, rather, an aid project. A clear understanding of the difference between the two concepts does not seem to exist among officials in Rason, making it difficult in particular for investors to raise any understanding of questions of profit generation and profit repatriation.

Finally, there is an assorted number of other investments in Rason, among these a small cigarette factory (Shinheung Cigarettes), which produces for the Chinese market and comes closest to the ideal of direct foreign investment. The most conspicuous investment is the aforementioned Emperor hotel and casino. The latter operated from 2000 until its closure in 2005 through Chinese pressure.[12] By 2010, however, a smaller casino had reopened on the upper floor of the hotel and seems to be tolerated by both Koreans and Chinese. While all this investment and the modest inflow of foreign people (among them those of non-Chinese origin) certainly led to change in the region, it was not enough for any form of viable economic upswing. The decision in 2001 to give up the special zone, therefore, did not much trouble the North Korean decision-makers. However, the rapid economic development of the Chinese border area, the Chang-Ji-Tu (Changchun, Jilin and Tumen) region, again changed the perspectives for Rason's development and led to renewed Korean interest in the zone. This time, Rason as a transport corridor was at the core of economic interest, as the next section shows.

---

[11] The main entrance to the hospital features in large Latin letters the name 'Rason International Catholic Hospital', but the Korean title is simply Rason People's hospital, and there are no religious symbols in the building, only the usual pictures of the leaders.

[12] According to information from the Rason Economic Administration, up to 600 people, among them around 300 Chinese, once worked in the hotel, which belonged to the Emperor group of Albert Yeung.

3 THE REBIRTH OF RASON AS A TRANSPORT CORRIDOR

From the moment the area was designated the Rajin and Sonbong Economic and Trade Zone, there had be the calculation that the port of Rajin might be attractive for Chinese companies exporting to Japan, South Korea or across the Pacific. However, as described above, the Chinese side of the border was as undeveloped as the Korean side. This situation, however, changed rapidly. The Chinese northeast had been one of the most industrialised areas of China for decades, but underwent a considerable decline during the 1980s and 1990s, when development in the coastal areas began. Later, however, development also extended to the northeastern region, partly through private investment, partly through foreign investment and partly through large-scale, state-sponsored development projects aimed at reducing the ever-growing divergence between the east coast of China and the peripheral regions. In the Yanbian Korean Autonomous prefecture with its up to two million ethnic Koreans, from the early 1990s South Korean investment also played an important role, with the growth of large exporting companies, for example, the car manufacturers of the Changchun region, but also of other exports and imports like coal and other raw materials.

From at least the mid-2000s, China began systematically to explore the possibilities of actively using Rason as an extension to the Chang-Ji-Tu region. Rason might not have been the first (or only) Chinese choice. A *China Daily* report of 28 April 2003 mentioned that the Russian Ministry of Communications was opposed to a proposed deal to lease for 49 years either the port of Zarubino or Posyet, both located directly on the Russian-Chinese border. At that time, the inflow of Chinese into the Russian Far East, which concurrently was experiencing a dramatic drop in the former Russian population, led to a fear that China could argue in favour of (re-)gaining those territories, which had been only relatively recent Russian acquisitions.

In 2005, for the first time the news made the rounds that China had acquired a 50-year lease of Rajin port. This information, however, proved to be premature, as well as did similar reports in later years. Negotiations were going on, but with unclear direction and sometimes with regional Chinese authorities (from Jilin province), sometimes at the highest level of state, e.g. during Kim Jong Il's visits to China. At one point, even, reports leaked out that China had leased the port of

Chongjin instead of Rason, in a move to overcome local Korean resistance.

Once China was determined to use a Korean port and economic zone, they systematically tried to prepare for the task. First, numerous delegations in the field of economy and transport visited the port and plans for development were drawn up, even in rather unrelated areas, such as agriculture. Yanbian University with its Institute for Northeast Asia and other related faculties played an important role in planning. Then, the bridge over the Tumen river, which was still the one put up by the Chinese in the early 1930s, was completely renovated (see Figure 3).

Figure 3 Reconstruction of Tumen river bridge

Reconstruction of the old bridge, dating from Japanese colonial times, began in 2010 with Chinese materials and heavy equipment.

All the material and machines for the construction came from the Chinese side, while North Korean labour participated in building the southern (North Korean) part of the bridge. After rebuilding the Tumen river bridge in 2010 and providing materials for improving the dirt road to Rajin (around 50 km from the border), in 2011 China started in earnest to reconstruct the road. This had been a constant danger and greatly inhibited trade: on the 48 km from the border village Wonjeong to Rajin the tracks were made of sand and dirt. In the autumn and winter, conditions were particularly dangerous, and almost every week there were severe accidents.

On the ground, the possible disagreement between China and North Korea regarding economic projects and the alleged postponement of the road construction opening ceremony mentioned in the press in April 2011 had no visible effect. In at least six camps more than 60 large construction machines (bulldozers, excavators, large concrete mixers, etc.) were already working on road construction. The workers for these machines were all Chinese, and some might have come from the military, as a North Korean guide mentioned. In addition, at one point North Korean soldiers were working on the road-building. Chinese workers lived in tents in the camps already mentioned. One camp seemed to be Russian (with Russian signposts). All signs at the construction site were bilingual, in Korean and Chinese. Both the building of the bridge in 2010 and the construction of the road in 2011 led to severe inconvenience in the form of restricted border-crossing times, partial closure and for some while a total closure of the road. The fact, however, that such drastic measures were possible shows how relatively unimportant trade through Rason still is for China.

When investment for the road began, the city of Rason also began to change somewhat. Neon lighting was added to 'beautify' the city, including a light-show at one roundabout. This indicated some improvement in electricity supplies, while access to water was still problematic in many restaurants and public places (including the Rason City administration building). By 2012, the road between Hunchun and Rajin was finished, allowing large trucks to pass much faster and more reliably than before along the road and paving thus the way to the use of the port.

In mid-2012, construction (or rather, extension) of the port was underway (see Figure 4). The port has originally been built in 1937 with three piers.[13] Plans exist for an extension to up to 12 piers. The harbour depth is 9.5 m and capacity is currently up to three million tons. In 2009, however, according to the port administration, turnover was only 200,000 tons. Existing cranes can carry loads of up to 30 tons. In 2008, Russia leased pier no. 3 of the port for 50 years with the aim of

---

[13] Communication from Kim Chun Il, director of the harbour, in May 2010.

building a new container terminal. However, no Russian investment has yet materialised. Russia first completed the railway connection to Rason and gave it a first trial run, though not yet any regular runs, in early 2012. China, on the other hand, though much more involved in trade through Rason than Russia, leased a pier (pier no. 1) only in 2011, for maybe 30 years according to different reports. Previously it had only leased a coal terminal at the pier. As of mid-2012, it was unclear when the terminal would be in full use, but the systematic way of approaching the problem—linking Yanji to Hunchun, rebuilding the bridge, reconstructing the road from Wonjeong on the North Korean border to Rajin, leasing the port and finally rebuilding it—is a sure indicator that China sooner rather than later will realise the use of the port as planned.[14]

Figure 4 Rajin port

The port, with its piers 1 and 3 leased to the Chinese and Russians respectively, is the greatest hope for the economic development of the special economic zone.

---

[14] For an extensive review of the transport linkages and needs in the area, see Jo and Ducruet (2007).

4 Does Chinese Investment Lead to Sustained Reform? Evidence from Recent Years

4.1 *The service structure for a special economic and transport zone*

Using Rason as a transport corridor means at first glance a rather low level of interaction of Chinese businesses within Rason special city. The transport corridor consists of the bridge, a road of only 48 km from Wonjeong to Rajin, meaning that journeys can easily be done in a day, with no need for accommodation in many cases, and the port itself, consisting mainly of a warehouse, future possible additional storage facilities, and cranes for loading and unloading. However, around this core business the slow build-up of a more comprehensive service structure can be expected. While technically, no overnight stay might be necessary, delays in loading and unloading, waiting times to avoid empty fares and other possible necessities for delay will lead to a surge in accommodation, as well as other services, including restaurants. Much of this service infrastructure is basically there, e.g. hotels, but for most of the year is idle. This might soon change, when Chinese transportation business sets up in earnest. Furthermore, gas stations, repair workshops and rest areas along the road and other services will develop. Currently, Chinese citizens can already enter the Rason zone in their own cars, and there is a taxi service for other visitors, though not one freely available for non-Chinese foreigners without North Korean guides. Local transportation will probably take an upswing, once more permanent or semi-permanent residents are in the city.

For Chinese officials and business people staying permanently or semi-permanently to oversee the import and export business, suitable accommodation is also necessary. The Wonjeong customs facilities, consisting presently of a far too small building for entry and exit, will have to be redesigned. Transport services also require improved communications, an issue on which Rason has already made considerable advances, although at the border between China and North Korea people still have to yield their cell-phones (on the Chinese side). There will, however, be increased pressure for business people to be allowed to use their cell-phones also in the zone, once import and export businesses are large enough. Additionally, a more sophisticated financial infrastructure might emerge. Most business is already being done in Chinese currency, but there might be demand for other services, including ATMs for Chinese currency. Not all of this pressure will indeed soon be successful, but if the plans to use Rason as a hub for Chinese investment are realised, then these service facilities also have to be in place. If not, despite the inconvenience of a much longer route, other ports will be more advantageous for export and import business by Chinese companies.

4.2 The administrative response: Rason Economic Administration as a 'one-stop shop'

Investment in North Korea is largely a process of political negotiation with few rules. Where rules exist, like the Rason special city law, they are easy to write but not easy to implement and even more difficult to uphold in times of disagreement. Nonetheless, there have been certain improvements with regards to Rason's legal situation. The most important change is that the responsibility for Rason is now, at least formally, completely independent from other organisations, including the central government in Pyongyang. Clearly, to some extent this would be fictitious should the central government want to intervene. But for average investment negotiations, which are small scale and not necessarily contentious, it is a great advantage that the zone can negotiate without a go-ahead from the central authorities. According to officials of the Economic Administration, responsibility extends to the zone being able even to set its own exchange rate with foreign currencies, independently from the rest of the country. Formerly, investment in existing plants was dependent on negotiations with the various economic organisations or committees to which those plants belonged. Now the Economic Administration claims that all Korean companies in the zone are administered by the zone itself. The zone actively seeks out investors, in particular in the field of infrastructure and energy, and there have been announcements that an airport is planned, although such announcements might not point to actual investment projects, but rather to vague intentions. Foreigners can lease land for from US$5 to US$40 per square metre according to contract and actual location. This is a one-time fee, to which are added annual user costs of around US$0.7 per square metre. Taxes are stated by the administration to be around 10 to 14 percent, less than the country average (though this average was not known to the official giving the information). The lower tax rates apply to companies in the fields of infrastructure and high-tech. The monthly average salary of workers was around US$110, which is higher than in Gaeseong. However, as mentioned above, actual small-scale investment projects often use completely different rates to these official rates mentioned, e.g. they may pay their workers in rice.

Whether the institutional environment for investments from abroad will really improve sufficiently cannot be answered at the moment. Certainly, international investors will not be interested in words of law or the assurances of government officials alone, but will look at the dismal track record of North Korea's handling of South Korean investment and other, less prominently discussed cases of crowding out of foreign investors after the initial investment has been made. Moreover, as Snyder (2010: 6) maintains, Chinese central government involvement might help to develop the zone, but might also help to maintain the uncertain status quo for investors instead of pressing for more reform and openness.

4.3 *Rason trade fair*

Among the activities indirectly related to the development of Rason special city is the trade fair. Until 2010, North Korea only knew the Pyongyang spring and autumn trade fair, and even they are of relatively recent origin. The 1st Rason International Trade Exhibition was held in a former art exhibition hall in Sonbong, part of the Rason Special Economic Zone from 22 to 25 August 2011. The exhibition was targeted at attracting foreign investors to the region and at creating networks with foreign and local companies. The products of 108 companies were exhibited in twelve rooms. Furthermore, there was a designated meeting room, a conference room for video presentations, and outdoor food stands. Next to the 22 exhibitors from the DPRK, there were 71 Chinese exhibitors and 15 from Russia, China, Australia, Italy, the United States and Taiwan (for list of participants see Appendix). The only European company besides the Russian companies was OTIM of Italy, a transportation company with a foothold in Pyongyang and regular appearances at the Pyongyang trade fairs. Products included electronics, pharmaceuticals, light and car industries and clothing, as well as foodstuffs, fishery products, books and household appliances. Some products, such as clothing and foodstuffs, were sold on the spot. On 24 August, the third day of the exhibition, about one-third of the booths were already empty, exhibitors choosing to rent a booth for the first two days only. A closing ceremony was held on 25 August at 11 am with congratulatory remarks for the organisers and diplomas for some exhibitors.[15]

Among the highlights of the fair was the 'forum on investment in the Rason Economic and Trade Zone'. About 150–170 visitors attended, overwhelmingly from China. Two video presentations with live commentary in Chinese were given, one about the development of the Rason Economic and Trade Zone, the other about future developments. Afterwards, there were breakout sessions, with smaller groups and discussions. The fact that such a trade forum took place is significant in itself. The presentation and slide show at the forum had had to be agreed upon with the Rason zone, and also with the central authorities in Pyongyang. It called for the development of a master plan for Rason. Though this plan looks extremely optimistic and, one might say, unrealistic about Rason's rosy future, its appearance was something new and important, since it is intended to create a vision of Rason based on external openness and trade. Still, the Rason trade fair is small and has a long way to go. The 15th Pyongyang Spring International Trade Fair held from 14 to 17 May 2012 in Pyongyang brought together 270 companies, among them representatives from Mongolia, Malaysia, Germany, the Netherlands, Taiwan, Italy, Austria, Bulgaria, Great Britain, Switzerland, Finland, Poland and Australia, plus China and North Korea (Kim 2012: 4). The Rason fair, with a much smaller number of exhibitors and visitors, had considerable difficulties in the arrangement of local transport and translation services and the organisation of events. However, Rason is working on this and the second trade fair, to be held in August 2012, promises some advances at least.

4.4 *Rason agricultural research centre*

Besides these larger developments, there are indications that there is indeed a 'trickle down' effect of foreign involvement and investment. For instance, in 2010 near Sonbong a new agricultural research centre was opened (or renovated) with obviously massive Chinese help, to

---

[15] Information on the fair comes from a visit and talks with exhibitors. The foreign exhibitors we talked to (Jiangsu Jinghai Transformer Co. and Jiangsu Xuemei Refrigerator, The Green Apple, New Lepo) were all either based in Rason already or based in China. According to them, the exhibition was well organised and visitor response was positive.

carry out research on around 20 ha of fields, including rice, maize (corn) and soy bean (see Figure 5). In hothouses erected by Jilin Provincial Agricultural Office (from China), two different kinds of mushrooms are being bred for export and domestic consumption. Equipment at the research centre includes two new tractors and other machines clearly brought in from China. The centre's main co-operation partner is the agricultural faculty of Yanbian University. This university has for many years been doing research on ways to integrate the small economy of Rason with the large and dynamically developing economy of northeast China. Another co-operation project has been started between Yanbian University and Rason Maritime College. In this way, various sectors—agriculture, marine products and fishing, and others such as processing—are slowly being affected. Moreover, university co-operation promises better education in Rason in the future, in particular sure access to information about the outside world, starting with technological issues, but also covering other fields. This might in the medium and long run have a very important impact on the way Chinese reforms are seen and, eventually, emulated.

Figure 5   Agricultural research centre, Sonbong

An investment showing that Jilin province's interest transcends the main goal of making Rason a transport hub for Chinese exports and imports.

5 CONCLUSION

Rason special city has narrowly escaped the fate of being completely written off after its first ten years of existence and, in recent years, has made a spectacular, though not much observed comeback. Although designed chiefly as a Chinese transport corridor, in the medium and long term this corridor should be capable of developing more comprehensive services for a modernisation of the economy and of enhancing the understanding of the importance of carrying out Chinese-inspired reforms. Nevertheless, to achieve this, Rason still has to go a long way. Among the urgent necessities for reform are the following four issues:

1. Improved communications:

While certain basic fixed-line telephone and cell-phone services are available, Rason has to be linked up completely through wireless and fixed-line connections. This requirement includes an exemption from the ban on the use of foreign-made cell-phones; at least foreigners should be able to use their own cell-phones. It should also mean the exemption of more officials from the ban on communicating with foreigners. Currently, all email and telephone contact goes through the representative's office in Yanji, but more direct communication must be made possible to ensure smoother business. Officials must be able to answer emails directly and speedily from potential or actual investors.

2. Training of officials:

Officials must not only be able to communicate, they also need a lot of additional training, starting with basic issues such as the differences between humanitarian aid, development projects and businesses, and leading to the education of specialised officials in sectoral and functional areas.

3. Regional integration:

Rason is an unusual project, since it is not politically motivated, but driven by Chinese (and, to a smaller extent, Russian) economic interests. This aspect, however, requires that it has not only strong bilateral ties with the adjacent regional entities, but also closer regional integration. Membership in the Greater Tumen Initiative, which was suspended in May 2009 after the second nuclear test and the subsequent censure by the UN Security Council, must urgently be renewed, to include co-operation in all transnational projects such as transport, environment, trade facilitation and tourism, since all of these are closely related to the fate of Rason.

4. Development of financial services:

This is a tricky issue, since it involves not only Korean activities, but also international negotiations. It is a fact that without a functioning financial system it will be difficult to expect Rason to grow smoothly. However, this requires among other moves the exemption of Rason from financial regulations imposed by the UN Security Council. Together with international agencies, Rason (and, behind it, Pyongyang) could try to negotiate a special financial regime for Rason catering for the needs of investors, which at the same time could not be abused for illicit transactions.

The next few years will be crucial for Rason's development as a new transport corridor and moreover as an area where a more comprehensive opening and reform of the country could start. As Kim and Abrahamian (2011) recently commented, the joint interest of China, North Korea and Russia 'sets the scene for a North Korean special economic zone with higher chances of success than perhaps ever before'. It is a development well worth watching and a vision well worth supporting.

References

China Daily (2003), 'Russian Media Play up the Tune of China's Port-renting', in: *China Daily* Online. Online: http://english.peopledaily.com.cn/200304/28/eng 20030428_115951.shtml (accessed 20 May 2012)

Cotton, James (1996), 'The Rajin-Sonbong Free Trade Experiment: North Korea in Pursuit of New International Linkages', Working Paper 9/1996, Department of International Relations, Australian National University, Canberra: Australian National University

Jo, Jin Cheol and César Ducruet (2007), 'Rajin-Seonbong, New Gateway of Northeast Asia', in: *Annals of Regional Sciences*, 41, pp. 927–50

Jones, Derek C., Cheng Li and Ann L. Owen (2003), 'Growth and Regional Inequality in China during the Reform Era', in: *China Economic Review*, 14 (2), pp. 186–200

Kim, Rye Yong (2012), 'Trade Fair Invigorates Business Dealings', in: *Pyongyang Times*, 19 May 2012, p. 4

Kim, John and Andray Abrahamian (2011), 'Why World Should Watch Rason', in: *The Diplomat*, 22 December 2011. Online: http://thediplomat.com/new-leaders-forum/2011/12/22/why-world-should-watch-rason (accessed 10 March 2012)

Kundra, Ashok (2000), *The Performances of India's Export Zones: A Comparison with the Chinese Approach*, New Delhi: Sage

Litwack, John M. and Yingyi Qian (1998), 'Balanced or Unbalanced Development: Special Economic Zones as Catalysts for Transition', in: *Journal of Comparative Economics*, 26 (1), pp. 117–41

Mauer, David C. and Steven H. Ott (1999), 'On the Optimal Structure of Government Subsidies for Enterprise Zones and Other Locational Development Programs', in: *Journal of Urban Economics*, 45 (3), pp. 421–50

Mossberger, Karen (2000), *The Politics of Ideas and the Spread of Enterprise Zones*, Washington DC: Georgetown University Press

Peverelli, Peter J. (2009), 'The Tumen River Project: Sensemaking in Multiple Contexts', in: *International Journal of Chinese Culture and Management*, 2 (4), pp. 323–36

Ragnitz, Joachim (2002), *Arbeitsangebot, Arbeitsnachfrage und ein Lösungvorschlag für das ostdeutsche Arbeitsmarktproblem*, Discussion Paper no. 168, Halle Institute of Economic Research, Halle: Institute of Economic Research

Ryan, Peter F. (1985), 'Successes and Failures in Industrial Export Processing Zone Development', in: *The Journal of the Flagstaff Institute*, 9 (1), pp. 60–67

Schweinberger, Albert G. (2003a), 'Special Economic Zones and Quotas on Imported Intermediate Goods: A Policy Proposal', in: *Oxford Economic Papers*, 55 (4), pp. 697–715

Schweinberger, Albert G. (2003b), 'Special Economic Zones in Developing and/or Transition Economies: A Policy Proposal', in: *Review of International Economics*, 11 (4), pp. 619–29

Seliger, Bernhard (2009), 'Shenzhen Special Economic Zone', in: Linsun Cheng (ed.), *The Berkshire Encyclopedia of China*, Gt Barrington MA: Berkshire Publishing, pp. 1962–64

Seliger, Bernhard (2006), 'Towards a North Korea Boom? Special Economic Zones in North Korea and their Effects on the North and South Korean Economies', in: Bernhard Seliger (with Oh Yean-Cheon, Lee Dalgon, Park Sung-Jo), *The Unification Research and Strategy in Korea and Germany: Affinity and Specificity*,

Seoul: Graduate School of Public Administration, Seoul National University, pp. 93–122

Seliger, Bernhard (2003), 'Die nordkoreanischen Sonderwirtschaftszonen – eine Wiederholung des chinesischen Erfolgsmodells?', in: Patrick Köllner (ed.), *Korea 2003 – Politik, Wirtschaft, Gesellschaft*, Hamburg: Institut für Asienkunde, pp. 262–85

Shoesmith, Dennis (ed.) (1986), *Export Processing Zones in Five Countries: The Economic and Human Consequences*, Hong Kong: Asia Partnership for Human Development

Snyder, Scott (2010), 'Rajin-Sonbong: A Strategic Choice for China in its Relations with Pyongyang', in: *China Brief*, 10 (issue 7), pp. 4–6

Sonin, Konstantin (2003), 'Provincial Protectionism', Working Paper no. 557, William Davidson Institute, Ann Arbor MI: William Davidson Institute

UNIDO (1998), *DPR Korea's Rajin and Sonbong Economic and Trade Zone, Investment and Business Guide*, Beijing: UNIDO/UNDP

Weisman, Jason (1998), 'An Economic Geography Model to Evaluate the Benefits of Special Economic Zones in Peripheral Regions', in: *Regional Science Review*, 17, pp. 57–70

Appendix

Companies participating in the 1st Rason Trade Fair

Australia Technical Development Company

Baishan City Energy & Carborundum Co., Ltd.
Baishang City Fengda Metal Products Factory
Baishan City Tianhe Trade Co., Ltd.
Baishan City Xinlei Trade Co., Ltd.

Changbai Korean Nationality Autonomous County Jinkun Border Economic & Trade Co., Ltd.
Changchun Aofeng Business Trade Co. Ltd.
Changchun Eurasia Group Co. Ltd.
China Yanbian Kangde Network Technology Co., Ltd.

Faw Siping Special Automobile Co., Ltd.
Feyinman Technology Co., Ltd.
Fusong Xing Shenghe Trade Co., Ltd.

Gongzhuling City Jinyou Special Vehicle Assembling Co., Ltd.

Helong National Mat Factory
Hunchun City Jian Industrial Co., Ltd.
Hunchun City Sanyuan Steel Co., Ltd.
Hunchun City Zhongcheng Economic & Trade Co., Ltd.
Hunchun Datong Economic & Trade Co., Ltd.
Hunchun Hongyuan Industry & Trade Co., Ltd.
Hunchun Yunda Knitting & Clothing Co., Ltd.

Jian City Fuxing Foreign Trading Co., Ltd.
Jian City Hongdi Import & Export Trading Co., Ltd.
Jian City Huangjia International Trading Co., Ltd.
Jian City Lushanzhou Native Products Processing Export Co., Ltd.
Jian City Unites & Strong Trade Co., Ltd
Jian City Yahua Import & Export Trading Co., Ltd.
Jian City Zhenzhong Trade Co., Ltd.
Jiaohe City Fengyuan Grains & Oils Co., Ltd.
Jiaohe City Songhuahu Wine Industry Co., Ltd.
Jilin City Chutian Business Trade Co., Ltd.
Jilin City Haiyang Electric Appliance Co., Ltd.
Jilin City Luiang Import & Export Co., Ltd.

Jilin City Luwang Pharmaceutical Co., Ltd.
Jilin City Ruitao Construction Equipment Co., Ltd.
Jilin City Shiji Pesticide Co., Ltd.
Jilin Daojun Pharmaceutical Co., Ltd.
Jilin Dongrui Cereals, Oils & Food Stuffs Co. Ltd.
Jilin Province & the Installation of Steel Structure Assembling Co., Ltd.
Jilin Province Changbai Economic Development Zone Border Trade Company
Jilin Province Lianduan City Textile Co., Ltd.
Jilin Province Liugu Agriculture Development Co., Ltd.
Jilin Province Northerneast Asia Pharmaceutical Co., Ltd.
Jilin Province Wanshida Industrial Co., Ltd.
Jilin Tianrong Import & Export Co., Ltd.
Jilin Tobacco Industrial Co., Ltd.
Jilin Yuntianhua Agriculture Development Co., Ltd.
Jingsu Jinghai Transformer Co., Ltd.
Jingsu Xuemei Refrigeration Equipment Co., Ltd.
Jinung Trading Corporation

Kanghung Technical Trading Company
Korea Daedonggang Battery Company
Korea General 8.20 Trading Corporation
Korea Jangsu Trading Corporation
Korea Publications Import & Export Corp.
Krahun Company (China)
KSM Dongfang (Changchun) Castings Co., Ltd.

Lianduan Chenyu Socks Co., Ltd.
Lianduan Tianma Songhe Socks Group Co., Ltd.
Lien Chiny Enterprise Co., Ltd.
Longjing Fengcheng Commerce Co., Ltd.

Olangdo Co., Ltd.
Otim Spa (Italy)

Pyongchon Koryo Medicines Factory
Pyongyang Trading Corporation

Rason Baeksok Joint Venture Company
Rason Daehung Trading Co.
Rason Dongmyungsan Hotel

Rason Drink Factory
Rason Food Processing Company
Rason Hyesong Trading Corp.
Rason Kontrans J.V. Co., Ltd.
Rason Mokryon Furniture Company
Rason Moran Trading Corp.
Rason Ogasan Tech Trading Company
Rason Orient Industry Company
Rason Paekho Trading Company
Rason Shoes Factory
Rason Shuchaebong Fishery Corporation
Royal Team Corporation
Russia Alpha-Omega Co., Ltd.
Russia Gamma Center
Russia Prize Company
Ryonha Machinery Corporation

Shandong Province Qingdao Yuchen Artifact Co., Ltd.
Shenyang International Trade Promotion Committee
Siping Fenlin Dedicated Auto Co., Ltd.
Sonbong Clothing Factory
Songyuan City Jisheng Zhongliang Export & Import Co., Ltd.

Taiwan City Social Welfare Clothing Factory
Tonghua City Yijia Food Co., Ltd.
Tuman Gangxin Industrial Trade Co., Ltd.
Tumen City Tianren Medicine Co., Ltd.
Tumen Fenzheng Commerce Trade Co., Ltd.
Tumen Wangda Food Products Co., Ltd.

Wangqing Longsheng Beer Co., Ltd.
White Stone Corporation Co., Inc. USA

Yanbian Baichuan Aquatic Product Processing Co., Ltd.
Yanbian Baolixiang Beekeeping Co., Ltd.
Yanbian Dongzheng Agricultural Products Co., Ltd.
Yanbian Enrich Auto Sales & Service Co., Ltd.
Yanbian Huihwa Xingye Automobile Sales Co., Ltd.
Yanbian Mingren Medicine Co., Ltd.
Yanbian Shengxin Medicine Co., Ltd.
Yanbian Wangqing Dried Vegetables Processing Co., Ltd.
Yanbian Wantong International Freight Forwarder Co., Ltd.

Yanbian Wearcard Hongxin Technology Products Co., Ltd.
Yanbian Weifeng International Economic & Trade Co., Ltd.
Yanbian Wenyuan Vehicle Trading Co., Ltd.
Yanbian Xianchun International Co., Ltd.

Outdoor exhibition:

China Faw Group Import & Export Corporation
Jilin Province Changfeng Industry Trade Co., Ltd.
Rason Jongang Processing Company
Rason Samdaesong Joint Venture Co., Ltd.
Yanbian Jiulong International Industrial Co., Ltd.

Source: Author's information according to the name board at the trade fair.

THE NORTH KOREAN PHILOSOPHY OF FOREIGNERS[1]

Tatiana Gabroussenko

Abstract

In the popular view, the North Korean attitude to foreigners is often reduced to an isolationist policy and the ideologically driven alienation of the North Korean people from the world community; but a closer examination of the cultural practices of the DPRK provides evidence that isolationism alone does not exhaust the North Korean foreign perspective. The official ideology of the DPRK approaches the issue of communication between North Koreans and people of different blood and cultures in more intricate and elaborate ways. The officially promoted North Korean philosophy of foreigners emerges as a complex phenomenon which combines wariness and distrust of foreigners with internationalism and the concept of 'foreign friends'. Basing itself on an investigation of the currently available literary, visual and oral primary sources, this article aims to reconstruct a fuller version of the North Korean discourse of foreigners including its least studied part, internationalism.

Key words: North Korean world vision, literature, culture, communism in Korea, communist propaganda

1 Introduction

As is indicated by the popular name of the 'hermit kingdom' for the Democratic People's Republic of Korea (DPRK—North Korea), an ideologically driven estrangement of North Korean people from the world community is commonly recognised as a defining feature of North Korean society. Western Koreanists, whose perspectives of the DPRK vary from harsh criticism to empathy, tend to describe the North Korean attitude to the foreign world in a variety of terms, such as 'xenophobic nationalism' (Suh 1988: 313), 'racism' (Myers 2010)

---

[1] Research for this article was supported by a grant from the Academy of Korean Studies.

or 'national solipsism' (Cumings 2005: 407). Yet academics appear to concur that North Korean people share far-reached anti-foreign biases brought about by the detrimental influence of North Korean ideology.

This opinion, however, contradicts the views of foreigners with extensive firsthand experience of life in the DPRK or long-term contact with North Koreans. Visitors from overseas who have worked or studied in the DPRK for a substantial period of time all describe North Koreans as people who have a strong sense of national dignity, but who are nevertheless friendly and hospitable to guests of their country and content to communicate with them when such a chance arises. A former student from a university in Moscow who had regularly been in touch with groups of exchange students from both the Republic of Korea (ROK—South Korea) and the DPRK, described North Korean students as being apparently more friendly, relaxed and open to contacts with the locals than students from South Korea. A number of North Korean refugees whom the author interviewed in 2011 all describe their fellow compatriots in the DPRK as limited in their knowledge about foreign cultures and customs, yet inquisitive about them.

This discrepancy in understanding of the North Korean attitude to foreigners would not surprise if one had a close look at the multilayered pattern of the overseas world which emerges in the array of North Korean cultural practices and texts regarding foreigners. Regrettably, so far no scholarly attempt has been made to investigate systematically these original sources with the purpose of reconstructing a fuller version of a North Korean philosophy of foreigners. The present article aims to approach this challenging task, tracing historical origins and present forms of patterns, messages and imagery in a variety of North Korean narratives of the non-Korean world.

The research is based on the following sources: firstly a range of representative samples of North Korean official propaganda regarding foreigners. It includes media materials, documentary, feature films and literary texts which have been published in state-run journals of the DPRK, such as *Chosŏn munhak*, *Ch'ŏngnyŏn munhak* and *Adong munhak*.[2] The second source is interviews with people who have had extensive first-hand experience of life in the DPRK. They have been surveyed on the subject of how the prescribed models of the DPRK's attitude to the overseas world correspond to the actual attitude of North Koreans to foreigners. Among the respondents are North Ko-

---

[2] All translations into English are the author's own.

rean defectors, foreign students who have studied at Kim Il Sung University, a former Pyongyang-based news reporter, employees of the Soviet/Russian embassy in Pyongyang, and various other persons.

The author recognises that while the suggested model of a North Korean philosophy of foreigners fills particular gaps in our knowledge of the North Korean world vision, it is far from being fully accomplished. The success of this academic undertaking is limited not only by the lack of open sources available outside the DPRK, but also by the rapid social changes which the country is experiencing. While the attempt has been made to include the most recent documents relating to the communications of North Koreans with the overseas world, the speed of these changes may be too challenging for an academic work to keep up. The suggested model of a North Korean philosophy of foreigners is thus open to further investigations, additions and corrections.

2 NORTH KOREAN DISCOURSE OF THE FOREIGN WORLD: POLITICAL ROOTS, CONFLICTING DEMANDS AND CHALLENGES

2.1 *Soviet-style internationalism: a complex pattern*

While the Soviet roots to many North Korean cultural practices are commonly recognised, the North Korean discourse about foreigners is often perceived as diverging from the Soviet origin or even as a polar opposite to the Soviet prototype (Myers 2010). However, Soviet and North Korean pictures of the world had shared much more in common than is often imagined. The reason why their similarities are often left unnoticed could be explained by a misconception of the Soviet discourse of the foreign world as being consistently driven by the communist principle of proletarian internationalism and the Marxist slogan, 'Workers of the world, unite!'[3]

However, the Soviet rhetoric of the foreign world was much more multifaceted. In normal times, the proletarian internationalism of Soviet ideology, which summoned the labouring classes of all races to

---

[3] This approach treated the concepts of nation and race in the context of class exploitation and forthcoming world revolution, which was intended to unit the working classes of all countries forever. See MIA: Marxists: Marx & Engels: Library: 1848: Manifesto of the Communist Party: Chapter Online: http://www.marxists.org/archive/marx/works/1848/communist-manifesto/ch04.htm (accessed 26 May 2011).

join the Soviet-centred progressive camp, served as a political balance between the conflicting demands of the various cultures and nations of multinational Soviet society. However, when political necessity arose, proletarian internationalism could be postponed in favour of the more efficient strategy of nationalism or ethnocentrism. For example, the onset of World War II brought about the need to mobilise the population of the country to fight an enemy (Gromov 1998: 320–24). In response to this political demand, Soviet official rhetoric acquired assertive nationalist overtones. Soviet wartime propaganda employed ethnocentric imagery pinpointing the Great Russian legacy of the Soviets[4] and vilifying the German adversary as generalised 'Germans', regardless of class.[5] However, with the increasing counterattack by Russian troops in 1943, anti-German tendencies became increasingly downplayed as unnecessary. In April 1945, Alexandrov (1945: 4), writing in *Pravda*, criticised 'equating all German people with fascists' as inappropriate, a shift that heralded a complete return to the proletarian internationalist model.

In Soviet international politics, proletarian internationalism went hand in hand with support of local nationalisms, simultaneously attracting them to the Soviet side. Even rigidly anti-Soviet authors recognise that the cultural policy of the newly formed communist governments resulted in a revival of historical national pride and the unprecedented rise of folk art in Soviet-dominated territories (Reisky de Dubnic 1960: 158–59). Thus it can be said that internationalism and nationalism co-existed in the Soviet discourse of the foreign world, complementing each other and pursuing different political objectives at different times.

These double-sided Soviet cultural patterns were widely broadcast in the DPRK in the late 1940s through Soviet books and films and necessarily influenced the North Korean picture of the world. The place of the DPRK within this picture varied according to political

---

[4] Great Russians constituted a majority in the Red Army, so the wartime propaganda appealed in particular to their patriotism and national pride. On 24 May 1945 during the Kremlin's banquet in honour of the victory over Germany, Stalin, a Georgian, toasted the 'health of the Russian people, the greatest people of all nationalities of the Soviet Union' (Stalin 1946: 196–97).

[5] The outstanding expression of this tendency became a slogan, 'Kill the German'. The slogan first appeared in the pamphlet by the distinguished Soviet Jewish writer and war correspondent Ilya Ehrenburg, titled 'Kill!'(1942). It contained the following passage: 'We have understood: Germans are not people. From now on the word "German" is the most terrible curse for us.' See Ehrenburg 1942.

requirements. From 1945 to the early 1950s, North Korea strove to fit into a Soviet-centred internationalist model of the world as one of the 'younger brothers' within communism. However, from the mid-1950s, when the DPRK began to develop an independent political course, North Korean propaganda began to proclaim the world-dominating status of the DPRK and its ideology—altogether in the mode of Soviet communist ideology (Gabroussenko 2011: 275–302). One of the first North Korean texts to reflect these burgeoning internationalist ambitions was a short story by Yi T'ae-jun, 'Dear People' (1951). A Chinese protagonist of this story, a volunteer in the Korean War, acquires his political consciousness not from the Chinese Communist Party, but from the leaders and people of North Korea. During the following decade North Korean propaganda solidified this approach, placing the DPRK at the spiritual centre of the universe and referring to *chuch'e* (*juche*) as the beam of hope for all progressive humankind.

However, three objective factors have held back the realisation of this new internationalist tendency in the DPRK: the political seclusion of the DPRK, 'national solipsism' in the North Korean mono-ethnic mentality, and a paradigm of unfinished war with the United States.

2.2 *Political seclusion of the DPRK*

The seclusion of the DPRK restricts contacts between North Korean propagandists and the rest of the world. Unlike Soviet 'engineers of the human soul', who had communicated with foreigners even at the most restrictive points of Stalin's era (Margulies 1968; Hollander 1981), thus enriching Soviet culture with realistic images and plots of foreign life, North Korean propagandists have had limited knowledge and experience of the non-Korean world. Of necessity, this decreases the volume of internationalist messages and hinders evolution of the relevant patterns and imagery in North Korean propaganda.

In North Korean creative writing, the notion of the 'foreign world' is regularly employed as a measuring-stick for the activities of North Korean characters. Achievements of a progressive North Korean scientist 'are admired even overseas'; a 'foreign professor' steals an anticancer medicine invented by a creative North Korean rural doctor (Yang Chae-mo 1998: 304–23) a modest North Korean engineer impresses people with his perfect knowledge of 'a foreign language' which he learns by himself (Kim Ki-pŏm 2008: 53–60). In a detective story, 'foreign' secret agents who hunt for some invention of a North Korean scientist are referred to as 'bastards' and their state as a '*** country' or 'the enemy state' (Ch'oe Yang-su 2000: 61–70). With their limited knowledge about non-Korean space, North Korean writers must avoid any particulars and operate with obscure definitions of the greater world.

North Korean policymakers seem to recognise this problem and try for some mid-point resolutions. Since the mid-1980s, sporadic flows of translated foreign films and literature have become available in the DPRK;[6] particular writers who depict foreign life in their texts are granted access to classified overseas materials.[7] Judging by the fact that North Korean journals often republish materials from popular Russian websites,[8] it can be assumed that some journalists have access to the internet. This policy can be described by a well-known saying of Kim Jong Il, 'Plant your feet on your own ground, but turn your eyes to the world', which illustrates a desperate endeavour to make North Korean culture more open while keeping society itself profoundly closed.

2.3 'National solipsism' in the North Korean mono-ethnic mentality

The ethnocentrism or 'national solipsism' (to use Bruce Cumings' expression; 2005: 407) in North Korean mentality and state policy can be regarded as a consequence of the mono-ethnicity of North Korean society. While in Soviet propaganda shifts to ethnocentrism were sporadic, the DPRK's policymakers regularly employ ethnocentrism in support of the maintenance of the integrity of North Korean society as racially homogeneous and undiluted by any 'drop of ink', or foreign blood. For this reason, international marriages are the subject of particular condemnation by North Korean officialdom. In a *Rodong Sinmun* enumeration (11 November 2003) of American crimes committed on South Korean soil,[9] marriages of American men to Korean women

---

[6] Personal communication with A. Zhebin and Ivan Zakharchenko, July 2011.

[7] Interview with Ch'oe Jin-i, 6 April 2011.

[8] One such example is a translated letter from a Russian emigrant to the United States, expressing doubts: 'Migugini toen gŏsŭl such'iro yŏginda' [I consider it a shame to become an American]. See *Ch'ŏllima* (2005).

[9] The *Rodong Sinmun* article referred back to memoranda issued in 2003 by the Committee for the Peaceful Unification of the Fatherland and the Research Centre for

and the birth of mixed race children are mentioned as being an especially serious charge, and the mothers of these children are habitually presented as victims of rape.

The 'drop of ink' metaphor emerged during talks between General Han Min-gu of the ROK and General Kim Yong-chul of the DPRK in 2006. In response to Han's remark about the contemporary rise of international marriages in South Korea as a consequence of the female depopulation of its rural areas, Kim expressed his concerns that Korean 'singularity could disappear'. Han responded dismissively that such a dilution of the bloodline was 'but a drop of ink in the Han River'; Kim, however, retaliated by saying that '[n]ot even one drop of ink must be allowed to fall into the Han River' (this exchange was reported in *Chosun Ilbo* online).[10] Following this conversation, Ch'oe Mun-il (2006), writing in *Rodong Sinmun* (27 April 2006), equated the tolerant attitude of the South Korean government in regard to multiracial and multinational marriages with treason against the interests of the Korean nation.

The attitude of North Korean officialdom to multinational marriages on its own territory has been generally negative. Such marriages were contracted with the representatives of 'friends of Korea' such as Russians or Chinese in the 1940s to the early 1950s; yet, with the strengthening of Kim Il Sung's cult in the mid-1950s most international marriages were forcibly terminated under different pretexts. There were, however, some exceptions. In 2000, *Koreya segodnya*, the Russian-language edition of *Korea Today*, published an article written by Yu T'aek-hŭi, a woman of Indonesian background. Yu described her happy family life with her Korean husband in Pyongyang where they moved after being repatriated from Japan in 1961. The article emphasised an absence of ethnic discrimination in Pyongyang, in contrast to the humiliation that Yu and her Korean husband had experienced in Japan (Yu 2000: 19–20).

Ethnocentrism and 'national solipsism' effectively shaped three features in the international discourse of North Korean propaganda. Firstly, it created restrictions on a positive presentation of any contacts between North Koreans and foreigners which entailed 'spoiling Ko-

---

the Unification of the Fatherland (Choguk P'yŏnghwa T'ongil Wiwŏnhoe Choguk T'ongil Yŏn'guwŏn Pimangnok).

[10] 'Two Koreas' Top Brass Resort to Racist Mudslinging', 17 May 2006. Online: http://english.chosun.com/w21data/html/news/200605/200605170016.html (accessed 7 September2009).

rean blood', such as romance and marriage. North Korean fiction condemns the slightest hints of romantic designs between a Korean and a non-Korean. When in 1951 Yi T'ae-jun in 'Dear People' depicted a Chinese volunteer secretly falling in love with a Korean nurse who soon afterwards was killed during the battle and never came to know of his feelings, Yi was criticised for the 'unsuitability' of a romantic theme in the context of the 'lofty subject of Korean-Chinese friendship' (Om 1952: 193–95). In rare contemporary works of North Korean fiction which depict a Korean character involved with a non-Korean partner, the relationship is presented as unhappy on the Korean side. For example, in Nam Sang-hyŏk's 'Two Women' (Nam 1991–92), a beautiful Korean woman marries an ugly Japanese man as her second husband; he later proves to be sadist, xenophobic and a sexual maniac.

Secondly, North Korean internationalist messages are aimed mostly at Korean recipients. When it comes to the visualisation of overseas followers of *chuch'e*, North Korean propaganda as a rule employs images of Korean nationals living overseas, mainly in Japan or South Korea. These personages are portrayed as people who have been forcefully expelled from the North Korean community, who suffer through their separation from the motherland and who by definition share a belief in the greatness of *chuch'e* and the North Korean leaders, no matter which part of Korea they originate from.[11]

Thirdly, North Korean creative writings provide few images of ethnic Koreans as enemies of the DPRK. Even such usual adversaries as conservative South Korean politicians, or Koreans in Japan who chose to leave Chongryun (Ch'ongryŏn) and assimilate, are normally portrayed as victims of an environment filled with vicious foreigners; often, the process of their awakening, remorse and rectification is depicted.[12]

2.4 *The paradigm of unfinished war with the United States*

The DPRK's perception of itself as a forcibly separated country in a state of unfinished war with the United States and its 'puppets' has

---

[11] Among examples of such narrations see Hyŏn 1999, Kang 2001, Ri Sang-min 2005, Pak Chong-sang 2004, and Kim Sŏn-hwan 1999 and 2003.

[12] For examples of such narrations see Kim Ch'ŏng-nam 2000, or Hong 2007–2009.

imbued the North Korean view with a characteristically militant drumbeat. As with other wartime propaganda, including Stalinist propaganda during World War II or the wartime writings of Chiang Kai-Shek (Jiang Jieshi) and Mao Zedong (Stevens 1964), the North Korean art of persuasion has aimed at motivating people to fight the foe and for that reason vilifies the image of the adversary by all possible means. In a standard North Korean narration 'American beasts' emerge as an evil monolithic entity stripped of any complexity and associated exclusively with an aggressive US international policy and war crimes committed on Korean soil. The essential anti-American fictional work presupposes a plot in which American sub-humans initiate a threat against North Koreans but, being intimidated by the moral and physical might of the DPRK and its leader, instead crawl on all fours and plead for mercy.[13]

At a personal level, Americans are normally portrayed as possessing cunning minds yet simultaneously being devoid of human feelings; their bestiality is particularly aimed at the weakest of Koreans. Earlier examples of this pattern can be traced in Yi T'ae-jun's 'The American Embassy' (1951) (see Yi T'ae-jun 1951/1995), in which Americans organise the mass murder of Korean women, children and the elderly, and in Han Sŏr-ya's *Jackals* (1951), where Americans inject a Korean boy with a deadly bacillus (see Han Sŏr-ya 2003), or in his *Love* (1960), in which Americans sadistically run over and kill a young Korean girl (Han Sŏr-ya 1960; for an analysis of *Love* see Myers 1994: 126–34).

The innate spontaneity and naivety of Koreans (the core qualities of North Korean self-identity which Myers defined as being a 'child race') (Myers 2008) make *all* Koreans vulnerable, unsuspicious victims of Americans. In Kim Tŏk-ch'ŏl's 'An Unusual Marriage Ceremony' (2000), Americans trick the fair-minded South Korean boxer Tŭk-ku into participating in a competition against an American rival. Tŭk-ku loses the match through a foul punch by his rival. While the boxer is unconscious, Americans place him in a hospital under the pretext of taking care of him, yet at the hospital they kill him by cutting vital organs out of his healthy living body to transplant into a wealthy American. According to the plot, the crime only occurred because the Korean boxer and his friends were too decent to see through

---

[13] Examples of such plots may be found in Kim Ch'ŏl-min 2007 or in Kim Tae-sŏn 2009.

the deceptive external respectability of the Americans and recognise their inner evil.

The external culture and internal bestiality of Americans are constantly contrasted. In Ri Chŏng-su's 'Conversion' (1977), a seemingly kind and sensitive female American teacher breaks the hand of a little Korean boy as punishment for the child's accidental damage to flowers in her garden. In Kim Ch'ŏng-nam's 'The Feel of Civilisation' (2000), an apparently intelligent employee of the American embassy in Seoul entertains himself by torturing animals and watching them die. The moral of such narrations is summarised in the words of a female protagonist in 'Conversion': 'All Americans are evil, no matter what they may look like' (Ri 1977: 58).

Rampant anti-Americanism fuelled with the sentiments of unfinished war should surely be considered within a context of unsettled historical scores and the necessity to maintain the required level of political awareness among North Koreans. However, it seems that fiction and art about 'American sadists' fulfills an additional role, spicing overall bland North Korean literature and the arts with a much-needed pinch of sensationalism. As an example, an extensive exhibition of pictures at the Sinch'ŏn museum, displayed on the Juche-Songun LiveJournal website, depicts tortures of Koreans at the hands of Americans in considerable graphic detail,[14] and comic strips about mad American sadists are regularly published in the only North Korean women's journal, *Chosŏn nyŏsŏng* (Korean Women). A typical character in such comics is an American doctor who seizes an unsuspecting Korean woman from off the street, lures her into hospital and cuts off her legs out of sheer sadistic pleasure.

Considering that anti-American narrations are placed at the forefront of today's North Korean propaganda as it relates to the overseas world it is tempting to conclude that in North Korean discourse 'real fraternity between pure (Koreans) and impure (foreigners) is impossible' and that 'all foreigners are inferior' (Myers 2010: 131). However, literature and the arts in the DPRK do provide a wide range of accounts which testify that the North Korean vision of the outside world comprises an ability to look at foreigners from an inclusive perspective.

---

[14] Shown under the title 'Koreiskie kartiny o voennyh prestupleniyah americanskogo imperialisma' [Korean pictures about war crimes of the American imperialists], 2 March 2011. Online: http://juche-songun.livejournal.com/40834.html (accessed 30 May 2011).

3 Tales of 'Good Foreigners' as a Special Genre in North Korean Fiction

One good example of complexity in the foreign discourse of North Korean propaganda is the depiction of the sworn enemies of Korea, the Japanese. While in North Korean fictional portrayals of the colonial period or the Imjin War, Japanese characters are vilified in a manner similar to racist anti-American propaganda (see, for example, Kang 2001), criticism of contemporary Japan and the Japanese takes the form not of racist denunciation of them as an 'inferior' or 'impure nation', but rather of an anti-capitalist critique of Japanese society in which Korean characters (Koreans in Japan) are forced to live (see, for instance, Ri Sang-min 2005). Even in their condemnation of the international policy of today's Japan, North Korean propagandists refrain from racist comments about contemporary Japanese. In Kim Ch'ŏng-su's 'My Arirang' (2002), Kim Il Sung warns his subordinates that 'we should separate militarism and the Japanese people' (14). North Korean writings about contemporary Japan often contain positive Japanese characters, such as those found in 'The Second Briefing' by Ryang Ch'ang-cho (2000) or 'The Flag of the Republic' by Kim Sŏng-ho (2008).

As in proletarian internationalist Soviet texts, an acceptance of the Japanese in these North Korean narrations is conditional: positive Japanese characters share or at least sympathise with the 'correct' ideology of the DPRK and with its personal embodiment in the shape of Kim Il Sung or Kim Jong Il. In fact, all North Korean narrations which employ positive foreign characters revolve around one major storyline: an individual foreigner encounters North Korea and its leader and falls in love with them, sometimes in contradiction to their previous political views.

3.1 *Exoticisation of foreign friends*

The primary goals of such stories are to enliven the artistic images of the DPRK, its people and its leader by presenting them from a position well beyond the ethnic Korean boundaries and to emphasise the universality of Korean values by transposing them onto those outside the North Korean cultural space.

For that reason, North Korean writers endeavour to portray 'foreign friends' as strikingly non-Korean. These characters have stereotypically non-Korean looks, such as blue eyes, pale skin, and blond or curly hair; however, unlike negativist presentations of the physical appearance of white Americans in works such as *Jackals* by Han Sŏr-ya,[15] these Caucasian features of 'good foreigners' are described in complimentary ways. A Soviet nurse in a Korean hospital from Kim Hong-mu's 'Marŭsya' is 'slim, with a moon-like shining face, big eyes as tranquil as a deep lake, and a clear forehead above which her blond hair is swept back in waves' and her beautiful smile 'shows snowy-white teeth' (Kim 1960: 35). Soviet engineer Fedya in Hwang Ju-yŏp's eponymous short story is a gentle giant with 'golden locks' (Hwang 1960: 50). A French boy, Julian, from 'Spring in Pyongyang' by Han Ki-sŏk is an 'extremely cute boy, with curly blond hair, astonishingly blue eyes, oval face and milky skin' (Han 2010: 9). In addition to these favourable descriptions of the unfamiliar physical features of foreign characters, North Korean texts provide exotic details of their native cultures, narrating them sympathetically, although far from accurately. Such, for instance, is the presentation of a contemporary Ecuadorian as an expressive believer in the Inca Sun God (Kim Myŏng-jin 2010) or the portrayal of a Soviet engineer of Kazak origins as constantly carrying an accordion around a construction site and singing old Kazak songs in a loud melodious voice (Hwang 1960).

3.2 *Koreanisation of foreign friends*

At the same time, the degree of Koreanisation of these essentially non-Korean individuals reaches considerable heights. A female doctor living in the remote Siberian wilderness in 1986 eats kimch'i and rice for supper and plays North Korean marches on the piano for pleasure (Yun 1986). An elderly German lady constantly advocates the benefits of Korean ginseng, which she drinks for 14 years for health reasons (Paek 2008: 11–22). Even an American protagonist in one short story cites a Korean proverb (Kim Myŏng-jin 2010: 46).

Apart from the primary propagandistic intention to claim the universality of Korean values, these fabrications often reflect the plain

---

[15] See the analysis of American images in North Korean fiction at Myers 1994, 126–34.

inability of Korean writers to imagine their positive characters behaving differently to familiar norms. A daughter-in-law of the German lady mentioned above is a typical example of this tendency. Although also German, this woman takes care of her mother-in-law in the typical fashion of a dutiful Korean daughter-in-law, with frequent bowing, massaging the feet of the older woman and serving tea to her and her guests (Paek 2008: 1–22).

'Good foreigners' in North Korean fiction who share Korean cultural values offer their love to the Korean leader with a spontaneity and naivety that bring them quite close to the pattern characteristic of the 'child race'. North Korean writers often directly compare their mature overseas characters to children. In one scene from 'The Fifteenth Year' by Paek Po-hŭm, a German female anti-fascist activist of 83 years links little fingers with the leader and makes him promise to live for one hundred years. The narrator relishes the 'sweetness' of the episode, fondly comparing the old lady to a 'little girl' (Paek 2008: 11–12).

The attachment of fictional foreigners to the leader, whether Kim Il Sung or Kim Jong Il, is based on an adoration of his personality rather than on any rational judgment of his activities. Overseas devotees rarely discuss the political values which he represents or the concrete material advantages of the state that was constructed under his guidance. At the very most, they praise the DPRK as a 'country of people' where 'there are no rich and poor' (Kim Myŏng-jin 2010: 43–45). Simultaneously, all narrations speak enthusiastically of the exemplary personal morality of the leader and the mystical appeal of his personality. A passing encounter with Kim Il Sung forces an old Ecuadorian Korea enthusiast, Umberto, to discard his lifelong belief in the Sun God and come to the conclusion that the real Sun God of our age is Kim Il Sung (Kim 2010: 42–46). After much deliberation over the reasons for the ecological bliss of the DPRK, an English biologist, John Haw, comes to understand that North Koreans have their own unique 'sun' which allows nature to thrive in the DPRK—their leader (Song 1988).

Just like fictional North Koreans who by definition cherish the motherland and their leader more than their blood relatives, the love of fictional foreigners for the North Korean leader, whether Kim Il Sung or Kim Jong Il, surpasses all other human feelings and attachments. A casual gesture of kindness from the leader, a tasty dinner together and a moment spent playing on swings causes a deeply depressed seven-year-old French boy from 'Spring in Pyongyang' to immediately forget about the death of his father and become happy (Han Ki-sŏk 2010). The Ecuadorian character Umberto is hospitalised with myocardial infarction after receiving news of the death of Kim Il Sung and refuses to undergo a necessary operation because he feels his life is empty now, after 'the Sun has set forever'. Only news about the rising genius Kim Jong Il is able to cure the inconsolable Umberto. Meanwhile, the near death of his only son in an accident does not force Umberto to postpone his next visit to the DPRK (Kim Myŏng-jin 2010: 42–48) The above-mentioned German admirer of Kim Il Sung, who survived the death of her spouse with exemplary stoicism, loudly mourns Kim's death, beating her chest and asking: 'Where did you go, why did you leave your Louise?' and her dutiful daughter-in-law in her early sixties joins her, 'sobbing like a child' (Paek 2008: 21).

The 'tributary' nature of North Korean texts about foreign friends of Korea which Myers has pinpointed with precision does not have any anti-foreign implications: the fictional relations of the Korean 'child race' with their leaders are portrayed as similarly tributary. In the framework of North Korean official philosophy, equality is ruled out from the relations of any human being with the leaders, as unconditionally supreme figures. On the contrary, the fact of recognising the greatness of one or other leader and thus sharing this symbol of faith with North Koreans and worshipping him in a Korean style equates people of non-Korean blood with North Koreans.

3.3 Foreign friends versus North Koreans

It must however be stressed that the texts about 'good foreigners' do not entirely deprive North Koreans of their perceived moral superiority. While the North Korean 'child race' is always depicted as unwaveringly moral, 'childlike' foreigners often have to go a long way before they learn to live as virtuously as Koreans. A typical example of such a narration is the short story 'Paeksŏl's Secret' by Song Pyŏng-jun (1988). The protagonist, an English biologist, John Haw, devotes his academic career to cultivating and protecting a rare tree species, but fails to achieve the outstanding results of his North Korean colleagues, who have succeeded in covering a vast tract of land with the rare species. John comes to understand that the Koreans' success is the result of an exceptional devotion to the cause, a devotion which he himself lacks. John humbly recognises that while he is thinking so much about personal fame and money, Koreans devote themselves to a cause selflessly and wholeheartedly. While he is alone in his research, John's North Korean colleagues receive support from the leader and the entire nation, including little children who help the adults to take care of the saplings. John is astounded to learn that during a battle in the Korean War, which had occurred on a mountain slope covered with the rare trees, a North Korean battalion commander refused to allow his unit to use artillery out of concern for the trees and consequently died protecting the natural heritage of his socialist motherland. John weeps at the thought of the exemplary moral nobility of North Koreans, whom he now perceives as 'the most loving, beautiful friends' (Song 1988: 24). This text acknowledges the higher morality of the North Korean people but substantiates this morality not by an implied purity of blood of the Koreans but by the Korean ideology of socialist patriotism, socialist collectivism and loyalty to the virtuous national leader. Similarly to the communist propaganda of China and the Soviet Union, the North Korean understanding not only places the 'progressive nation' of North Koreans ahead of other people, but it also illuminates a path to this same bliss though the acquisition of a proper 'progressive' worldview.

All North Korean writings about 'good foreigners' which I have encountered so far consistently emphasise that the social and political advantages of North Korea's 'socialism of our style', such as collectivism and nationalism or patriotism, are attainable by outsiders. The only exception is the figure of the leader, whose uniqueness is not questioned. However, North Korean propagandists make it clear that paradise is open for those foreigners who choose to cherish Kim Il Sung and Kim Jong Il.

In many North Korean accounts, the leaders are depicted as being ready to protect people of non-Korean blood, in a similar manner to their own people. Most stories about overseas admirers in which foreign characters personally contact Kim Il Sung or Kim Jong Il reproduce normal patterns of communication of the father leader with his Korean 'children'. In 'Spring in Pyongyang' (Han Ki-sŏk 2010), the interaction of Kim Il Sung with the French boy Julian, the son of one of Kim's recently deceased followers, is strikingly reminiscent of North Korean texts in which the leader cares for the offspring of his deceased revolutionary friends. The story emulates even such a popular pattern as the leader marrying off sons and daughters of his deceased revolutionary comrades by finding suitable partners for them from families of good reputation. Kim Il Sung secretly inspires beautiful Mi-yŏng, the daughter of a North Korean diplomat, to 'accidentally' meet and make friends with the lonely French boy and thus distract Julian from his depression.

Thus, within the framework of North Korean propaganda, even a foreigner whose physical appearance and cultural background are strikingly non-Korean can be treated as equal under the following conditions: he or she must love Korea unconditionally, share the symbols of faith with North Koreans, and worship the leader as an embodiment of North Koreanness, with the sincerity of the 'child race'. Characteristically, tales of 'good foreigners' portray thinking, emotions and behaviour characteristic of the 'child race' as attainable by those outside the North Korean cultural space. This aspect of North Korean international propaganda demonstrates similarities with many ideologies that might be termed world consolidating, such as communism, Christianity, Buddhism and Confucianism. All of these accept people of other races under the condition of their sharing of basic values of the respective teaching.

4 AMERICANS AS 'GOOD FOREIGNERS': CASE STUDY OF KIM CHUN-HAK'S 'ENCHANTMENT'

Considering the set role of the United States as a mortal enemy in North Korean military-first propaganda, one would not expect Americans to be the subjects of narrations about 'good foreigners'. However, North Korean propagandists have proved that when political goals change, they are able to discard this fixed racist paradigm and fit Americans into the mould of a standard narration of 'good foreigners'. One example is the short story by Kim Chun-hak (1998) entitled 'Enchantment' ('Maehok')—a fictional representation of the events of 1994 when the former US president Jimmy (James) Carter, accompanied by his wife Rosalynn, visited North Korea in order to convince Kim Il Sung that he should freeze the development of nuclear weapons in exchange for concessions from the US. This story represents a striking contrast with previous North Korean narrations about Carter, such as Kim Ik-ch'ŏl's essay (1979), 'History is watching', which was written at the time when Carter was president of the United States. A detailed analysis of 'Enchantment' demonstrates how radically just one twist in political relations between the DPRK and the US was able to change imagery that for decades had been anti-American in North Korean propaganda.

In his book *Our Endangered Values* (2005), the former American president recalls his visit to Pyongyang as one of innumerable meetings with various political leaders of the world, which formed a regular part of his long political career. In hindsight, Carter expresses his firm conviction that at the time 'the combined forces of South Korea and the United States could defeat North Korea' (Carter 2005: 110), but that the casualties in such a potential war would be too enormous for the US ally, South Korea. He states his belief that 'good-faith diplomacy between the United States and North Korea is necessary' for the stability of the region (111). Carter mentions Kim Il Sung in a neutral tone, seemingly unconcerned about the exalted stature of the North Korean leader, whom he refers to as 'president', and briefly describes Pyongyang's octogenarian as 'vigorous' and 'alert' (Oberdorfer 1997: 334). Carter speaks in a matter-of-fact manner of the several years of invitations from Kim Il Sung prior to the visit and Kim's 'promise' to have diplomatic discussions with the US ally, the ROK. For the former leader of the world's superpower, this cool and confident approach to what Carter obviously perceives as a minor nuisance rather than a major international problem and one which in addition does not represent any direct threat to the United States, is rather predictable. Yet the fictional commentary on this meeting provided by the North Korean side paints an entirely different picture of events.

While Carter's unorthodox gesture was treated as a sign of appeasement by some of his American colleagues (Oberdorfer 1997: 326–36), North Korean official propagandists did not depict the event according to the fixed conventional schema of the 'bestial Americans plead for mercy from the humane Koreans'. Instead, Kim Chun-hak portrays the Carter visit through the concept of 'love which conquers all'; that is, love for Kim Il Sung that allegedly conquers the hearts of the Carters, forcing them to discard their lifelong advocacy of gunboat diplomacy and to fall in love with North Korea. 'Enchantment' focuses on the Carters' impressions of Kim Il Sung and depicts the various emotional states of Rosalynn and her husband before, during and after their meetings with the Great Leader. The rhetoric that the author uses to describe these emotional states is particularly interesting.

In his image of Kim Il Sung, Kim Chun-hak reinforces a common practice of portraying the leader by merging militant clichés with soft, sentimental expressions. He portrays Kim Il Sung as a mighty but gentle giant, customarily comparing him to the sun ('the Chairman warmed up the surroundings as the sun heats the cold soil') or, alternately, to a god who 'decides the fate of the US' (Kim Chun-hak 1998: 33). On the one hand, Kim Il Sung is

> an experienced Marshal who had once destroyed with one blow the UN forces under the leadership of the US, and who openly named their homeland, America, 'the ringleader of the world's imperialists' and struggled with America. [He] was an indomitable anti-imperialist fighter who openly summoned the world's people to fight the US ... Marshal Kim Il Sung, if necessary, would not hesitate to engage in a mortal struggle that would erase America from the face of the world (Kim Chun-hak 1998: 23).

He is a 'self-confident rebel who feared neither sanctions nor war' (25). On the other hand, Kim's smile is 'shining and charming' and his manners 'poised' (24). He is a 'politician who wipes the tears of his people' (33), a person of 'rich human beauty of the soul and a broad mind' (26). The approaching smile of the Chairman makes 'the flowers bloom more fully and butterflies and bees fly more happily' (28). Whilst explaining why Kim Il Sung has remained in power in the DPRK despite his advanced years, the narrator points out that 'in the same way there is no particular term in office for God in heaven, there is no term in office for Kim Il Sung on earth. The fact that he remains in office is his kind service to the people' (33).

In its turn, the presentation of the Carters breaks out of the usual anti-American convention and reproduces instead the convention of fiction about 'good foreigners'. In contrast to the usual pattern of Americans as cunning, heartless creatures, Kim Chun-hak robs his protagonists of common sense and the advantages of their rich life experiences and infantilises them along the lines of North Korean gender stereotypes. The veteran spouses of high-level politics have been transformed into a pair of teenagers: a 'cute girl' and a 'naughty boy'.

4.1 *The 'teenage girl'*

In 1998, Rosalynn Carter was a former first lady of mature age, an indispensable helpmate to Jimmy Carter in his long political career—an activity which naturally required a pragmatic mind, general sensibility and level-headedness. Kim Chun-hak acknowledges that in everyday political activities, Rosalynn is indeed known as a 'steel magnolia' (Kim Chun-hak 1998: 23), implying a contrast between her delicate appearance and her strong personality. Yet in 'Enchantment' this experienced person undergoes an extreme mental transformation during her few days' visit to the DPRK. A meeting with Chairman Kim Il Sung allegedly turns this mature, assertive, rational and self-confident former first lady into an emotionally unstable schoolgirl whose 'feelings betray her reasoning' (23) and who unquestionably 'follows the will' (25) of the Great Leader.

Rosalynn is portrayed as being totally confused by the new North Korean scenery and by her own mixed feelings towards Kim Il Sung—'she has lost herself in Pyongyang' (31), 'she did not understand herself', 'her whole body was wrapped in unknown emotions' (24). Together with her husband, Rosalynn blushes in front of her idol, stiffens at the slightest deviation from diplomatic etiquette, smiles awkwardly in order to hide her embarrassment and shyness before Kim Il Sung, runs excitedly towards the Chairman to meet him in her room, 'shakes', 'trembles' and 'shivers' because of her uncontrolled feelings (27–28), and suffers from emotionally driven insomnia and her inability to stop thinking of her idol; she plays the piano at night in a vain attempt to calm herself down. Several times throughout the text the author openly compares Rosalynn to a happy young girl—'her face was brightened with romantic feelings, like the face of a girl' (24). As if to stress further Rosalynn's resemblance to an excited schoolgirl, Kim Chun-hak dresses his mature heroine in a light-purple frock which floats gracefully as Rosalynn, thrilled and excited, walks with fast steps in her garden deep in thought of the Great Leader (22). 'Her whole soul was trembling with joy' (26) when she beheld the beautiful Kim Jong Il flowers sent by Kim Il Sung to her room.

Instead of applying logical reasoning to the actions of Kim Il Sung, as a mature individual would, the childlike Rosalynn carefully watches his gestures and listens to the sound of his voice, rather than contemplating the meaning of his words. In the typical mode of an excited teenager who falls in love with a rock star at the first sound of his guitar, Rosalynn completely defines the personality of the Chairman at the first sound of his voice, which miraculously exposes to her such qualities of Kim Il Sung as 'good will and friendliness, softness and delicacy, open-heartedness and depth, the vitality and energy of a man in the prime of his life' (27). To the fictional Rosalynn, the butterflies and flowers that surround Kim Il Sung's palace in Kŭmsusan are sufficient evidence that the DPRK is a civilised country which 'has nothing to learn from others' (27). In the view of Kim Chun-hak, the presumed absence of logical reasoning makes Rosalynn the most objective observer of the famous meeting, for she listens to the Great Leader 'through feelings' (29).

Rosalynn not only behaves like a child but she also considers herself a child in comparison with the adult figure of Kim Il Sung. She feels that the Chairman lives for his people, while Jimmy and herself are 'like schoolchildren who have just started to learn the first letters of the special political handbook of the Chairman, who regards his people as exalted as heaven' (32). Rosalynn feels too that comparing any American president, including her husband, to Kim Il Sung was 'like comparing a little boy with God, or rather comparing the glow of a firefly with that of the sun' (33).

4.2 A 'naughty boy'

The ex-president of the United States feels and behaves in a similarly childish manner, striving to hide his shyness before the Chairman under an 'unnatural smile' or by suddenly becoming 'as stiff as a stone Buddha' (Kim Chun-hak 1998: 27). However, Jimmy's perceived childlike behaviour, like that of the contemporary American administration he represents, has different implications. While Rosalynn embodies the idea of naivety and the unconditional belief of a foreigner in the Great Leader, Jimmy's immature conduct is instead related to his naughtiness and insignificance. When, for example, on the first day of their meeting, Kim Il Sung announces that it is time to break for lunch, Jimmy's facial expression is as happy as that of 'a schoolboy who has been luckily spared by the sudden school bell from answering a difficult question from his strict teacher or showing his homework' (25). Like Rosalynn, Jimmy is aware of his own insignificance in comparison to the Great Leader: during discussions, the former president was unable 'to raise even one single objection to the words of the Chairman'. Kim Il Sung's unexpected mercy and the success of the negotiations left Jimmy feeling 'dizzy with excitement' (23). After a few days of contact with the Chairman, however, the first signs of conscience awakened in the soul of Carter, the 'naughty boy'. He began to feel the 'love and inner beauty' (27) of the Chairman and felt shame for America and his compatriots. Discussing the US administration with the Chairman, Jimmy acts 'like a parent whose children have been caught in a stranger's garden and who has to apologise to the owner' (25).

4.3 *Kim Il Sung and the fictional Carters—mutual sensuality*

In addition to the childhood metaphors of the Carters' feelings towards Kim Il Sung, their fictional relationships are permeated with a characteristic underlying sensuality, thus reproducing the conventions of standard North Korean writing about the love of the people for their leader. In North Korean cultural discourse, expressions like 'the leader is the lover of all Koreans' or images of a girl who tosses in bed at night, enwrapped in thoughts of the Great Leader, are stereotypical. The poet Ri In-mo, for example, writes: 'I sleep under a warm blanket/But suddenly wake up and think/I think about love which knows everything:/The Love of the Great Marshal' (Kim Tong-gi 2005: 64).

'Enchantment' follows this same line in terms of its portrayal of the relationship between the Carters and Kim Il Sung in scenes which, if taken out of the North Korean cultural context, could be perceived as bordering on impropriety. For example, at one point, Rosalynn confesses to Kim Il Sung that his smile is the most beautiful in the world—even in comparison to the smile of her husband! (Kim Chun-hak 1988: 25). Jimmy, in his turn, playfully comments that the Chairman has carried away his wife's heart. Thinking about the Chairman, Rosalynn feels estranged from her husband and 'embarrassed and strangely resistant' (25) to his behaviour and political actions. While the real Rosalynn is a strict Catholic and no longer a young woman, the fictional Rosalynn desires to touch her idol physically, for example 'to put her small hand to the wide chest of the leader and feel the beat of his mighty heart filled with love for his people' (33). Jimmy seems to be so enwrapped in 'the love and human beauty' (34) of the Chairman that he forgets his wife, thus making her envious (29). The Chairman seems to encourage the relationship, joking about taking Jimmy away from Rosalynn because her husband is so beautiful, about Rosalynn's youthful looks (29), and so forth.

No matter how odd these scenes might appear to a foreign reader, they indicate that Kim Chun-hak has endeavoured to humanise his American characters by applying to them a common framework of

North Korean literature: the spontaneous eruption of emotions at the expense of logical reasoning. Another testimony that the fictional Carters emerge as good characters is the positive descriptions of their appearances. The pale skin and slight build of Rosalynn Carter are emphasised to stress the spirituality and delicacy of the American heroine (22; 30), unlike anti-American narrations such as *Jackals* or 'Conversion', in which these attributes are otherwise popular negative signs of the 'American beasts'. Jimmy Carter's appearance is also referred to as 'beautiful', 'youthful' and 'attractive' (25).

Because the rhetoric of unfinished war largely defines the contemporary North Korean concept of the US, (Pak Sŏng-guk (2003) provides a characteristic example), texts like 'Enchantment' constitute a minority of North Korean representations of Americans. However, a body of narrations that defy the standard vilifying pattern of Americans does exist in the North Korean discourse. To return to the former president Jimmy Carter, an image of him as an admirer of Kim Il Sung who understands the leader 'through feelings' can be found in the short story 'The Fifteenth Year', mentioned above. In this text, Jimmy Carter is reported as declaring in front of journalists that 'at the very moment of meeting with Chairman Kim Il Sung, I was completely enchanted by him because I understood how sincerely the Chairman loves peace. Kim Il Sung is greater than the three greatest American presidents, the Founding Fathers: George Washington, Thomas Jefferson, and Abraham Lincoln' (Paek 2008: 12). The claim is also made that meeting with Kim Il Sung allegedly taught Carter, who was famous for his 'soft and fragile smile', to smile broadly and sincerely. Carter, who came to Pyongyang 'with a scared soul', began to relax and smile 'ecstatically, like a person who has received the help of Christ or enlightenment from Buddha' (Paek 2008: 12). This episode depicts the American ex-president not as a regular 'beast' but as a human being who, in order to act and feel like a 'normal' North Korean and as a good foreigner, simply requires some additional information.

5 FOREIGNERS AS KOREAN HEROES

A notable part of the North Korean conception of the foreign world is the practice of including foreigners in the category of Korean national heroes. Understandably, they constitute a minority in the North Korean pantheon and normally belong to politically allied nations, such as Russia or China.

The most celebrated foreign figure is Yakov Novichenko (1914–96), a Soviet officer who in 1946 saved Kim Il Sung from assassination by catching a hand grenade thrown at the North Korean leader by members of a right-wing terrorist group (the White Shirt Society, *Paekŭisa*). Novichenko lost an arm after the grenade exploded (Lankov 2002: 25; Mal'tseva 2009; see also 'Zhizn' za vozhdya' 2010[16]). During one of his visits to the Soviet Union in 1984, Kim Il Sung found his saviour, expressed his gratitude and bestowed on him the highest award of the DPRK, 'Hero of the DPRK'. Kim showered Yakov and his family with expensive gifts, and every year invited them to Pyongyang for a visit. During his 2001 visit to Russia, Kim Jong Il also brought Yakov's widow and children a suitcase of expensive presents.[17]

In 1985, Yakov was the subject of a Soviet-North Korean film titled *A Second for an Exploit* (*Secunda na podvig*, 2011), the scenario of which was written by a distinguished author Paek In-jun; and in 1987, the North Korean sculptor Yi P'yŏn-il created the statue 'Novichenko the Internationalist', showing the Russian flying like an angel, his military coat flapping like wings, towards the deadly grenade. Novichenko's popularity in Pyongyang is said to have eventually risen to such a height that some Koreans named their children in his honour.

Another well-known person among Soviet liberators of Korea in 1945 is a 19-year-old nurse, Maria Zshukanova, who was captured by the Japanese and died at their hands after brutal torture. In 1987, work began on a joint Soviet-Korean film about this heroine; however, to the extent of the author's knowledge this project has not been accomplished, most probably because of political reasons.

Among the Chinese who fought for Korea's liberation the most prominent is Mao Anying, the eldest son of Mao Zedong, who volun-

---

[16] The story of Novichenko's exploit and the details of the film about him, of Yi P'yŏn-il's sculpture and of his popularity in North Korea are told in 'Zhizn' za vozhdya ili istoriya Yakova Novichenko' [Life for the leader or a story of Yakov Novichenko], 18 October 2010, available at the pikabu.ru website. Online: http://pikabu.ru/view/zhizn_za_vozhdya_ili_istoriya_yakova_novichenko_186114 (accessed 18 April 2010).

[17] This story is available at the lenta.ru website, 31 July 2001: 'Kim Chen Il privez chemodan podarkov sem'e ofitzhera, spasshego ego ottsa' [Kim Jong Il has brought a suitcase of gifts to the family of the officer who rescued his father]. Online: http://lenta.ru/russia/2001/07/31/kim/ (accessed 29 January 2012).

teered for the Chinese People's Volunteers (CPV) and died during an American bombing raid. Mao was buried in Pyongyang, in the Cemetery for the Heroes of the CPV. Another particularly respected Chinese is Luo Shengjiao, who died on Korean soil while saving a Korean boy from an icy river. A North Korean primary school is now named after Luo. (His story is relayed on the Juche-Songun LiveJournal website for 20 October 2011.[18])

The exploits of these foreigners have often become the subjects of Korean art and films which emphasise in particular the human side of foreign characters. Heroic foreigners are presented as smiling to Korean civilians, giving brotherly hugs to Korean soldiers or holding Korean babies. This stereotype is visible in a picture depicting Luo Shengjiao's exploit or in the monument devoted to Soviet soldiers in Pyongyang. Russian tourists to the DPRK speak admiringly of the perfect condition in which the Soviet war cemetery in Pyongyang is maintained; they are particularly touched by the warm words of gratitude, in Korean and in Russian, on the gravestones. Among all the fluctuations in the North Korean relationships with the Soviet Union and China, the position of these foreign characters in North Korean discourse has remained unchanged.

6 Conclusion

The narrative of the foreign world plays an important role in North Korean propaganda, serving as a measure for the achievements of the DPRK and the challenges it poses. The North Korean international discourse has undoubtedly evolved under the influence of Soviet international approaches which combined proletarian internationalism with wartime ethnocentrism and support of local nationalisms.

While the pattern of North Korea's relations with the world is described in the nationalistic rhetoric of self-sufficiency, this pattern simultaneously reveals North Korean ambitions towards some kind of world consolidation. North Korean ideologists offer *chuch'e* and North Korean 'socialism in our style' as beams of hope for the progress of mankind. Yet the policy of isolationism, the mono-ethnic

---

[18] 'On dumal tol'ko o mal'chike' [He thought only about the boy], 20 October 2011. Online: http://juche-songun.livejournal.com/304310.html#comments (accessed 17 June 2011).

framework of the North Korean mentality and the paradigm of unfinished war with the United States have put their limitations on internationalist messages in North Korean discourse.

As we find with communism, Christianity, Buddhism and Confucianism, the North Korean version of internationalism has a provisional recruitment system. It accepts persons of other races as 'us' under the condition of their sharing basic North Korean values, such as cherishing the state and its leader. Didactic works in North Korean literary fiction about 'good foreigners' demonstrate how foreigners are supposed to think and behave in order to be treated as equals in the DPRK. In such narrations, a strikingly non-Korean foreigner opens his or her heart to basic North Korean values with the wholesomeness of the 'child race', often overcoming previous doubts and inhibitions. The reward which an enlightened neophyte receives is the obtainment of a new, real meaning of life and the love and care of the leader. 'Good foreigners', moreover, can also be Japanese or American. North Korean propagandists take such characters out of the political context of unsettled historical scores and ascribe to them qualities which are normally attributed to 'good foreigners', including physical attraction and a praiseworthy emotionality.

While the proposed model of North Korean relationships with the outside world can hardly be described as realistic or fair (few Europeans or Americans would like to associate themselves with the subservient fictional figures of John Haw, Louise or the Carters), it delivers messages that have actual positive effects on the North Korean mentality. For all its North Korea-centred positioning, North Korean internationalist propaganda takes its recipients out of their seclusion and widens their mental horizons. The tales of 'good foreigners' include positive, albeit overstated, references to the cultures out of which their foreign characters emerge, to their beautiful physical looks, or to exotic features of unusual foreign life styles, thus drawing the attention of North Koreans to the non-Korean world. These narrations idealise foreigners by endowing them with positive qualities that are normally associated with North Koreans, thus building the trust of North Koreans in people of different blood. While North Korean discourse does not allow the 'spoiling' of Korean blood by international marriages, it presents other ways for North Koreans to interact with representatives of overseas communities. The North Korean philosophy of foreigners thus not only warns North Koreans against the dangers of the overseas world but also steers them towards those parts of the world community that are rendered responsive.

References

Alexandrov, Georgii Fedorovich (1945), 'Tovarisch Ehrenburg uproschaet' [Comrade Ehrenburg oversimplifies], *Pravda*, 18 April 1945
Carter, Jimmy (2005), *Our Endangered Values: America's Moral Crisis*, New York; London: Simon and Schuster
Ch'oe, Mun-il (2006), 'Taminjok, tainjongsahoeronŭn minjokaksallon' [The theory of multinational and multiracial society is the theory that is killing our nation], in: *Rodong Sinmun*, 27 April, p. 5
Ch'oe, Yang-su (2000), 'Isanghan moksori' [Strange voice], in: *Chosŏn munhak*, 8 (634), pp. 61–70 [This and other North Korean journals cited here are given an additional numeral indicting their issue number in a consecutive series.]
Ch'ŏllima (2005), 'Migugini toen gŏsŭl such'iro yŏginda' [I consider it a shame to become an American], 2 (73)
Cumings, Bruce (2005), *Korea's Place in the Sun: A Modern History*, New York: W.W. Norton
Ehrenburg, Ilya (1942), 'Ubei!' [Kill!], in: *Krasnaya Zvezda*, 24 July 1942. Online: http://vivovoco.rsl.ru/VV/PAPERS/HISTORY/ERENBURG/KILLHIM.HTM (accessed 24 December 2011)
Gabroussenko, Tatiana (2011), 'From the "Soviet Era" to the "Russian Renaissance": Evolution of the Narrative about Russia and Russians in the North Korean Cultural Discourse', in: Rüdiger Frank, James E. Hoare, Patrick Köllner, Susan Pares (eds), *Korea 2011: Politics, Economy and Society*, Leiden: Brill, pp. 275–302
Gromov, Evgenii (1998), *Stalin: vlast' i iskusstvo* [Stalin: power and the arts], Moscow: Respublika
Han, Ki-sŏk (2010), 'P'yongyangŭi pom' [Spring in Pyongyang], in: *Adong munhak*, 4 (660), pp. 9–17
Han, Sŏr-ya (1960), 'Sarang' [Love], in: *Han Sŏr-ya sŏnjip* [Collected works by Han Sŏr-ya], vol. 12, Pyongyang: Chosŏn Chakka Tongmaeng Ch'ulpansa
Han, Sŏr-ya (2003), 'Sŭngnyanggi' [Jackals], in: *Chosŏn munhak*, 8 (670), pp. 44–64 [first published 1951]
Hollander, Paul (1981), *Political Pilgrims: Travels of Western Intellectuals to the Soviet Union, China, and Cuba, 1928-1978*, New York, Oxford: Oxford University Press
Hong, Sŏk-jung, *P'okp'ungi k'ŭn toch'ŭl p'yŏlch'inda* [The storm fills the big sail], serialised in: *Ch'ŏllima*, 5 (2007)–1 (2009)
Hwang, Ju-yŏp (1960), 'Hueja' [Fedya], in: *Chosŏn munhak*, 5 (153), pp. 50–59
Hyŏn, Sŏng-ha (1999), 'Hyanggi' [Aroma], in: *Chosŏn munhak*, 5 (619), pp. 49–57
Kang, Kui-mi (2001), 'Tonjigap' [The wallet], in: *Chosŏn munhak*, 12 (650), pp. 35–45
Kim, Ch'ŏl-min (2007), 'Hoidaphal ttaega toiyŏtta' [It is time to answer], in: *Chosŏn munhak*, 7 (717), pp. 41–53
Kim, Ch'ŏng-nam (2000), 'Munmyŏng kamgak' [The feel of civilisation], in: *Chosŏn munhak*, 8 (634), pp. 71–80
Kim, Ch'ŏng-su (2002), 'Naŭi arirang' [My arirang], in: *Chosŏn munhak*, 4 (654), pp. 9–19
Kim, Chun-hak (1998), 'Maehok' [Enchantment], in: *Chosŏn munhak*, 9 (611), pp. 22–34
Kim, Hong-mu (1960), 'Marŭsya', in: *Chosŏn munhak*, 1 (149), pp. 35–45

Kim, Ik-ch'ŏl (1979), 'Ryŏksa nŭn chikhyŏpogo itta' [History is watching], in: *Chosŏn munhak*, 11 (385), pp. 78–80
Kim, Ki-pŏm (2008), 'T'oekŭn kilesŏ' [On the way home], in: *Chosŏn munhak*, 11 (733), pp. 53–60
Kim, Myŏng-jin (2010), 'Ŭiji' [Will], in: *Chosŏn munhak*, 8 (754), pp. 42–48
Kim, Sŏng-ho (2008), 'Konghwakuk kibal' [The flag of the republic], in: *Chosŏn munhak*, 9 (731), pp. 61–68
Kim, Sŏn-hwan (1999), 'Suhak ryŏhaeng' [Study travel], in: *Chosŏn munhak*, 5 (619), pp. 73–77
Kim, Sŏn-hwan (2003), 'Sae ach'im' [New morning], in: *Chosŏn munhak*, 12 (674), pp. 61–69
Kim, Tae-sŏn (2009), 'P'yŏnghwaŭi chogŏn' [Condition of peace], in: *Ch'ŏngnyŏn munhak*, 7 (608), pp. 7–13
Kim, Tŏk-ch'ŏl (2000), 'Ryutarŭn kyŏlhonsik' [An unusual marriage ceremony], in: *Chosŏn munhak*, 3 (629), pp. 69–75
Kim, Tong-gi (2005), 'Sarange taehan saenggak' [A thought about love], in: *Chosŏn munhak*, 9 (695), p. 64
Lankov, Andrei (2002), *From Stalin to Kim Il Sung: The Formation of North Korea, 1945–1960*, New Brunswick NJ: Rutgers University Press
Mal'tseva, Olga (2009), 'Koreya s severa na yug' [Korea from the north to the south]. Online: http://www.all-korea.ru/novye-proekty-1/novicenko---geroj-kndr accessed 15 February 2012
Margulies, Sylvia (1968), *The Pilgrimage to Russia: The Soviet Union and the Treatment of Foreigners, 1924–1937*, Madison, Milwaukee, and London: The University of Wisconsin Press
MIA: Marxists: Marx & Engels: Library: 1848: Manifesto of the Communist Party: Chapter 4. Online: http://www.marxists.org/archive/marx/works/1848/communist-manifesto/ch04.htm (accessed 26 May 2011)
Myers, Brian (1994), *Han Sorya and North Korean Literature: The Failure of Socialist Realism in the DPRK*, Ithaca NY: Cornell University
Myers, Brian (2008), 'Ideology as Smokescreen: North Korea's Juche Thought', in: *Acta Koreana*, 11 (3) (December 2008)
Myers, Brian (2010), *The Cleanest Race: How North Koreans See Themselves and Why It Matters*, Hoboken NJ: Melville House Publishing
Nam, Sang-hyŏk (1991–1992), 'Tu nyŏin' [Two women], parts 1, 2 and 3, in: *Chosŏn munhak*, 11 (529) (1991), pp. 51–58; 12 (530) (1991), pp. 55–62; 1 (531) (1992), pp. 51–62
Oberdorfer, Don (1997), *The Two Koreas: A Contemporary History*, London: Little, Brown and Company
Ŏm, Ho-sŏk (1952), *Munye kibon* [The basis of literature and the arts], Pyongyang: Kukrip ch'ulp'ansa
Paek, Po-hŭm (2008), 'Yel tasŏt pŏnchche hae' [The fifteenth year], in: *Chosŏn munhak*, 7 (729), pp. 11–22
Pak, Chong-sang (2004), 'Sosaeng' [Resuscitation], in: *Chosŏn munhak*, 12 (686), pp. 62–68
Pak, Sŏng-guk (2003), 'Sŭngnyanggi onŭldo saraitta' [Jackals are alive today], in: *Chosŏn munhak*, 9 (671), p. 77
Reisky de Dubnic, Vladimir (1960), *Communist Propaganda Methods: A Case Study on Czechoslovakia*, New York: Frederick A. Praeger
Ri, Chŏng-su (1977), 'Chŏnhwan' [Conversion], in: *Chosŏn munhak*, 8 (358), pp. 49–59

Ri, Sang-min (2005), 'Manp'ungnyŏn' ch'angga' [A song in praise of good harvest], in: *Chosŏn munhak*, 5 (691), pp. 54–57
Rodong Sinmun, 11 November 2003, p. 5, 'Mije ka Namchosŏn inmindŭl ege chŏjirŭn chŏndae mimun ŭi taebŏmjoe rŭl yŏlsanhanda' [Enumerating the vast, unprecedented crimes of American imperialists against the South Korean people]
Ryang, Ch'ang-cho (2000), 'Tupŏnchchae kija hoekyon' [The second briefing], in: *Chosŏn munhak*, 2 (628), pp. 55–63
Song, Pyŏng-jun (1988), 'Paeksŏrŭi pimil' [Paeksŏl's secret], in: *Chosŏn munhak*, 7 (489), pp. 17–25
Stalin, Joseph (1946), *O velikoi otechestvennoi voine Sovetskogo soyuza* [On the Great Patriotic War of the USSR], Moscow: Progress
Stevens, Charles (1964), 'A Content Analysis of the Wartime Writings of Chiang Kai-Shek and Mao Tse-Tung', in: *Asian Survey* 4 (6), pp. 890–903
Suh, Dae-Sook (1988), *Kim Il Sung: The North Korean Leader*, New York: Columbia University Press
Yang, Chae-mo (1998), 'Nop'ŭn mokp'yo' [Lofty goal], in: *Pinnanŭn rojong* [A brilliant course], Pyongyang: Munhak yesul chonghap ch'ulp'ansa, pp. 304–23
Yi T'ae-jun (1951/1995), 'Dear People' [Kogwihan saramdŭl], in: *Yi T'ae-jun munhak chŏnjip* [Complete works of Yi T'ae-jun], vol. 3, Seoul: Kip'ŭnsaem, pp. 147–59
Yi, T'ae-jun (1951/1995), 'Miguk taesagwan' [American Embassy], in: *Yi T'ae-jun munhak chŏnjip* [Complete works of Yi T'ae-jun], vol. 3, Seoul: Kip'ŭnsaem, pp. 141–46
Yu, T'aek-hŭi (2000), 'Ochag moego stchastia' [The hearth and home of my happiness], in: *Koreya segodnya*, 9, pp. 19–20
Yun, Kyŏng-ju (1986), 'SSibiriŭi pulgŭn changmi' [Red roses of Siberia], in: *Chosŏn munhak*, 8 (466), pp. 10–18

ABOUT THE AUTHORS AND EDITORS

Sabine Burghart
is a Ph.D. candidate and research assistant to the chair of East Asian Economy and Society at the department of East Asian Studies, University of Vienna. She holds an M.A. in political science from the University of Leiden. Between 2004 and 2007, she served as project coordinator at the Korea office of the German Friedrich Naumann Foundation for Freedom (FNF) in Seoul. She was in charge of the foundation's training programmes and capacity-building projects in the DPR Korea. In 2010, she pursued her research in Seoul supported by a scholarship from the Institute for Far Eastern Studies of Kyungnam University. In 2011–2012, she temporarily returned to the voluntary sector to facilitate co-operation projects between the FNF and the DPRK.
Email: sabine.burghart@univie.ac.at

Patrick Flamm
is a graduate student in political science at Goethe University Frankfurt. His research interests include the foreign and security policy of South Korea, regional affairs in Northeast Asia and post-structural approaches to international relations. From October 2011 to September 2012 he was a research assistant at the GIGA German Institute of Global and Area Studies, Hamburg.
Email: flamm.patrick@googlemail.com

Rüdiger Frank
is chair and professor of East Asian Economy and Society at the University of Vienna, also an adjunct professor at Korea University and the University of North Korean Studies (Kyungnam University) in Seoul. He holds an M.A. in Korean Studies, Economics and International Relations and a Ph.D. in economics. In 1991/1992, he spent one semester as a language student at Kim Il Sung University in Pyongyang and has been researching North Korea ever since. Visiting professorships have included Columbia University New York and Korea University, Seoul. In addition to membership in and association with a

number of Korea- and East Asia-related societies, he is a council member of and for the period 2011–2013 secretary of the Association for Korean Studies in Europe. He is also an executive board member and for 2010–2012 a steering group member of the European research network 'EastAsiaNet'. In 2012, he became vice-president of the US- and Hong Kong-based Asia Pacific History Association. Professor Frank is deputy chief editor of the A-ranked *European Journal of East Asian Studies*, co-editor of the series *Korea: Politics, Economy and Society* published annually since 2007, member of the editorial board of the book series *Brill's Korean Studies Library*, an associate at *The Asia Pacific Journal*, member of the editorial board of *Korea Review of International Studies*, co-founder and member of the editorial board of the *Vienna Graduate Journal of East Asian Studies* and *Vienna Studies on East Asia*. He is also the founding editor of a new book series at Brill titled *Security and International Relations in East Asia*. His major research fields are socialist transformation in East Asia and Europe (with a focus on North Korea), state–business relations in East Asia, and regional integration in East Asia. His most recent books are: (with S. Burghart, eds), *Driving Forces of Socialist Transformation: North Korea and the Experience of Europe and East Asia*, Vienna: Praesens 2010; and (ed., 2011), *Exploring North Korean Arts*, Nuremberg: Verlag fuer Moderne Kunst. Professor Frank is regularly consulted by governments, media and businesses on North Korea and East Asia. Most recently, this included consultancy work and a background policy paper for the visit by former presidents Martti Ahtisaari, Jimmy Carter and Mary Robinson, and former prime minister Gro Brundtland to the Korean peninsula and China. In 2011, he joined the World Economic Forum, Global Agenda Council on Korea.
For more information, see http://wirtschaft.ostasien.univie.ac.at
For publications, see http://univie.academia.edu/RuedigerFrank
Email: ruediger.frank@univie.ac.at

Tatiana Gabroussenko
graduated from the Far Eastern State University (ex-USSR), where she majored in Korean history. She obtained her Ph.D. in East Asian Studies at the Australian National University. She is currently an adjunct lecturer in Korean Studies at University of New South Wales in Australia and an assistant professor in North Korean Studies at the Faculty of Korean Studies at Koryo University, Korea. She is the author of a number of articles devoted to contemporary North Korean

culture, literature and propaganda. Her most recent book, *Soldiers on the Cultural Front: Developments in the Early History of North Korea Literature and Literary Policy*, was published by University of Hawai'i Press in 2010. The book has been selected for inclusion in Choice annual list of Outstanding Academic Titles in 2011.
Email: t.gabroussenko@unsw.edu.au

James E. Hoare
Ph.D., retired from the British Diplomatic Service in 2003. He was posted to Seoul and Beijing, and his last appointment was as British Chargé d'Affaires and Consul-General in Pyongyang. He now writes and broadcasts about East Asia. Among his recent publications are *A Political and Economic Dictionary of East Asia* (Routledge 2005) and *North Korea in the 21st Century: An Interpretative Guide* (Global Oriental 2005), both written with his wife, Susan Pares. He is a senior teaching fellow at the School of Oriental and African Studies, University of London, where he teaches a course on North Korea, and an honorary departmental fellow in the department of International Politics, Aberystwyth University. He lives in London.
Email: jim@jhoare10.fsnet.co.uk

Patrick Köllner
is director of the Institute of Asian Studies, GIGA German Institute of Global and Area Studies, and professor of political science, with a focus on political systems in East Asia, at the University of Hamburg. He holds a Ph.D. and a *venia legendi* in political science. Between 1996 and 2006 he was sole editor of the German-language predecessor of the *Korea Yearbook*. His research focuses on Japanese and Korean politics and political regimes, parties and other organisations more generally. He has published in journals such as *Japan Forum*, *Japanese Journal of Political Science*, *Journal of East Asian Studies*, *Politische Vierteljahresschrift*, and *Social Science Japan Journal*.
Email: koellner@giga-hamburg.de

Mark Morris
is university lecturer in East Asian Cultural History at the University of Cambridge and a Fellow of Trinity College. His main teaching and research interests concern Japanese modern fiction and film, and South Korean cinema. He is an associate of the online journal *The*

Asia-Pacific Journal: Japan Focus, where some of his recent work has appeared.
Email: mrm1000@cam.ac.uk

Susan Pares
has worked in the Research and Analysis Department of the Foreign and Commonwealth Office and, since 1987, as an editor and writer on East Asian subjects. She edited *Asian Affairs*, 1997–2001, and between 2000 and 2007 the *Papers of the British Association for Korean Studies*. She served in the British Embassy in Beijing, 1975–76 and accompanied her husband, James Hoare, on postings to Seoul (1981–85), Beijing (1988–91) and Pyongyang (2001–02). They are co-authors of several books dealing with East Asian and specifically Korean affairs. The most recent is *North Korea in the 21st Century: An Interpretative Guide* (2005).
Email: spares@myway.com

Martin Petersen
is assistant professor in Korean Studies at the University of Copenhagen. He completed his Ph.D. in Comparative Cultural Studies at the University of Copenhagen in 2009 with the thesis 'Collecting Korean Shamanism—Biographies and Collecting Devices'. His recent publications include 'Collecting Korean Shamanism for the National Museum of Denmark' in *Nordisk Museologi*, 2011 (2). 'A New Deal' is part of an ongoing research project on the North Korean graphic novel medium and its politics. Articles are forthcoming in *Korean Studies* and comic/graphic novel journals.
Email: mpe@hum.ku.dk

Bernhard J. Seliger
is currently resident representative of the Hanns Seidel Foundation in Korea, based in Seoul, which offers consultancy services to NGOs, academic and public institutions on questions of unification. He frequently travels to North Korea, where the Hanns Seidel Foundation implements training programmes in the fields of economics, organic agriculture, sustainable forestry and the clean development mechanism under the Kyoto protocol. He also is associate editor and book review editor of *North Korean Review* as well as founding editor of the website www.asianintegration.org.
Email: seliger@hss.or.kr

Dong-min Shin
is a Ph.D. candidate in the department of War Studies at King's College London. His main areas of research are the Republic of Korea (ROK)'s foreign and security policy and North Korean issues. Mr Shin is currently 2nd secretary in the Ministry of Foreign Affairs and Trade of the ROK. He obtained his B.A. and M.A. from the department of International Relations of Seoul National University.
Email: dong_min.shin@kcl.ac.uk

MAP OF THE KOREAN PENINSULA

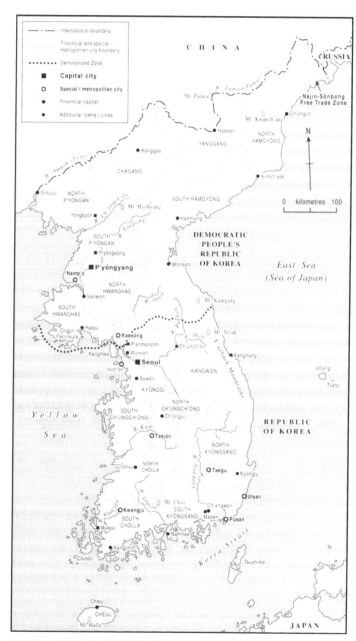

Design and Imaging Unit, Durham University.